Church and State in
the Roberts Court

Church and State in the Roberts Court

Christian Conservatism and Social Change in Ten Cases, 2005–2018

Jerold Waltman

McFarland & Company, Inc., Publishers

Jefferson, North Carolina

LIBRARY OF CONGRESS CATALOGUING-IN-PUBLICATION DATA

Names: Waltman, Jerold L., 1945– author.
Title: Church and state in the Roberts court : Christian conservatism
and social change in ten cases, 2005–2018 / Jerold Waltman.
Description: Jefferson, North Carolina : McFarland & Company, Inc.,
Publishers, 2019 | Includes bibliographical references and index.
Identifiers: LCCN 2019003379 | ISBN 9781476671475
(paperback : acid free paper) ∞
Subjects: LCSH: Church and state—United States. | Church and
state—United States—Cases. | Freedom of religion—United States. |
Christianity and politics—United States. | Conservatism—United States. |
Roberts, John G., 1955– | United States. Supreme Court.
Classification: LCC KF4865 .W35 2019 | DDC 342.7308/527—dc23
LC record available at https://lccn.loc.gov/2019003379

BRITISH LIBRARY CATALOGUING DATA ARE AVAILABLE

ISBN (print) 978-1-4766-7147-5
ISBN (ebook) 978-1-4766-3514-9

Front cover images © 2019 Shutterstock

Printed in the United States of America

*McFarland & Company, Inc., Publishers
Box 611, Jefferson, North Carolina 28640
www.mcfarlandpub.com*

Table of Contents

Acknowledgments

Anyone who has written a book knows that there are both general and specific acknowledgments that ought to be mentioned. Who first stirred our interest in writing? Who provided the intellectual impetus to become interested in a given area of inquiry? When we reach a certain age, they are, of course, from the distant past, and are often even deceased; nevertheless, they are still important for us to keep in mind. I especially recall, for example, Mr. L.E. Storey, my undergraduate constitutional law professor.

Regarding more recent days, David Clinton, my department chair, deserves a special note of thanks. Along with providing encouragement for the project, he graciously arranged my teaching schedule to allow time for research and writing. Librarians at both the Baylor Law School and the university's Moody Library met my frequent requests for materials with efficiency and good humor. Sinai Wood was especially helpful when it came to navigating me through the pathways of internet access to academic journals. The administrative staff of the Department of Political Science, Jenice Langston and Melanie Pirelo, as always, helped me solve various computer problems.

John Duddington, the editor of the British journal *Law and Justice*, encouraged me early on to write a couple of articles that laid the groundwork for the book. In addition, he was always a superb intellectual conversation partner.

Finally, my students, both graduate and undergraduate, are constantly stimulating me to rethink how the Supreme Court deals with the contentious issues surrounding the religion clauses. To them, I owe a good deal of thanks.

Preface

Supreme Court decisions are ordinarily influenced by three factors. There is, first, the judicial and political philosophies of the justices. Judges are not engineers applying a mathematical or mechanistic set of principles to the cases before them. They are human beings with strongly held values both about the role of courts in our governmental system and specific policy issues. Of course, all judges deny that their own values affect their decisions—that they only "apply the law"—but no informed observer takes that seriously. People who follow the Supreme Court often disagree, naturally, about exactly what Justice X's judicial and political philosophy is, and how consistently she applies it. And oftentimes, especially in the popular press, we find overly simplistic labels, such as "liberal" and "conservative." Nevertheless, even these labels can be informative, and are usually a good starting point for more careful analysis. What cannot be doubted is that justices' judicial and political philosophies matter, and that the collective judicial and political philosophy of a majority of justices in a given case is a crucially important element in determining how a decision comes out.

Second, there is the weight of precedent. No case comes to the Court, that is, on a blank slate. Our common law system with its decision rule of *stare decisis*—stand by the decision—means that judges should look to the rules established in previous decisions and render holdings in line with them. This gives an important stability to the law that it would lack if each case was considered *de novo.* There are several important qualifications, though, that in theory and practice make *stare decisis* more a guideline than a rigid framework. For one thing, few cases are exactly like previous ones. The facts are often different enough that an exception to the general rule is called for. For another, there are often multiple precedents and therefore several possible lines of decisions to follow. At times, the lines of precedents may actually be contradictory. Often, moreover, if

1

not most often, there are nuances and shadings surrounding a general principle. A judge will consequently have to select among precedents or lines of precedents to formulate the rule for deciding the case before him. Finally, courts have the power to overrule precedents set by a court of parallel authority, as is always the case at the Supreme Court. *Stare decisis*, therefore, is not a binding rule. Nonetheless, there is an inherent tendency among judges to accord significant weight to precedents, not determinative to be sure but significant. Consequently, when a case reaches the Supreme Court, it is always instructive to examine what has come before.

The third factor that influences Supreme Court decisions is the social, economic, cultural, and intellectual currents of the times. Society is not static, and neither is the law, constitutional or otherwise. Developments in the wider society affect the Supreme Court in two ways. First, the justices themselves are products of their age. They have been reared and educated in a certain milieu, where both spoken ideas and unspoken assumptions have molded their outlook. Furthermore, they are intelligent and widely read people. They cannot help but be influenced by the intellectual currents and social changes that are occurring outside the courtroom. Justice Benjamin Cardozo said long ago "The great tides and currents which engulf the rest of men do not turn aside in their course and pass the judges by."[1]

Second, social, cultural, and economic trends go far in shaping the types of cases that end up on the Court's docket. Active political groups— and such groups are always in flux—win or lose political battles in Congress, state legislatures, or local government bodies, and the losers rush to the Court. Consider recent disputes over affirmative action, gun control, and gay and lesbian rights, for example. Fifty years ago, none of these issues would have been seen at the Court because no powerful interest group pushed for such policies in the political arena, a fact rooted in the attitudes of the times.

The first two factors have been studied extensively. There are hundreds of books analyzing the judicial and political views of individual justices and groups of justices. Likewise, there are shelves of books tracing the development of legal doctrines. The third, however, has been given much less attention.

In the following work I analyze the church-state cases decided by the Roberts Court from the appointment of John Roberts as Chief Justice in 2005 through Justice Neil Gorsuch's early days in 2018 in light of the changes occurring in the society at large. Of course, no one-to-one correspondence, or causal arrow if you will, can be drawn between social developments and specific Supreme Court decisions. The enterprise is necessarily speculative (which is a major reason it is seldom done). However, simply because it is speculative doesn't make it any less important. I hope to show that the religious changes that have taken place in American society in the last two decades have indeed had an influence on the drift of church-state jurisprudence.

In all, ten church-state cases were decided by the Supreme Court in these years. I opted to take them up chronologically rather than divide them into establishment clause and free exercise categories. Part of the reason is that some of them, especially one of the most important (*Hosanna-Tabor Lutheran Church and School v. Equal Employment Opportunity Commission*), raised both sets of issues. Another part is that following a historical narrative approach gives an important window onto the development of religious liberty jurisprudence in general.

In the first chapter, I lay out the religious changes that have occurred in American society over the last two decades: the astounding growth of religious diversity, the increase in secularism, the rise in the legitimacy and political power of gay and lesbian groups, and the resulting reaction by more conservative Christians to these three developments. In the second chapter, I explain why the Roberts Court is usually called conservative, discuss briefly what conservatism means in the context of church-state relations, and set out the background of establishment clause and free exercise jurisprudence the Roberts Court inherited. Then, I take up each of the cases in turn, asking whether and how they were influenced by these changes. Finally, I draw the threads together and offer some concluding thoughts on both Supreme Court jurisprudence and the state of religion and politics more broadly in the United States today.

A note on citations: To save the clutter of countless footnotes, I have opted not to give the detailed legal citations to the various cases. They are easily looked up online by anyone interested.

CHAPTER 1

A Changing Religious Landscape

To be sure, it is fair to say that the American religious landscape has been continually changing since 1607. Each decade has witnessed the arrival of a wide variety of immigrant groups bringing new religious bodies to the country; meanwhile, any number of exotic homegrown religions have sprung up, and these have often grown and endured. The result has been an ever-changing kaleidoscope of religious groupings. Nevertheless, there are periods when change is more acute, and carries more social and political consequences, than at others. The era since 1990 has unquestionably been one of those times. In large measure, there have been four major trends that have characterized these years, and therefore form the backdrop for contemporary church-state relations. The first is a growing religious diversity; the second a marked growth in secularism; the third the emergence of gay and lesbian groups as legitimate parts of society; and, the fourth, the reaction to these three trends among conservative Christians, especially evangelicals.

Growing Diversity

Despite the country's always harboring a large degree of religious diversity, from the beginning most Americans have identified as Protestants.[1] During the entire period of colonization, there was, for example, a scattering of Catholics and Jews, but they were decidedly small in number. So prevalent was Protestantism from then through the early days of the Republic, public identity, public institutions, and the law, almost unthinkingly, reflected that fact. To choose but one example, when Horace Mann set the curriculum for the first public schools in the country, he said that "[O]ur system earnestly inculcates all Christian morals; it founds its morals on the basis of religion; it welcomes the religion of the Bible; and in receiving the Bible it allows it to do what it is allowed to do in no other system—to speak for itself."[2] An almost perfect capsule of nineteenth-century Protestant theology.

By the middle part of the nineteenth century, however, Catholic immigration, coming at that time mostly from Ireland and Germany, had altered the religious landscape. In fact, by 1860 Catholicism was the largest single denomination in this country, although it was still subsumed within the large Protestant majority. In 1900, for instance, fully 80 percent of Americans still claimed a Protestant identity.[3] The papal opposition to liberalism and democracy during these years put the American Catholic Church in an awkward position. As a result, tensions with segments of the Protestant majority flared occasionally, but over time the Catholic Church became thoroughly Americanized,[4] with anti–Catholic sentiment largely disappearing by the beginning of the twentieth century. Anti-Semitism, too, found occasional outbursts. Yet, this too declined in the twentieth century.

By the mid–twentieth century, in fact, American pundits were celebrating the unity of the three faiths in an American "civil religion." Will Herberg's widely read 1955 book *Protestant, Catholic, Jew* was the handbook of this position. Herberg wrote that while some differences remain, all three major traditions recognize "a need and a responsibility that overrides, if it does not dispel, all suspicions and doubts." In fact "the interfaith idea has become one of the accepted aspects of the American Way of Life."[5] This sentiment was, at the time, widely embraced by all concerned: religious leaders, political figures, and the broader public, as historian Kevin Schultz has carefully documented.[6] Nevertheless, as Joseph Bottum has stressed, Protestantism continued to form the subtext.

> In truth, all the talk, from the eighteenth century on, of the United States as a religious nation was really just a make-nice way of saying it was a Christian nation—and even to call it a Christian nation was usually just a soft and ecumenical attempt to gloss over the obvious fact that the United States was, at its root, a *Protestant* nation. Catholics and Jews were tolerated, off and on, but "the destiny of America," as Alexis de Tocqueville observed in 1835, was "embodied in the first Puritan who landed on those shores, just as the whole human race was represented by the first man."[7]

In the 1960s, however, dramatic changes were underway. In part, this was sparked by a renewed interest among native-born Americans in Eastern religions, in particular Buddhism and Islam (in the latter case primarily among African-Americans). But more than that, it came as a byproduct of the Immigration and Nationality Act of 1965.[8] Beginning in the 1920s, the United States had followed a highly restricted immigration policy, only admitting immigrants by the percentage of the population already here. As a result, people from Europe generally, and especially Western

Europe, were highly favored. The 1965 act abolished these quotas and opened the door without racial or ethnic restrictions. The effects have been dramatic. Comparing the 1950s to the 1990s, European immigrants fell from 53 percent to 15 percent of the total, whereas those entering from Asia and Latin America grew from 31 percent to 78 percent. While many of the Latin American immigrants replenished the ranks of Catholics leaving the Church (and contributed a not-inconsequential number of new Protestants, particularly Pentecostals), those from Asia brought a variety of non–Western religions to the country.

Paul Numrich and his colleagues reported that in Chicago in 2003 there were 400,000 Muslims, 150,000 Buddhists, 80,000 Hindus, 7,000 Jains, 6,000 Sikhs, 2,000 Bahá'ís, and 700 Zoroastrians.[9] These numbers reflected national trends as well. The Council on American-Islamic Relations reported that the 962 mosques in the country in 1994 had grown to 2,106 by 2011. As one might expect, the most populous states contain the most: New York with 257, California with 246, and Texas with 166. Nevertheless, there are mosques in every state, with places like Alabama having 31, Iowa 17, and Mississippi 16. Parallel to this, the number of regular participants in mosque activities rose from 500,000 in 1994 to 2,600,000 by 2011.[10] Estimates of the total Muslim population in the United States range up to six million, with about a quarter of those being African Americans.[11]

Buddhists' numbers have also increased, although exact figures are hard to come by.[12] Despite the fact that the first Buddhist temple in the United States was erected in 1853, and Chinese and Japanese immigration steadily added to the Buddhist presence, the numbers remained small. In the 1960s, converts became more common; then when the 1965 immigration law went into effect a stream of Asian immigrants brought even more Buddhists here. Current estimates by the Pluralism Project range from 2.45 to four million Buddhist adherents; of these, approximately 800,000 are believed to be converts. At the moment, there are reportedly 2,228 Buddhist centers in the country.

Hindus, hailing chiefly from India, had few fellow religionists when they began to come to the United States in the 1960s. Before 1965 there were only about 15,000 immigrants from the entire Indian subcontinent. A trickle began in the late 1960s, but by the 1980s that had become a steady stream. According to the Hindu American Foundation, there were only 1,700 Hindus in the country in 1900. By 1980, there were 387,000 and by 1997 1.1 million. This had more than doubled by 2008 to 2.3 million.

Naturally, the growth in these religious bodies has affected the position of Christians in general and Protestants in particular. In 1948, 91 percent of Americans called themselves Christians, compared to 77 percent in 2008.[13] By 2014 that had slipped further to 71 percent.[14] While this shrinking percentage is in part attributable to the growth in non–Christian numbers, it is also the result in the shrinkage in the absolute numbers of people identifying as Christians. Between 2007 and 2014 the number of Christian adults fell from 178.1 million to 172.8 million. Within Christianity, two groups, Catholics and mainline Protestants, have been hit especially hard. The number of adults asserting Catholic identity decreased from 54.3 million in 2007 to 50.9 million by 2014; undoubtedly, there would have been an even steeper drop had immigrants from Mexico and other Latin American countries not entered the pews. An even sharper decline, in both absolute numbers and percentage terms, has occurred among mainline Protestants. From 41.1 million adult identifiers in 2007 their numbers fell to 36.0 million in 2014, a 12.4 percent drop. Two groups—historically black churches and evangelicals—have fared somewhat better. The former has held almost steady in absolute numbers, while the latter has actually shown a slight increase; in both cases, though, they have become a slightly smaller percentage of the population. For the country as a whole, in fact, in 2014, Protestants had become a minority, now making up only 47 percent of the population.

Both the increasing religious diversity and the decline of Protestantism can be seen in the realm of public institutions. There is now, for example, both a Muslim and a Hindu member of Congress. The New York public schools are the latest (joining districts in Massachusetts, Michigan, and New Jersey) to add two Muslim holidays to its school calendar (with Hindus pressing for the same recognition).[15] In the 2012 elections, none of the four candidates from the two major parties for president or vice president was a white Protestant. Until Neil Gorsuch came to the bench in 2017, no member of the Supreme Court had been a Protestant since John Paul Stevens had retired (in 2010). Andrew Koppelman is certainly right to say that "The 1950s idea of Judeo-Christian America is untenable for the same reason that the idea of Protestant American became untenable over a century ago. Demographics have changed."[16]

Secularization

The decline in the percentage of Christians in the population is not only attributable to an increase in the numbers of non–Christians. There has been an increasing secular trend in society that is also responsible.

There is a large debate about what secularism means and whether it is growing as much as is widely claimed. Without probing into the myriad of books and articles on the subject, it will be helpful for our purposes to draw a distinction between what I will call *secularity* and *secularism.* By the former, I mean a position that merely has no connection to organized religion, little interest in religious matters, and only faint, if any, commitment to religion in general. The latter refers to a religious-like embrace of secularism as an ideology. Those in the latter category, which we might call *secularists,* are often far from neutral toward religion, and even frequently exhibit an active hostility to it, although to varying degrees it must be said. For that reason, we might usefully further divide them into passive and active secularists.

Numbers tell part of the story. In the latest Pew Research Center survey, 55.8 million adults said they were "religiously unaffiliated" (often labeled "nones"), a larger number than either Catholics or mainline Protestants. Moreover, between 2007 and 2014, their ranks had increased from 36.6 million, a 52 percent increase. Furthermore, if one examines the age cohorts, it seems this group is only likely to grow. Table 1 shows the breakdown of affiliation of people born in various time periods. The later one was born, it is abundantly clear, the more likely one is to be a "none." Thus, even if the percentage of people saying none stayed the same among those born after 1996, their overall percentage of the population would increase as the older generations pass from the scene. Additionally, few people gravitate to religion who have not been raised in a religious household. As the Pew researchers put it, "[F]or every person who has joined a religion after having been raised unaffiliated, there are more than four people who have become religious 'nones' after having been raised in some religion."[17] As the younger cohorts have children, therefore, it seems more than likely that more and more people with no religious connection will be produced over time.

Table 1: Religious Affiliation by Date of Birth

	1928–45 %	1946–64 %	1965–80 %	1981–89 %	1990–96 %
Evangelical Protestants	30	28	25	22	19
Mainline Protestants	22	17	13	10	11
Historically African-American Protestants	5	7	7	6	6
Catholics	24	23	21	16	16
Unaffiliated	11	17	23	34	36

SOURCE: Pew Research Center, *America's Changing Religious Landscape*, May 12, 2015, 11.

Yet it is not just the growth in the number of "nones" that is important; it is their composition. At one time, hardly any Americans told pollsters they were atheists, or even agnostics. In 2007, however, 25 percent of those selecting "none" in the Pew Survey said they were atheists or agnostics; tellingly, by 2014 that number had risen to 31 percent.

This growth in the number of people willing to self-describe themselves as atheists and agnostics has been accompanied, not surprisingly, by a sharper advocacy of secularism as an ideology. A spate of books, headlined by Richard Dawkins' *The God Delusion*,[18] has put forth the case for atheism and urged that religion be removed from society. Secularism on steroids, or hard secularism, is an apt description of this position. Its adherents, as noted above, can be called active secularists. A softer version, and the one most prominent among Americans, is more areligious than anti-religious. These are the passive secularists referred to above. They take the view, that is, that religion and non-religion stand on an equal footing. Religion, in this view, is merely another "lifestyle choice," akin to the decision of New Yorkers whether to support the Yankees or the Mets. Religion, from this perspective, is free to exist, and may even need protection, as long as it remains a purely private matter. Public institutions must be denuded of any and all religious preferences and support, even symbolic ones. As Steven Smith has said, these people feel that if everyone could only agree that religion is strictly a private matter, then we could all get along.[19] Some constitutional scholars, in fact, endorse this view, contending, either openly or by implication, that the religion clauses of the First Amendment are outdated and superfluous, and that protection for religious people and institutions can be guaranteed by the protections for freedom of speech, the right of association, and the requirements of equal protection.[20]

Alongside the emergence of intellectual movements supporting both hard and soft variants, there has been a blossoming of groups dedicated to the public pursuit of secularism. Noteworthy in the public policy realm are the Freedom from Religion Foundation, now claiming 21,500 members and the Secular Coalition of America.[21] The former spends a good bit of its energy filing lawsuits, one of which we will encounter later. The latter is dedicated mostly to lobbying activities, for example urging the adoption of legislation providing for Humanist chaplains in the armed forces.[22]

As but one measure of the growth of public secularism in America, when President Obama issued the usual proclamation celebrating Religious Freedom Day in 2014, for the first time he explicitly included atheists and agnostics: "Today, America embraces people of all faiths, and of no faith. We are Christians and Jews, Muslims and Hindus, Buddhists and Sikhs, atheists and agnostics."

Compare this with Franklin D. Roosevelt's radio address in June 1944. As American troops were approaching the Normandy beaches, he asked the nation to join him in prayer. A shortened version of what he said was this:

> Almighty God: Our sons, pride of our Nation, this day have set upon a mighty endeavor, a struggle to preserve our Republic, our religion, and our civilization, and to set free a suffering humanity.
>
> Some will never return. Embrace these, Father and receive them, Thy heroic servants, into Thy kingdom.
>
> As we rise to each new day, and again when each day is spent, let words of prayer be on our lips, invoking Thy help to our efforts.
>
> With Thy blessing, we shall prevail over the unholy forces of our enemy.
> Thy will be done, Almighty God.
> Amen.

Of course, we all fervently hope that we never face another situation like D-Day. Nevertheless, for our purposes it is important to look at the symbolism and the substance of his act. It was, first, a prayer, led by the president himself. Second, quite apart from the King James Version terminology of "Thy," the broad Protestant themes are evident.[23] Ask yourself: Can you picture a liberal, Democratic president leading the nation in such a prayer today, whatever the circumstances?

Changed Attitudes Toward Homosexuality

There are few instances in American—and probably other countries'—history in which public attitudes have changed as swiftly and dramatically as they have toward homosexuality. In 1987, 75 percent said homosexual activity was always wrong, paired with 12 percent who said it was not wrong at all.[24] By 2010 the former number had fallen to 44 percent and the latter had climbed to 41 percent. When asked if homosexual couples should have the right to marry each other, in 1988, three percent strongly agreed and eight percent agreed; in contrast, 44 percent strongly disagreed and 24 percent disagreed. In 2001, 57 percent still opposed allowing homosexuals to marry each other and 35 percent favored.[25] A mere 14 years later, however, those figures were reversed: 55 percent supported the right of gays and lesbians to marry each other with 39 percent opposed.

While there were still significant differences among various segments of the population, it is interesting that the support for gay marriage rose in every demographic group. Take age, for example. Among those born after 1980 support climbed from 51 to 70 percent. Yet, even among the cohort born between 1928 and 1945, support rose from 21 percent to 39 percent. Similarly, backing (or at least tolerance) for gay marriage increased among all religious groups. Among the unaffiliated, the support in 2015 was a full 82 percent, compared to only 24 percent of white evangelical Protestants. But seen from a time perspective, support in the former group went up from 61 percent in 2001 while it rose from 13 percent among the latter, an almost 100 percent increase among white evangelicals. Thus, even with static numbers, the natural replacement of generations would lead to further change; yet it is also important to note that the actual attitudes of lagging groups is changing in the same direction. The same trends show up, in fact, when the population is broken down by political party, ideology, and gender.[26]

Both as a result, and perhaps as a cause, the portrayal of gays and lesbians on television, in the movies, and in the news media has shifted dramatically. Today, gay characters are a mainstay of television series and in the movies, usually depicted in a positive light. (Think, for example, of Cameron and Mitchell on the award-winning *Modern Family.*)

Moreover, the newfound public acceptance of homosexuality has been accompanied by a growth in the political power of and significant policy victories by gay and lesbian groups. Bans on gays in the military fell, as did any number of discriminatory policies in other institutions such as schools and colleges. Sexual orientation has been added to anti-discrimination statutes in a number of states and in local government ordinances as well. And, of course, there have been profound victories in the courts, such as the overturning of the federal Defense of Marriage Act in 2013.[27] Most dramatically, of course, was the 2015 Supreme Court decision mandating that the states allow gays and lesbians to marry.[28]

The Push Back from Traditional Christians

All three of the above trends make traditional Christians, especially those who identify as evangelicals, but also to a degree conservative Catholics, uncomfortable at the least. In many ways, it amounts to something akin to feeling of being under a state of siege. They see a familiar world becoming strikingly unfamiliar. Certainly there is a dose of nostalgia here, an imagination that things were once largely aright when in fact reality was more complicated. But there is also a great deal of truth in their observations. Until the 1960s, we did have an underlying social consensus. Mayberry may not have represented reality, but the real world was recognizable from there.

Moreover, as stressed above, a broad, moderate Protestantism was a central component of that consensus, and represented a value system supported by virtually all the pillars of society. Just to choose one example, in at least one episode of *Leave It to Beaver*, Wally and the Beaver talked off-handedly about going to Sunday school. No television show does that today.

In short, we had a deeply religious society. Of course, not everyone ascribed to the ethos, and a goodly number of elites were never sold on its tenets. Too, there was a good bit of hypocrisy. Still, though, it was more than a veneer, and it had a far from trivial impact. In some ways, the fact that we had a religious society made a secular state possible. No one argued that the state should promote a specific denomination, but it was a given that it would be benign to religion in general, especially the mainline Protestant version. Furthermore, few saw any need to worry about religious liberty, since it was written into the political DNA. I do not want to overstate the degree of consensus or the disagreements surrounding the debates about religion in the immediate postwar period. Of course, there were disputes over various issues, such as state aid to parochial schools and released time programs, but they did not go to the heart of the nation's character.

Today, though, the world appears differently, with evangelical Protestants holding views markedly at variance with the country at large. In a 2012 Public Religion Research Institute poll, 56 percent of Americans said they do *not* believe that religious liberty is under any threat. However, 61 percent of white evangelicals believe that it *is*.[29] In the same vein, a 2015 Barna Research poll found that 41 percent of all adults and 52 percent of practicing Christians believed that "religious freedom in the U.S. has grown worse in the past 10 years." But 77 percent of evangelical Protestants thought that it had. Similarly, only 27 percent of adults said they were "very concerned about religious liberty becoming more restricted in the next five years." Nearly half, 48 percent, of practicing Christians thought so, but 68 percent of evangelicals answered yes. When asked whether they agreed that "religious freedom has become more restricted in the U.S. because some groups have actively tried to move society away from traditional Christian values," 51 percent of the population at large and 70 percent of practicing Christians answered in the affirmative. In contrast, fully 96 percent of evangelicals believed this to be true. Asked if "the gay and lesbian community is the most active group trying to remove Christian values from the country," 68 percent of evangelicals agreed, compared to 49 percent of all practicing Christians and 30 percent of all adults. Finally, when queried whether "traditional Judeo-Christian values should be given preference in the U.S.," 76 percent of evangelicals thought they should. Only 26 percent of adults agreed while 51 percent of all practicing Christians did.[30] Keep in mind that the "all adults" and "practicing Christians" included evangelical Protestants. Removing evangelicals from those categories would magnify the differences even more.

Another poll, conducted in 2014, that does break out these groups more specifically furnishes an even clearer picture.[31] Among those with no religious affiliation, 62 percent indicated that they believed religious liberty is under no threat. Standing against that view, 55 percent of Catholics, 53 percent of white mainline Protestants, and 50 percent of minority Protestants are inclined to believe that it is. White evangelical Protestants, though, are even more deeply concerned about religious liberty, with fully 83 percent of them believing that it is under threat.

In a still more recent poll, 68 percent of all Protestants and 54 percent of Catholics maintained that Christianity is under attack in the U.S. Yet, the numbers shot up to 81 percent when the question was posed to evangelicals.[32]

While, therefore, evangelical Protestants are far more worried and more uneasy about religious liberty and the status of traditional values than their mainline Protestant and Catholic counterparts, they are not alone in voicing concerns. In April of 2012 the United States Conference of Catholic Bishops felt the need to issue a statement on religious liberty entitled "Our First, Most Cherished Liberty." It reads in part:

> Catholics in America have [long] been advocates for religious liberty, and the landmark teaching of the Second Vatican Council on religious liberty was influenced by the American experience. It is among the proudest boasts of the Church on these shores. We have been staunch defenders of religious liberty in the past. We have a solemn duty to discharge that duty today.
>
> We need, therefore, to speak frankly with each other when our freedoms are threatened. Now is such a time. As Catholic bishops and American citizens, we address an urgent summons to our fellow Catholics and fellow Americans to be on guard, for religious liberty is under attack, both at home and abroad.

Seven examples follow, accompanied by a lengthy essay explaining the Bishops' position and urging all Americans to join them.

Any number of anecdotes could be offered to reinforce the poll data. To take but one example, when the Muslim community in Murfreesboro,

Tennessee wanted to build a new mosque, local evangelicals rose in defiance.[33] The televangelist Pat Robertson said Muslims were trying to take over the city. A lawyer representing the evangelical community filed a lawsuit claiming that the Muslims could not claim the protection of the free exercise clause since Islam was not a genuine religion. The federal courts, of course, thought otherwise and ordered the city to grant the construction permit.

As we examine the cases that have landed on the Supreme Court's docket between 2005 and 2018, we will try to assess the way the Court's decisions reflect the changed religious landscape of American life. Before we can do that, though, we need offer some comments on the philosophy of the Roberts Court and the precedents it inherited.

CHAPTER 2

Ideology and Baggage

The Ascendancy of Conservatism

Virtually all observers agree that the Supreme Court under Chief Justice John Roberts should be labeled "conservative." In fact, it is usually thought that it is even more conservative than its predecessor, the Rehnquist Court (1986–2005), which itself clearly leaned in a pronounced conservative direction. The reason for this conclusion stems from Justice Samuel Alito's replacement of Justice Sandra Day O'Connor in 2006. First, Alito is a much more forthright and more consistent conservative than was O'Connor. She tended to be conservative, to be sure; however, her jurisprudence was more piecemeal and she often voiced any number of qualifications in her opinions. Second, while O'Connor was on the Court she was often the "swing" justice, sitting between the Court's liberal and conservative blocs. When she left the Court, Justice Anthony Kennedy became the swing justice. And, with the exception of gay rights (which is an important exception, of course), he is noticeably more conservative than was Justice O'Connor. Thus, the rightward stance of the contemporary Supreme Court is strikingly clear. As an aside, there have been four other replacements on the Supreme Court during Chief Justice Roberts' tenure: Sonia Sotomayor for David Souter, Elena Kagan for John Paul Stevens, Neil Gorsuch for Antonin Scalia, and Brett Kavanaugh for Kennedy. However, in the first two instances it was replacement of liberals by liberals and in the third of a conservative by a conservative. Hence, the ideological balance of the Court was not altered by those changes.

However, simply to say that the Roberts Court is conservative and close the book on further analysis vastly oversimplifies. To begin with, broadly speaking, there are two variants of conservatism, and in more than one area they can come into conflict with each other. One strand is traditional conservatism. It is rooted in the philosophy of Edmund Burke, and is personified in its American version by Russell Kirk.[1] Its central tenet is a respect for a society's traditional values, and the need to transmit those from one generation to the next. Social institutions—including government—should both reflect and seek to reinforce those values, for they are the glue that holds societies together. People can and should be taught, that is, to be virtuous. The other strand is libertarianism, a school of thought whose leading intellectual parent is Frederich Hayek.[2] Libertarianism is above all concerned with individual liberty; each individual should be given the maximum amount of autonomy to pursue whatever goals she wishes and however she defines them. It therefore teaches that a minimal state is to be preferred under all (or almost all) conditions. Governmental power, no matter how exercised, even benignly, is always a danger. It is better to live with the consequences of minimized state power than run the risk of an overweening state. These two sets of ideas can lead to significant differences in a variety of policy areas, including church and state.

Another complication is that jurisprudential doctrines do not match up perfectly with "conservative" or "liberal" political positions. Supreme Court justices are not simply politicians in black robes (although they are sometimes accused of that). Constitutional theory and precedents are important in judicial decision making. Now, justices try to convince us (and perhaps themselves) that constitutional theory and precedents are *all* that matter, that their decisions are always apolitical. However, no thoughtful court watcher buys that. The difficulty is that constitutional theory and the lessons one can draw from precedents are inextricably intertwined with political ideology. They are not, however, identical to political ideology. It is too cynical to believe that any justice simply looks at a case, chooses who he or she wants to win, then crafts an argument to support that view. Nevertheless, the method of constitutional interpretation a given justice utilizes will be heavily influenced by, if not grounded in, a political orientation (if ideology is too strong a word). Thus, it becomes impossible to assign an unassailable weight to the role of political, as opposed to judicial, theory. Still, though, as intimated above, we often end up with liberal and conservative blocs on the Court, and also we end up being able to say with confidence that the Court in one era is more liberal or more conservative than it was in another.

Another layer of complications is added when we turn to the religion clauses of the Constitution. The First Amendment contains two religion clauses, and while they both attempt to create a general system of religious liberty, they prohibit different types of actions by government. Further, at a certain point the clauses can come into conflict with each other.

The precise wording of the First Amendment is "Congress shall make no law respecting an establishment of religion, nor prohibiting the free exercise thereof." What would the conservative position be on the establishment clause? Traditionalists would want to read it very narrowly, to mean, for example, only that government may not establish a national church. Government should be free, though, to help inculcate traditional religious values, both symbolically (by erecting religious symbols on public property, for example) and through specific policies, such as having students recite prayers in the public schools. Of course, there would always be lingering debate about what exactly the content of those traditional values should be. Nevertheless, most modern traditional conservatives tend, it seems, to see them as embodying a kind of generic Christianity, or slightly more inclusively, a broad monotheism.

Libertarians are much more skeptical about the establishment clause and prefer a broader reading. For them, when the state tries to teach values it becomes paternalistic, undermining individual autonomy and individual responsibility. By attempting to tell people what they should think, they believe the state enters a dangerous realm. Thus, the two strands of conservatism take rather different and decidedly conflicting views concerning the establishment clause.

The libertarian position is clear regarding the free exercise clause. Granting each individual the maximum freedom to believe as he or she chooses and to act on those beliefs as far as possible sits comfortably with libertarianism. Obviously, libertarians would support restrictions on religious liberty when given acts might do harm to others or threaten public order. However, the preference should always be for more rather than less religious liberty. And, further, this religious liberty should be available to all equally. No one, that is, can judge the validity of anyone else's religious beliefs, meaning the traditional and the nontraditional stand on the same footing.

Traditional conservatives become a bit more ambivalent when the discussion turns to free exercise. They certainly support religious liberty in the abstract. However, when nontraditional religious groups claim religious liberty, especially if their practices are seen as undermining traditional values, they become uneasy. They begin to argue that the state should regulate behavior they see as undermining the society's attachment to traditional values. At the same time, if political groups hostile to traditional values win control of legislative institutions, traditional conservatives will quickly turn to claims of free exercise for themselves. Consequently, there are times when traditional conservatism can almost find itself at war with itself concerning free exercise.

There is yet another complication regarding how the religion clauses should be applied. Who should decide where to draw the lines? This is usually couched as a conflict between judicial activism and judicial restraint. That is, should legislative bodies set the contours after democratic debate? Or, should the Supreme Court police when the establishment or free exercise clauses have been violated? This quandary is often called the "counter-majoritarian difficulty."[3] In a democratic society, should an unelected and largely unaccountable judiciary be empowered to overturn decisions made by majoritarian political institutions? A stentorian political ideology, such as a strong version of either traditional or libertarian conservatism (or, conversely, any variant of political liberalism as well), would care little about this issue and only be concerned with outcomes. However, this issue is a vital one in judicial philosophy. To make matters more difficult, all justices claim to follow judicial restraint. However, some are clearly more devoted to that principle than are others. Furthermore, almost every justice varies in his or her commitment to judicial restraint depending on the particular issue on the table.

John Roberts became Chief Justice in 2005, upon the death of William Rehnquist. The next year Justice Samuel Alito, as mentioned above, joined the Court, replacing Sandra Day O'Connor. Two liberal justices, David Souter and John Paul Stevens, were subsequently replaced by two other liberals, Sandra Sotomayor and Elena Kagan. Thus, it is fair to view the Roberts Court's liberal wing as being more or less stable. At the same time, because of the Alito-O'Connor dynamic, it is also fair to designate it overall as a decidedly conservative court. The conservative shift has, so far, not seemingly been affected by the ascendancy of Neil Gorsuch to Antonin Scalia's seat, and it is too early to determine the impact of Kavanaugh's appointment.

The State of Establishment Clause Jurisprudence in 2005

One of our most insightful of establishment clause scholars has argued that it was largely a "milk and water" proviso from the beginning.[4] It was only meant to prohibit, that is, the federal government from creating a publicly endorsed religion. Another well-known writer has said that the amendment was essentially jurisdictional in intent.[5] What it was designed to do, he thinks, was protect established churches in those states that then had them. (As we shall see, Justice Clarence Thomas has adopted this view.)

Several states, in fact, had established churches in 1791, the date the First Amendment was ratified. The last to give up this arrangement was Massachusetts, in 1833. But should whatever the amendment's drafters intended be the controlling factor today, or should more modern developments be accounted for when interpreting the clause?

At this point, it is important to enter a clarifying note on the applicability of the Bill of Rights, the first eight amendments, to the states. (Often the first 10 amendments are called the Bill or Rights; however, numbers nine and ten are not concerned with specific rights.) The First Amendment clearly states that it applies only to Congress, while the wording of the other seven is ambiguous. In 1833, the Supreme Court clarified the matter, saying that none of the Bill of Rights apply to the states. The ratification of the Fourteenth Amendment in 1868 altered this, however. It seems clear from recent scholarship that the drafters of this amendment intended it to make the first eight amendments apply to the states.[6] However, the Supreme Court was slow to adopt this approach, and has never said that the entire Bill of Rights applies to the states carte blanche. Nevertheless, the Court has held on any number of occasions that the First Amendment, including the religion clauses, apply equally to the federal government and the states.

Whatever the original intent of the amendment's authors, two broad general approaches have undergirded most establishment clause jurisprudence. On the one hand is the strict separation school. In this view, a high and rigid wall must be erected and maintained between church and state. Neither may intrude into the affairs of the other, and it is up to the courts to police the barrier, and to do so diligently. The other framework is usually known as "accommodationism." This position holds that, while clearly no government may establish an official church, when it comes to general public policies, as long as government does not discriminate among religious groups, there is no violation of the establishment clause.

Although there have been some other rather peripheral types of cases, for the most part the establishment clause has generated three different but related sets of issues: whether public monies can be spent to support parochial schools; the legitimacy of religious exercises in the public schools or other public forums; and whether religious symbols may be placed on public property.

The Roberts Court only decided one case involving public aid to religious elementary and secondary schools, and, as we shall see, in that instance reverted to the issue of standing, thereby avoiding facing the matter directly. A second case, involving public finding of safety materials to be used on a church related pre-school's playground, did raise similar issues, though. It is impossible to understand the drift of cases and the Supreme Court's holdings without a bit of historical context. At one time, this whole matter was heavily influenced by the fact that almost all parochial schools were Catholic, and, further, that being Catholic in America meant belonging to an important subculture. In the nineteenth century, in large part responding to Protestant suspicions of their Catholic neighbors, to ensure that Catholic schools could not tap into public funds a number of states passed "Blaine amendments," which prohibited public monies from being diverted to Catholic schools. With the growth of Catholic voting strength, though, and the increasing cost of maintaining Catholic schools, especially after World War II, there was growing pressure on public officials to find some way of supporting the parochial school system. By the 1980s a new factor entered the equation. A number of committed conservatives argued that the public schools were failing and that the private sector could do a better job of educating children. (In large measure this was based on a preference for market institutions over government ones in general.) Public funding, they argued, did not necessarily mean public ownership and operation of the schools. They were joined by a number of analysts who advocated for the same plans because they felt low-income parents should have the same choices as their more affluent counterparts. Nevertheless, the fact remained that any program to send public funds to private schools would mean that a good bit of the money would go to religiously affiliated schools. It is also perhaps pertinent that by the 1980s a number of Protestant churches, especially evangelical ones, were also operating elementary and secondary schools.

The first case in this area was *Everson v. Board of Education*, decided in 1947. New Jersey passed a law allowing local school districts to add transportation services for parochial schools to their already established systems if they wished. Accordingly, Ewing Township's board of education provided vouchers to all students within the district that allowed them to ride the public bus system to any public or Catholic school within the district. The Court's opinion is unusual in a sense, for the framework it establishes seems at variance with its holding. The majority justices spent a good bit of time pointing out how important it was to the American colonists to separate church and state. "A large proportion of the early settlers of this country came here from Europe to escape the bondage of laws which compelled them to support and attend government-favored churches." After summarizing similar practices in the colonies, they said that "These practices became so commonplace as to shock the freedom-loving colonials into a feeling of abhorrence." The result, the Court said, was the First Amendment, and, adopting a phrase of Thomas Jefferson's, averred that we must maintain a "wall of separation" between church and state. In fact, that wall must be "high and impregnable." Nevertheless, the bus program had not "breached" this wall. To support this conclusion, the Court drew an analogy with police and fire protection. The bus vouchers, that is, were merely a public service, akin to the fire department putting out a fire at the Catholic (or Presbyterian or whatever) church.

This decision breathed life into the movement to secure state funding for Catholic schools in some indirect fashion. The landmark case of *Lemon v. Kurtzman* came to the court in 1971. Pennsylvania had enacted a complex statute in which the state "purchased" the services of teachers in parochial schools to teach secular subjects. (The argument was that math, say, would be taught the same way in a public school, for which the state would have to pay.) Provisos were added to ensure that religion did not enter the courses taught by these partially publicly funded teachers. The Court granted that there were no hard and fast or easily discernible lines that could be drawn. "[W]e can only dimly perceive the lines of demarcation in this extraordinarily sensitive area of constitutional law." To guide them here, the justices adopted a three-pronged test that has become known as the *Lemon* test. "First, the statute must have a secular legislative purpose; second, its principal or primary effect must be one that neither advances nor inhibits religion; finally, the statute must not foster 'an excessive government entanglement with religion.'" (The internal quotation is from *Walz v. Tax Commission* [1970] which upheld property tax exemptions for religious institutions.) While the Court granted that the Pennsylvania law met the first two criteria, it faltered on the third. Insuring that the funds were spent as required would mean that auditors would have to come to the parochial schools and demand to see the books, a deeply entangling activity.

Following these cases, the Supreme Court faced a number of instances in which either (1) some type of indirect or technical aid was given to parochial schools (secular textbooks, maps, audio-visual equipment, payments for building repairs, etc.) or (2) a state tax system was manipulated in such a way as to provide a subsidy to parents who chose parochial schools. The Court followed a meandering path in these cases, applying the *Lemon* test, but sometimes upholding and sometimes striking down these programs. Even experts had trouble finding a consistent rationale for the decisions. In a 1995 case, for example, dealing with another issue Justice William Rehnquist offered a litany of inconsistencies, including that "a State may lend to parochial school children geography textbooks that contain maps of the United States, but may not lend maps of the United States for use in a geography class. A State may lend textbooks on American colonial history but it may not lend a film on George Washington, or a film projector to show it in history class." Then, in 1997, in *Agostini v. Felton* the Court announced that it was abandoning the third prong of the *Lemon* test and, in effect, loosening the second prong. (Only occasionally in this area of establishment clause jurisprudence have the justices had much trouble finding that statutes met the first prong.)

Five years later, in 2002, came the landmark case of *Zelman v. Simmons-Harris*. Cleveland's public school system was clearly failing, and that failure heavily penalized poor children. The state took over the system in 1995 and established a voucher plan. Basically, parents who opted out of the public school system were to be given a voucher which they could "spend" at any nonprofit private school (or any public school in an adjacent district, if the school elected to participate in the program, which none did). The school would then submit the voucher to the state and obtain payment. The vast majority of nonpublic schools in Cleveland, 82 percent, were religiously affiliated and the vast majority of students whose parents opted for the vouchers (96 percent) would be attending these institutions. The Supreme Court made two important holdings. First, the program was neutral as between religious and nonreligious schools and between religious schools affiliated with various religious bodies. Second, the funds that were funneled to the schools resulted from the private choice of individuals, not a direct government grant. "We believe the program challenged here is a program of true private choice ... and thus constitutional."

In essence, the Court had now moved away from the *Everson* doctrine of strict separation to a more accommodationist stance. Further, it was seeming to say that any program based on private choice would be sustainable, even if the practical effect was to provide public funds directly to parochial schools. For the moment, at least, the Court stood on the ground that these issues should be worked out in the political arena.

Turning to the question of prayer and other religious exercises in the public schools, the Court first ventured into this area in 1962 and 1963. In *Engel v. Vitale* it struck down a "nondenominational" prayer used in some New York public schools; in *Abington Township v. Schempp* it did the same for daily Bible reading exercises in Pennsylvania. The Court's logic seemed to rest on two propositions. First, because these exercises were being done at the behest of public officials there was an official "endorsement" (although that specific term was not used) of religion or even a certain version of religion (the Pennsylvania statute, for example, mandated that the King James translation be used). Second, the activities were being done in front of impressionable children. Although the pair of decisions generated a huge amount of controversy, even leading to periodic calls for a constitutional amendment overturning the holdings, the Court stuck to its position. Lower courts followed the guidelines established by the Supreme Court and repeatedly struck down similar exercises elsewhere.

The next landmark case occurred in 1985, and was *Wallace v. Jaffree.* Alabama's legislature passed a bill setting aside a moment of silence at the beginning of each school day for "meditation or silent prayer." The Court majority applied the *Lemon* test and found that the law failed the first prong. The legislator who sponsored the bill had said that it was an "effort to return voluntary prayer" to Alabama public schools. This led the Court to muse "that the enactment of [the statute] was not motivated by any clearly secular purpose; indeed, the statute had *no* secular purpose" (emphasis in original). The concurring and dissenting opinions in the case deserve a brief note. Justice O'Connor argued that the Court should lean more heavily on the "endorsement test," which, as we shall see, had been developed the previous year in *Lynch v. Donnelly.* For her, this was to be the guiding principle in all establishment clause cases. Justice Rehnquist's sharp dissent advocated abandoning the *Lemon* test altogether. In his view, accommodationism was the original intent of the establishment clause and that approach should govern contemporary cases (which would have allowed the Alabama law to stand).

In 1992 the Court had to deal with a slightly different issue, the propriety of prayers at middle school and high school graduation ceremonies. The case, *Lee v. Weisman,* originated in Providence, Rhode Island. The school district allowed principals to invite local clergy to offer a nonsectarian prayer at graduation ceremonies. The nonsectarian character was specifically outlined in a pamphlet the principals provided to the various clergy. Attendance at the ceremony was ostensibly voluntary, but as the Court pointed out, students were under parental, school, and peer pressure to attend. During the prayer, offered in the year under review by a rabbi, students were asked to stand.

The Court found that "[T]he government involvement with religious activity in this case is pervasive, to the point of creating a state-sponsored and state-directed religious exercise in a public school." Therefore, the policy violated the second prong of the *Lemon* test. Moreover, the Court turned to psychological studies to argue that a student who did not wish to participate in the exercise was put in an "untenable position." If she stood, she would be tacitly endorsing a religious position with which she did not agree. If she did not stand, she would be noticed by her peers. Either way, she would suffer psychological harm. The state cannot "place primary and secondary school children in this position."

The 2000 case of *Santa Fe (Texas) School District v. Doe* involved a prayer even further removed from the classroom, at high school football games. A school board policy provided that the students at Santa Fe High School would vote, first, whether to have prayer at the opening of games and, second, if that passed to elect a student chaplain who would offer the prayer, which had to be "nonsectarian and nonproselytizing." The school board argued that there is a sharp distinction between graduation cere-monies and athletic events, in that attendance at the latter is entirely vol-untary. Moreover, the fact that the students chose whether or not to have the prayer and selected the student who would give it made it "private speech," and therefore protected by the rules governing what is known as "limited public forums." The Court, however, found that the school district had not distanced itself far enough from a religious exercise by its two-step process. Call it what you will, the Court said, it amounts to an endorsement of religion. Consequently, the policy has no secular purpose, putting it at odds with the first prong of the *Lemon* test. As for the limited public forum argument, the Court denied that this was an instance of pri-vate speech, akin to an argument for or against political, or other, propo-sitions. Interestingly, the Court did stretch the voluntary attendance aspect, noting, without much proof, that going to athletic events is impor-tant in many communities, and one might actually feel compelled to attend.

When it comes to religious symbols on public property, the Court has had to draw some very difficult lines. The initial modern decision is *Stone v. Graham*, decided in 1980. The Kentucky legislature stipulated that the Ten Commandments were to be displayed in every classroom in the state. Trying to avoid at least the first criteria of the *Lemon* test, they attached the following note: "The secular application of the Ten Com-mandments is clearly seen in its adoption as the fundamental legal code of Western Civilization and the Common Law of the United States." Despite these words, the Court had no difficulty finding that there was no secular purpose to the legislation. "The preeminent purpose for posting the Ten Commandments on schoolroom walls is plainly religious in nature." The Court was signaling that it would look behind the formal words a legislative body might adopt.

Four years later the landmark case of *Lynch v. Donnelly* arrived on the Supreme Court's docket. Pawtucket, Rhode Island had long had a Christmas display at a downtown park. It included an array of secular images of the season, such as Santa Claus, reindeer, and so forth. However, it also included a crèche. The American Civil Liberties Union contended that the crèche's inclusion violated the establishment clause.

The majority justices invoked the *Lemon* test, as usual. However, they gave it an accommodationist slant. They began by saying that "In every Establishment Clause case, we must reconcile the inescapable tension between the objective of preventing unnecessary intrusion of either the church or the state upon the other, and the reality that, as the Court has often noted, total separation of the two is not possible." Following this generality, the Court held that the Constitution does not "requite complete separation of church and state; it affirmatively mandates accommodation, not merely tolerance, of all religions, and forbids hostility toward any." They then offered a survey of the history of how government has accommodated religion in the past, by presidential proclamations, for example.

Turning to the specifics of the *Lemon* test, they said that a governmental practice must be "motivated wholly" by religious goals to be invalid. The city in this instance was merely helping celebrate the holiday season (and helping downtown merchants). As for the second prong, any benefit to religion by displaying the crèche was remote. Thus, there was no primary effect of aiding religion. Finally, there was no administrative entanglement between church and state, as the city owned all the displayed material. In short, all three parts of the *Lemon* test were met.

Justice Sandra Day O'Connor wrote an oft-cited concurrence. Seeking to "clarify" the *Lemon* test, she proposed that the Court examine whether or not a governmental action "endorsed" or "disapproved of" religion. She famously said that "Endorsement sends a message to nonadherents that they are outsiders, not full members of the political community." "What is crucial is that a government practice not have the effect of communicating a message of government endorsement or disapproval of religion." Given the specific facts here, Pawtucket was doing neither in her view. But more important was how others were to come to see this test as a central part of establishment clause doctrine.

In *Allegheny County v. American Civil Liberties Union of Greater*

Pittsburgh (1989), the Court turned to the endorsement test rather than focusing strictly on the *Lemon* framework. As is often the case, details became important. Two different buildings and two different displays were at issue. At the county building, a crèche was erected annually at Christmas time by the Holy Name Society, a Catholic organization. It stood alone at a central location inside the building with a plaque attached indicating the sponsoring organization. Outside an adjacent building owned jointly by the city and the county, a menorah (a symbol indicating the Jewish holiday of Chanukah) was included in a display alongside a Christmas tree and a sign praising liberty. In a lengthy opinion, the Court held that the county had crossed over the line allowed by *Lynch* but that the menorah, being part of a more general display, was acceptable.

Finally, the Court decided two cases on the same day in 2005 that, on the surface at least, appear rather similar. A close inspection of the details, though, as before, explains why the justices went different ways in the two. In *McCreary County v. American Civil Liberties Union*, a Kentucky county had made several attempts to place the Ten Commandments on a courthouse wall. When local protests were made, the county twice modified the display by including various other documents. The second effort included several that, such as a letter from Abraham Lincoln, contained religious references. The third attempt inserted ones that serve, along with the Ten Commandments, as the foundations of the American legal system. These included Magna Carta and the Declaration of Independence, for example. A closely divided Court held, however, that looking at this history it was impossible not to see the religious purpose at work here. Thus, lacking any discernible secular purpose, the display had to come down. *Van Orden v. Perry* likewise dealt with the Ten Commandments. In 1961 the Fraternal Order of Eagles had presented the state of Texas with a monument containing the Commandments. The state placed it on the grounds of the state capitol, among 17 other monuments and 21 historical markers devoted to various aspects of Texas and American history. Again, the Court split 5–4 but upheld the validity of this monument. It said, first, that the *Lemon* test was not appropriate here, without explaining exactly why. "Instead, our analysis is driven both by the nature of the monument and by our Nation's history." Finding that the monument did not really show that the state was promulgating religion, and that many public places include monuments with religious themes, this one would pass muster. Apparently, the longevity of the monument and the fact that it had stood for over forty years without protest made it sharply different from the Kentucky display.

The Contours of Free Exercise Jurisprudence in 2005

The free exercise clause was clearly designed to protect individuals and religious bodies from government impinging on their liberty to worship as they pleased. With time, the clause has come to be understood to encompass much more than worship though.[7] Today, it is rare, although it does occasionally happen, for government policies to regulate worship. Rather, the usual case involves what are called "generally applicable laws." An individual or a religious group claims that they should be exempt from a law that applies to everyone else because if they are forced to obey the law it will entail violating their religious beliefs.

The seminal case is *Reynolds v. United States*, which came to the Court in 1879, following an attempt by the federal government to eradicate the Mormon practice of polygamy in the Utah Territory. The Court said that a distinction must be drawn between belief and action, and that while one could believe anything whatever, action could be constrained by government. The principle should be that you cannot assert free exercise to violate the criminal law. The door was left open, however, indirectly, to pursue this matter further. The Court explained that polygamy was such a deep affront to Western civilization that it had to be regulated. What, though, about less fundamental statutes?

The next major case did not come until 1963.[8] A Seventh Day Adventist in South Carolina was laid off from her job and filed for unemployment payments. She was offered other jobs but they all entailed her working on Saturday, her Sabbath. When she turned them down, the state denied her the unemployment benefits. In the ensuing case, *Sherbert v. Verner*, the Court held that the state must show a "compelling interest" to override her free exercise claims. In this instance, they found no compelling interest and ordered the state to pay what she was due. Thus, those wishing to assert a free exercise claim now had a stronger judicial ruling on which to rely.

Nevertheless, in the years following *Sherbert* very few free exercise claims were successful. Aside from several other cases involving unemployment insurance (such as a pacifist turning down a job at an arms factory [*Thomas v. Review Board of Indiana Employment Security Commission*, 1981]) and the Amish being allowed to take their children out of school before they reached the state's compulsory age for school attendance (*Wisconsin v. Yoder*, 1972), governments were usually able to show that they had a compelling interest in uniformly enforcing a particular law or regulation. A Jewish Air Force officer, for example, was not allowed to wear a yarmulke with his uniform; Native Americans were not allowed to block the Forest Service's plans to build a road through sacred land; a prison did not have to reshuffle work schedules to accommodate Muslim inmates' need to attend Friday worship services; a private university lost its tax exemption because it practiced racial discrimination despite its claim that its position was based on religious principles; and so forth.

In 1990 the Supreme Court took a step that generated most of the contemporary controversies over free exercise. In a case that seemed to everyone involved at the time to be a standard unemployment compensation case, the Court overturned the compelling interest test. In *Employment Division, Department of Human Resources of Oregon v. Smith*, two Native American drug counselors were dismissed from their posts because they ingested small amounts of peyote during a religious ceremony, as was customary in their religious tradition. When they filed for unemployment compensation, because peyote was illegal in Oregon, their applications were denied. In a 6–3 vote, the justices said that any future exemptions from generally applicable laws would have to be granted by the legislature.[9] Moreover, they would no longer apply the compelling interest test and would henceforth return to the belief versus action principle enunciated in *Reynolds.*

An immediate outcry came from virtually every religious body in the country, with petitions and pleas to Congress to "do something" about the decision. After several hearings and numerous discussions, Congress passed nearly unanimously (unanimously in the House and 97–3 in the Senate) the Religious Freedom Restoration Act (RFRA) in 1997. It ordered the Court to reinstate the compelling interest test in all free exercise cases, whether they came from local, state, or the federal government. Actually, it went one step further. In some areas the Court has applied what is known as the "strict scrutiny" test. This is a two-step test requiring that government show that it has a compelling interest in uniform enforcement of the law in question *and* that it has employed the least restrictive means to accomplish its goals. This constitutes a very high hurdle, which, while not impossible to scale, is very difficult to do. RFRA's provision stipulated both of these, thus moving beyond compelling interest alone.

It is perhaps necessary to briefly explain why Congress thought it had authority to order the Court to modify, or essentially overturn, one of its cases. This, in fact, was the central problem that engaged congressional experts as RFRA was under consideration. Recall first that the Fourteenth Amendment makes the First Amendment applicable to the states. Section five of the Fourteenth Amendment says that "Congress shall have power to enforce this article by appropriate legislation." Did this grant of authority include the power to overturn judicial interpretations of the amendment, and by implication the First Amendment also? Congress clearly thought so.

That belief was tested in 1997, at least as RFRA applied to state and local governments. A dispute over proposed modifications to a historic church which violated a city preservation ordinance in Boerne, Texas ended up at the Supreme Court in *City of Boerne v. Flores*. The church claimed that the city was violating RFRA by refusing it a building permit. The Court ruled that the law was unconstitutional because (1) it violated principles of federalism that the Congress which adopted the amendment wished to leave intact and (2) it was the job of the Supreme Court, and the Supreme Court alone, to interpret the Constitution. Later (in *Gonzales v. O Centro Espirita Beneficente Uniao do Vegetal*, 2006), the Court held that RFRA was valid as it applied to the federal government.[10] Congress, that is, could tie its own hands any way it wished.

When the *Boerne* decision was announced, many members of Congress were outraged. Intense discussions began about re-enacting RFRA but finding some alternative constitutional provision to base it on. As the so-called Religious Liberty Protection Act wound its way through Congress, though, a new development occurred. Gay and lesbian groups had secured antidiscrimination laws regarding employment and housing in several cities and states and feared, not entirely without reason, that such a law would give employers and landlords standing to challenge the new statutes. Their allies in Congress managed to block the new law. In the end, a compromise was worked out, with Congress enacting a law which would apply only to zoning and prisons. The Religious Land Use and Institutionalized Persons Act of 2000 (RLUIPA) mandated the strict scrutiny test in all free exercise cases in those two areas, regardless again of the level of government involved. (The main constitutional foundation, incidentally, was the taxing and spending clause. Since state and local governments receive federal grants, the federal government could attach conditions. The secondary one was the commerce clause, applicable here because religious bodies engage in commercial transactions that cross state lines.) RLUIPA's prison portion was upheld as constitutional in 2005 in *Cutter v. Wilkinson*. Several lower courts have also upheld the constitutionality of the land use provision, and the Supreme Court has left those decisions undisturbed, presumably making it constitutional as well.

Conclusion

Although demarking Supreme Court eras by the service of chief justices is always a bit artificial, the Court often does assume a definable tenor under a given chief. Thus, we conventionally refer confidently to the Warren Court and the Burger Court, for example. So it is with Chief Justice John Roberts. Without question, its defining ethos is "conservatism." Moreover, it is a conservatism that became more pronounced with the appointment of Samuel Alito to replace Sandra Day O'Connor, something that resulted in the move of Justice Anthony Kennedy to the role of "swing justice." We will have ample opportunity to observe the importance of Justice Kennedy's place on the Court in several of the cases we examine in the following chapters.

Yet, church-state issues do not easily beak down into the conventional categories of conservative and liberal, as there are several crosscurrents. To be sure, we will discover the conservative/liberal voting dichotomy in several cases. At the same time, though, we will see unanimous opinions in some others. Further, we will sometimes find the conservative and liberal blocs split up in unusual fashion. That is why to understand how the Roberts Court has handled church-state issues it is important to take up the cases one by one, a task to which we now turn.

CHAPTER 3

Challenging President Bush's Faith-Based Initiative

Hein v. Freedom from Religion Foundation

The first church-state case the Supreme Court faced after Chief Justice Roberts' appointment did not deal directly with the religion clauses. Instead, it was decided on the issue of standing. Nevertheless, it is an important case, for standing is a major question when it comes to the establishment clause. Stated simply, the essence is Who can bring a challenge to a law that purportedly violates the establishment clause?

The traditional view of standing is that a person (or other entity, such as a business firm) must have suffered, or is in danger of suffering, some direct loss if the statute or governmental practice at issue is implemented. This can be seen most clearly in the area of criminal justice and the strictures contained in the fourth, fifth, sixth, and eighth amendments. If my trial violated any of these, I will obviously suffer—a fine, prison, or perhaps even execution. Or, consider the First Amendment's free speech clause, barring government from impinging on my right to speak out on matters of public concern. Less dramatically, but still importantly, if I own a business and a particular law or regulation will raise my costs and thereby lower my profits, I am being harmed. In any of these cases, I have clear standing to bring a suit attempting to overturn the governmental action.

Standing and the Establishment Clause

The establishment clause is more complicated, however. How does someone claim an injury? One possibility, if some type of government funding is involved, is a taxpayer suit. The 1786 Virginia Statute for Religious Freedom, authored by Thomas Jefferson, contains the proposition on which such a suit could rest: "[N]o man shall be compelled to ... support any religious worship, place or ministry whatsoever." Until the 1960s, nevertheless, the Supreme Court looked askance at taxpayer suits of any kind. The signal case was *Frothingham v. Mellon,* decided in 1923. There, a taxpayer challenged a federal appropriation for a public health program on the grounds that it violated the tenth amendment,[1] because it intruded on a policy area allegedly reserved to the states. Refusing to consider the merits of this argument, the Supreme Court held that:

> [I]interest in the moneys of the Treasury ... is shared with millions of others; is comparatively minute and indeterminable; and the effect upon future taxation ... so remote, fluctuating and uncertain that no basis is afforded for an appeal to the preventive powers of a court...
>
> The administration of any statute, likely to produce additional taxation to be imposed upon a vast number of taxpayers, the extent of whose several liability is indefinite and constantly changing, is essentially a matter of public and not of individual concern.

In short, the remedy for Mr. Frothingham, and any other aggrieved party, is to petition Congress, not come to the courts.

Echoing this position, the Court reiterated in 1952 (this time, importantly, in an establishment clause case, *Doremus v. Board of Education of Hawthorne*) that "the interests of a taxpayer in the moneys of the federal treasury are too indeterminable, remote, uncertain and indirect to furnish a basis for an appeal" to the courts.

In 1968, though, under the leadership of Chief Justice Earl Warren, the Court, in the case of *Flast v. Cohen,* lowered the standing requirements considerably. Here, too, this was a case that dealt directly with the establishment clause. A group of taxpayers was seeking to have the portion of federal funds allocated to religious schools under the Elementary and Secondary Education Act of 1965 declared invalid. Allowing the taxpayers to have standing, the justices claimed that they were only creating a narrow exception to the previous holdings. Technically, that was true; but the practicality was that many more taxpayer suits now had a chance of at least getting in the courthouse door. Furthermore, we should perhaps add, given the increasing secularism of the Warren Court, they also had a greater chance of success on the merits.

Returning to the matter of standing, what the Court said was that to obtain a hearing, a plaintiff had to successfully assert two propositions:

> First, the taxpayer must establish a logical link between that status and the type of legislative enactment attacked. Thus, a taxpayer will be a proper party to allege the unconstitutionality only of exercises of congressional power under the taxing

> and spending clause…. It will not be sufficient to allege an incidental expenditure of funds in the administration of an essentially regulatory statute…. Secondly, the taxpayer must establish a nexus between that status and the precise nature of the constitutional infringement alleged. Under this requirement, the taxpayer must show that the challenged enactment exceeds specific constitutional limitations imposed upon the exercise of the congressional taxing and spending power and not simply that the enactment is generally beyond the powers delegated to Congress….

This rule may sound as though it imposes a high barrier, but in practice it is accordion like. Loosely applied, it opens the door to any number of challenges; strictly applied, it can serve as almost as high a fence to scale as the old test. In this instance, the Court allowed the challenge, and in subsequent cases found the test met also. At the same time, parallel rules were applied when it came to state and local expenditures.

For several years, therefore, the broad interpretation of *Flast* held sway. Think of the establishment clause cases we discussed in the previous chapter, for example. However, it was never a blanket welcome mat and the Court periodically adopted a more restrictive reading, barring the pathway to the judicial forum. As early as 1982, for example, it ruled that an action by the executive branch, as opposed to Congress, could not meet the *Flast* test. This, too, was an establishment clause case, involving the transfer of surplus federal property to religiously based institutions of higher education. Thus, the law of standing regarding the establishment clause was in something of a state of flux when *Hein v. Freedom from Religion Foundation* came to the Court in 2006.

The Bush Administration's "Faith-Based Initiative"

The federal government provides funds to a wide variety of social welfare agencies to bolster their work. For many years, though, there was a hesitancy to allow religiously based organizations to participate in these programs, for fear of violating the establishment clause. Many critics have long argued, however, that institutions connected to religious bodies do admirable work and do it effectively and efficiently. If they could obtain federal funds for their work, therefore, public policies would be more effectively administered and probably at lower cost. Both of these propositions are undoubtedly true.

Opponents of having church related organizations participate in federal social welfare programs make several counterarguments however. One group, militant secularists, not surprisingly, are against any amount of public monies going to any religious body whatever. More moderate analysts, though, worry about the entanglement that would ensue should public funds be given to religious groups. How would public authorities make sure that the money was spent as appropriated? Some type of auditing would be necessary to make that assurance. Having public officials entering religious buildings and demanding to "see the books" is worrisome on several fronts. Recall the third prong of the *Lemon* test. Further, money is fungible and what government gave to a religious social welfare organization would free up other money for more explicitly religious purposes. Indirectly, then, government would be supporting religion. Others, usually thoughtfully and sincerely, argued that one of the reasons religious organizations are so successful is that they combine social welfare work with religious proselytizing. If they jettison that aspect of their programs, they will become just like any secular social welfare organization, and everyone will lose rather than gain. Others, especially many within the religious community, have pointed out that taking the state's money is always dangerous. The state may not start out demanding that you meet all its regulatory demands but the requirements will inevitably creep in. What about antidiscrimination in hiring statutes when it comes to sexual orientation, for example? What about advocating alternatives to abortion? And on and on. Taking money from the federal spigot will, these people maintain, stifle religious bodies' ability to remain independent.

President George W. Bush and his administration took the position that faith-based organizations could compete for federal funds without impairing either the secular character of the programs or the ability of the organizations to maintain their religious character. Less than two weeks after entering office, by executive order the president created the White House Office of Faith-Based and Community Initiatives. Funding was obtained from general executive branch appropriations. These are monies that Congress grants the executive branch to use without specifying what exactly they should be spent for. In addition to creating this office, the president also established a number of "centers" in five federal departments that had a similar purpose. Both the White House Office and the centers were to see that religious groups "have the fullest opportunity permitted by law to compete on a level playing field, so long as they achieve valid public purposes" and maintain "pluralism, nondiscrimination, evenhandedness, and neutrality." Obviously, it was federal money that was at issue, and the president ordered that no "organization should be discriminated against on the basis of religion or religious belief in the administration or distribution of Federal financial assistance under social service programs." To publicize the new policies, the administration dispatched several officials to give public speeches in various forums and also held a number of conferences and grant-writing workshops around the country, to which leaders of social welfare organizations, both religious and secular, were invited. The speeches and conferences were both financed through the White House Office for Faith-Based and Community Initiatives.[2]

The whole enterprise, but especially the speeches and conferences, was challenged by the Freedom from Religion Foundation (FFRF). Their contention was that these activities promoted religion and were therefore violations of the establishment clause. But the first stumbling block was standing.

The Foundation took the position that its members were federal tax-payers and therefore met the *Flast* test. A Federal District Court in Wisconsin, however, took a different view. It held that the activities engaged in by the administration were executive in character and "not exercises of congressional power." Consequently, the first prong of the *Flast* test had not been met. The FFRF therefore had no standing to bring the case. The Court of Appeals reversed this holding, since in its view the programs rested on financing from a congressional appropriation, even if it was indirect. Accordingly, as long as any one taxpayer's stake in the program is greater than zero, he/she can bring a suit seeking a ruling on an establishment clause violation. The government appealed to the Supreme Court.

The Opinion of the Court

The Court split 3–2–4 in this case. Justice Alito wrote the plurality opinion of the Court, holding that the FFRF lacked standing, but only Roberts and Kennedy endorsed his approach. Kennedy, in fact, even filed a separate concurring opinion elaborating his views. Justice Scalia also filed a concurring opinion, which agreed that the government should win, but sharply disagreed with Alito's conclusions. Justice Thomas signed on to his opinion. Justice Souter wrote a dissenting opinion, which was joined by Justices Ginsburg, Stevens, and Breyer.

Justice Alito begins his opinion by noting the demands of Article III—the section of the Constitution constructing and empowering the federal judiciary—that matters brought to the courts must be in the guise of a "case or controversy." In essence, this means that abstract questions of law, unless raised by a specific set of facts in an actual case, will not be considered. He quotes from the venerable 1803 case of *Marbury v. Madi-*

son that the courts will not pass on "the constitutionality of an act ... unless obliged to do so in the proper performance of our judicial function, when the question is raised by a party whose interests entitle him to raise it." He then reviews *Frothingham* and stresses that that case is still the appropriate precedent.

Flast, he emphasizes, was but a narrow exception to *Frothingham*'s general proposition. "The expenditures challenged in *Flast* ... were funded by a specific congressional appropriation and were disbursed to private schools (including religiously affiliated schools) pursuant to a direct and unambiguous congressional mandate." That link, however, is missing in the current case. FFRF does "not challenge any specific congressional action or appropriation; nor do they ask the Court to invalidate any congressional enactment or legislatively created program as unconstitutional." Lacking that, their petition must fail for lack of standing.

Three previous cases buttress this point, he says. One was the 1982 case we mentioned earlier, *Valley Forge Christian College v. Americans United for Separation of Church and State.* There, the transfer of some federal property to a Christian college was being challenged. But, as noted above, crucially according to the Court, the transfer had been made by an executive agency; thus the taxing and spending clause was not involved, making the *Flast* exception inapplicable.[3] In an even earlier case, *Schlesinger v. Reservists Committee to Stop the War*, decided in 1974, an attempt to have the Court declare that members of Congress could not simultaneously hold commissions in the Armed Forces Reserves was turned aside. Again, because it was within the purview of the executive to appoint reserve officers, the plaintiffs had no standing as taxpayers. (The basis of the challenge was the "incompatibility clause," which forbids members of the legislature from holding an executive office.[4]) In a similar vein, a group of taxpayers in another 1974 case (*United States v. Richardson*) sought to force the executive to publish the budget of the Central Intelligence Agency. Certainly, here there was a colorable claim that moneys were being appropriated by Congress but hidden from public view inasmuch as CIA expenditures are embedded in the budgets of other agencies by congressional order. Nonetheless, the Court held that Congress could not be compelled to order the executive to publish the budget via a taxpayer suit.

One case seemed to lean the other way, and the FFRF stressed it in its argument before the Court. In *Bowen v. Kendrick* (1988), the Court had allowed taxpayers to challenge grants to religious groups made under the Adolescent Family Life Act. The plaintiffs were successful despite the fact that the funds themselves were given out by the executive branch. But, Alito contended, the money was being spent to carry out a specific congressional mandate. "Unlike this case, *Kendrick* involved a 'program of disbursement of funds pursuant to Congress' taxing and spending powers.'"

FFRF acknowledged that if *Flast* were read too loosely it would allow almost unlimited standing, which they knew the Court would not go along with. The Court of Appeals had gone almost that far with its anything above zero marginal cost to a taxpayer postulate. What FFRF asked the Court to do was adopt a "traceability" rule. That is, if an expenditure by the executive branch could be reasonably traced to a congressional enactment, then the taxpayers had standing. Alito, however, says this would be in practice an illimitable rule, demolishing the *Flast* requirements. Furthermore, it would raise serious separation of powers issues, as the Court would be called on to police the entire federal budget.

While maintaining the legitimacy of the *Flast* test, he, and presumably the other two justices who joined his opinion, nevertheless indicated that it was not entirely satisfactory. Even with its limitations, it might not give adequate weight to separation of powers concerns. Giving weight to this issue would argue even more strongly for a narrow reading of the case. Seemingly, even while they were allowing *Flast* to stand then, the plurality was suggesting that it could be denuded of meaning in the future. In short, *Flast* would remain a controlling precedent, but it would be read very narrowly and certainly would not be expanded.

As an aside, this is a clear instance of what is known as "judicial minimalism." Judges should, according to this maxim, decide cases on the narrowest possible grounds, thereby keeping the law stable and avoiding overturning precedents. This will, it is said, allow the law to develop more slowly and more incrementally.[5]

Concurring and Dissenting Opinions

Justice Kennedy, while joining Alito's opinion, wrote a concurrence. He wished to stress the separation of powers issues that would arise should the plaintiffs prevail. The Supreme Court is not, he contends, the only oracle on the meaning of the Constitution.[6] It is up to the president and Congress to perform their duties in light of the Constitution.

> It must be remembered that, even where parties have no standing to sue, members of the Legislative and Executive Branches are not excused from making con-

stitutional determinations in the regular course of their duties. Government officials must make a conscious decision to obey the Constitution whether or not
their acts can be challenged in a court of law and then must conform their actions
to these principled determinations.

Justice Scalia's persuasive concurrence embodies the clear logic and
flowery flourishes for which he was famous. In his view, the proper way
to decide this case was to straightforwardly overrule *Flast.*

He begins by setting up two differing ways that taxpayers might con-
ceivably be "injured" by alleged establishment clause violations: "wallet
injury" and "psychic injury." Since wallet injury always involves such
minute sums to an individual taxpayer, the Court has, without really
spelling out why, resorted to a version of psychic injury. This has led to
two basic problems. "We have never explained why Psychic Injury was
insufficient in the cases in which standing was denied, and we have never
explained why Psychic Injury, however limited, is cognizable under Article
III."

If we look closely at a comparison between *Frothingham* and *Doremus*
on the one hand and *Flast* on the other, we can see that *Flast's* two prongs
were designed to evade the other two cases. The first prong supposedly
differentiated *Flast* from *Doremus* but in reality it failed to do so. The
Flast majority tried to say that the congressionally mandated expenditures
in the Elementary and Secondary Education Act were not the same as the
"regulatory statute" that required Bible reading in *Doremus* but surely,
Scalia says, "If taxpayers upset with the government giving money to
parochial schools had standing to sue, so should the taxpayers who disapproved of the government paying public-school teachers to read the
Bible," and similarly so with *Frothingham* and the second prong. The lim-
itation on government spending imposed by the establishment clause is
no more important than other limitations the Constitution contains. So
why give weight to one and not the others? He then takes up the subsequent taxpayer standing cases and argues that "coherence and candor
fared no better" there.

The truth is, of course, that the expenditures at issue here are for all
material purposes like those in *Flast.* The psychic injury claimed by the
members of FFRF is no less because the actual checks were written from
a general rather than a specific appropriation of Congress. Thus, the only
logical course of action is to either grant the taxpayers standing here or
overrule *Flast.* Scalia acknowledges that "[m]inimalism is an admirable
judicial trait" but stresses that it should not be followed when "it comes
at the cost of meaningless and disingenuous distinctions that hold the

sure promise of engendering further meaningless and disingenuous distinctions in the future."

Because *Flast* relies on psychic injury, the answer has to be that it was a mistake and should be overruled. "Is a taxpayer's purely psychological displeasure that his funds are being spent in an allegedly unlawful manner ever sufficiently concrete and particularized to support Article III standing? The answer is plainly no." An individual taxpayer has no "particularized" grievance that is different from the interests of all other citizens, which means such matters are best settled in the political arena. Furthermore, *Flast* did not give adequate weight to separation of powers concerns, something even the plurality at least hints at. As "damaged goods" it therefore needs to be consigned to the waste bin.

He then makes a further nod to the virtues of minimalism but argues that they should not apply here.

> Overruling prior precedents, even precedents as disreputable as *Flast,* is nevertheless a serious undertaking, and I understand the impulse to take a minimalist approach. But laying just claim to be honoring *stare decisis* requires more than beating *Flast* to a pulp and then sending it out to the lower courts weakened, denigrated, more incomprehensible than ever, and yet somehow technically alive. Even before the addition of the new meaningless distinction devised by today's plurality, taxpayer standing in Establishment Clause cases has been a game of chance.

Justice David Souter penned an enlightening dissenting opinion, joined by Justices Stevens, Ginsburg, and Breyer. He argues, first off, that the plaintiffs here are in no different position from those in *Flast*. Granting them standing would not, as the plurality avows, extend *Flast* but merely apply it. The fact that the executive spent the money from a discretionary fund is immaterial. Surely, he points out, if the Department of Health and Human Services built a chapel with discretionary monies, there would be no doubt that a challenge could be mounted.

As for precedent, *Bowen* should be the controlling case here. It was less important there than Alito wants to claim that the funds came from a direct congressional appropriation. The executive was actually making the expenditures and the Court granted the taxpayers standing, as should be done here.

But his more important point moves beyond how *Flast* and *Bowen* should be read. He brings up the rationale behind the establishment clause. Its whole purpose was to prohibit government from supporting religion, and which branch of government might be at fault in a given instance is irrelevant. If the Court denies taxpayers standing to question such governmental actions in court then "Establishment Clause protection would melt away."

Conclusion

If we shift to the actual outcome in this case, it can be viewed from several different perspectives. As for a study in Supreme Court decision making, as mentioned, it is a classic case of judicial minimalism. Justice Alito and the other members of the plurality were clearly trying to avoid overturning a long-standing precedent and did so by stressing a legalistic—in the worst sense of the word—distinction between money spent in accordance with a specific as opposed to a general congressional appropriation. However, pursuing this is not our chief concern.

On the matter of substantive jurisprudence, Scalia and the dissenters are surely correct: either *Flast* should have been followed or overturned. Whether it should be or not is a hugely important issue in constitutional jurisprudence. The consequence of discarding the case's precedential value, would, as Souter said, be that challenges to establishment clause violations (at least those involving federal funds) will largely disappear from the courtroom. No one will have standing to bring them. A prohibition on government action embedded in the Constitution will be all but free from judicial invalidation. This would wade into the matter of whether constitutional issues should always be adjudicated by the Supreme Court, an issue that has lately attracted increased attention.[7]

On judicial ideology, it is easy to see that, despite Scalia's and Thomas's disagreement with the plurality, the decision itself split exactly along conservative/liberal lines. The five conservatives voted to uphold a policy desired by traditional religious groups while the liberals stood by the secularists. If we are keeping a box score of wins and losses, this one unmistakably goes to the traditional religionists.

What, though, about the actual impact of the case? In practical terms, Alito has all but emasculated *Flast* without overruling it. This means that for this type of establishment clause cases at least, where the expenditure of federal funds is at issue, the matter is transferred to the elected branches, to be subject to the vagaries of electoral politics and the constitutional judgments of Congress and whoever the sitting president is. For example, less than a month after entering office President Obama modified the thrust of this program. He renamed the office within the White House the Office of Faith Based and Neighborhood Partnerships. Its "top priority" was to make "community groups an integral part of our economic recovery and poverty a burden fewer will have to bear when recovery is complete." Further, its work will be done "in a way that upholds the Constitution...." The White House also took pains to note that "separation of church and state is a principle President Obama supports firmly...." Later, in November 2010, Obama issued an executive order placing further restrictions on religious groups that took federal funds; however, he did not end their ability to discriminate in hiring, something a number of secular groups wanted. While not dispensing entirely, therefore, with the encouraging of religious groups to solicit federal grants, the wording of the initial order and the actions taken subsequently speak of a much different approach. What FFRF and its allies could not gain in court, they largely obtained through having a friendlier occupant in the White House. Of course, this could have been done even if *Hein* had gone the other way. Importantly, though, should another president decide to return to the Bush approach, if *Hein* stands, he or she will be free to do so. As of this writing, the Trump administration has not abolished the office, but has not named someone to head it and its website is no longer active.

CHAPTER 4

Who Can Put a Monument in a Public Park?

Pleasant Grove City v. Summum

This case bears some resemblances to the previous one but also has some important differences. Like *Hein*, it was decided on the basis of another constitutional provision, here the free speech clause, rather than the religion clauses, even though for all intents and purposes it was an establishment clause case, something Justice Scalia again unhesitatingly pointed out. Like *Hein*, too, it was a victory for traditional religion. In contrast to *Hein*, however, this was a unanimous decision. Justice Alito once again wrote the majority opinion and he was joined by seven of his fellow justices. Of note, though, three of these other justices in the majority—Stevens, Scalia, and Breyer—felt moved to pen concurrences, adding their elaborations and qualifications. Only David Souter demurred from endorsing the majority opinion, and he too explained his reasons in a concurrence.

The Facts of the Case

The city of Pleasant Grove, Utah, was home to a public park in which stood 15 monuments, including one which bore the Ten Commandments. It had been donated to the city in 1971 by the Fraternal Order of Eagles, the same organization that had been responsible for erecting the Ten Commandments monument on the Texas state capitol grounds at issue in *Van Orden v. Perry*. A Salt Lake City religious group known as Summum asked permission to place a monument in the park setting out the "Seven Aphorisms of Summum." The city council announced that it only considered monuments for the city park that either directly related to the history of Pleasant Grove or were sponsored by groups with "longstanding ties" to the community. Summum's proposed monument fitting neither of these, the request was rejected. This action was upheld by the District Court. However, the Court of Appeals reversed this decision and ordered the city to accept the monument. The city, in turn, appealed this ruling to the Supreme Court.

The Opinion of the Court

Focusing on the free speech clause, Alito recognized that there were two lines of precedents that might be applied, and that this particular set of facts had not come to the Court before. On one side, there is a long stream of cases involving "traditional public forums." In such a setting, reasonable "time, place, and manner" restrictions may be adopted by the government responsible for the public forum, but the content of an individual's or group's speech may not be regulated. Public streets and areas such as public parks have always been viewed as such forums, meaning government may not favor one viewpoint over another there. On the other side, there are a number of cases addressing the issue of government speech. That is, what are the rules when an entity of government itself "speaks"? Although there are some restrictions, such as the prohibitions of the establishment clause and the equal protection clause, by and large government is exempt from the First Amendment's free speech clause under these circumstances. In essence, government may speak its own mind without censure from the Courts. Presumably, political checks will serve to keep government from going too far in such speech. Was the Ten Commandments monument, therefore, one that gave the Eagles a privilege of speaking in a public forum, or was it, since it was formally accepted by the city council, government speech? The Court of Appeals held that the traditional public forum analysis was the correct one, and applying "strict scrutiny" (that government had to show a compelling interest in the policy at issue and that it had adopted the least restrictive means to accomplish its goals) found for Summum. Alito, however, felt that the Supreme Court had to address the question anew. Here is how he laid out the issue.

> No prior decision of this Court has addressed the application of the Free Speech Clause to a government entity's acceptance of privately donated, permanent monuments for installation in a public park, and the parties disagree sharply about the line of precedents that governs this situation. Petitioners [the city] contend that

the pertinent cases are those concerning government speech. Respondent [Summum], on the other hand, agrees with the Court of Appeals panel that the applicable cases are those that analyze private speech in a public forum. The parties' fundamental disagreement thus centers on the nature of petitioners' conduct when they permitted privately donated monuments to be erected in Pioneer Park. Were petitioners engaging in their own expressive conduct? Or were they providing a forum for private speech?

He begins by stating that governments have the right to speak for themselves, and retain that right even when they are receiving "assistance from private sources for the purpose of delivering a government-controlled message." Coming down clearly on the side of the city, he says that "Permanent monuments displayed on public property typically represent government speech."

To buttress this conclusion, looking to history, he points out that governments have from ancient times used monuments to convey various messages. As for the question of private funding, he argues that when government accepts the monument, it is endorsing the message it is designed to send. Throughout American history governments have followed a policy of "selective receptivity" in accepting donated monuments. He offers some examples of local governments turning down monuments when they did not wish to be seen as supporting the message of the monument. "The monuments that are accepted, therefore, are meant to convey and have the effect of conveying a government message, and they thus constitute government speech."

Prepared for this argument, Summum proposed that each time a monument is donated to a government for placement on public property that the appropriate public body formally adopt a resolution "embracing" the message of the proposed monument. This would force the government to skate awfully close to, if not over, the line drawn by the establishment clause. Alito's response was that monuments can convey more than one message. The Vietnam Memorial, for example, or the monument with John Lennon's "Imagine" in Central Park in New York, have different meanings for different people. Further "when a privately donated memorial is funded by many small donations, the donors themselves may differ in their interpretation of the monument's significance." Indeed, the meaning of monuments may change over time. For example, the Statute of Liberty has stood for several different viewpoints since it was donated by France to the American people. Consequently, a requirement that government formally embrace the specific meaning of a monument would pose too stringent a rule for practicality.

The difference between monuments and the traditional public forums of public parks also overrides a rule stipulating that all parks must adopt "content neutral" policies with regard to privately donated monuments. As a traditional public forum, a public park can accommodate any number of speakers or demonstrations. A monument, though, occupies space permanently, limiting the number that can be erected. No public park can have an unlimited number of monuments, which would be necessary if government were forced to be truly neutral among various groups. "The obvious truth of the matter is that if public parks were considered to be traditional public forums for the purpose of erecting privately donated monuments, most parks would have little choice but to refuse all such donations."

In sum, the monuments placed in Pleasant Grove's park are government speech, and the city is not obligated to accept any and all privately donated monuments.

The Concurring Opinions

Justice Stevens, with whom Justice Ginsburg joined, wanted to restrict the government speech doctrine, lest it become a wide door for government to escape judicial oversight. It is, he stresses, of relatively recent vintage, and should not be made rigid before subsequent cases are heard. He thought that "the reasons justifying the city's refusal would have been equally valid if its acceptance of the monument, instead of being characterized as 'government speech,' had merely been deemed an implicit endorsement of the donor's message." Although the opinion in the decision at hand does not expand the government speech doctrine, some of the precedents hint at that, and that could become worrisome. For the moment, political checks are adequate safeguards against abuse of the government speech doctrine, but governments need to be warned that the establishment clause and the equal protection clause could be grounds for challenging government speech in the future.

Justice Scalia (in a concurring opinion joined by Justice Thomas), displaying his usual penchant for separating the wheat from the chaff, was wont to point out that even though this case was argued and decided under the free speech clause, and that he endorsed the Court's opinion "in full," it was "obvious that from the start, this case has been litigated in the shadow of the First Amendment's *Establishment* Clause." (Emphasis in original.) The city, aware of the precarious position it might be in, was trying to avoid "associating itself too closely with the Ten Commandments monument." If it did so, it might be charged with an establishment clause violation. If fact, had Summum's proposal, requiring Pleasant Grove to specifically endorse the monument's meaning, been imposed on the city, it would have been hard to avoid the establishment clause's reach, something undoubtedly behind the idea in the first place.

In Scalia's view, *Van Orden v. Perry* should govern here. The Pleasant Grove monument shared all the characteristics of the one involved in Texas—a message with historical content, its placement with other monuments, its funding by a private organization, and its longevity—which had led the Court to reject an establishment clause challenge there.[1] Thus, no part of the First Amendment is offended by Pleasant Grove's allowing this monument in their park. "The city can safely exhale. Its residents and visitors can now return to enjoying Pioneer Park's wishing well, its historic granary—and, yes, even its Ten Commandments monument—without fear that they are complicit in an establishment of religion."

Justice Breyer is keen to stress that the Court must exercise care about applying categories regarding free speech without considering the purposes behind the speech. Decisions should rest on whether a disproportionate burden is placed on free speech compared to the pursuit of "a legitimate government objective." Here, granted, Pleasant Grove's action restricts Summum's free speech rights to a degree. However, they are not being denied use of the park to engage in speech, say, by holding a rally or other act. Thus, the restriction is not disproportionate. The city is merely reserving some spaces in the park to "further other than free-speech goals. And that is perfectly proper."

Justice Souter, the only member of the Court not to sign the majority opinion, was worried about how the government speech doctrine would interact with establishment clause jurisprudence in the future. Citing Justice Stevens' point about the newness of the government speech doctrine, he urged caution. Clearly, he says "there is no doubt that this case and its government speech claim has been litigated by the parties with one eye on the Establishment Clause."

Specifically, in light of the majority opinion in this case, a wise government will want to be sure that it has a number of non-religious monuments near any religious ones it accepts. But if there are a multitude of monuments, then it will be "less intuitively obvious that the government is speaking in its own right simply by maintaining the monuments." Moreover, if there are several monuments standing on public property, suspicions might well surface "that some of the displays were not government speech at all (or at least had an equally private character associated with private donors)." If so, then another establishment clause issue would arise: the prohibition on government preferring one religious viewpoint over others. Could merely labeling the placing of a monument on public property government speech free it from this stricture? Souter did not propose answers. He merely wanted to stress that "It is simply unclear how the relatively new category of government speech will relate to the more traditional categories of Establishment Clause analysis." It is not time to decide these matters now, he said, but it is important to "keep the inevitable issues open."

A good starting point, in his view, would be to utilize Justice O'Connor's endorsement test. Would a "reasonable and fully informed observer" see a particular monument as "government speech, as distinct from private speech the government chooses to oblige by allowing the monument to be placed on public land."

As for this case, adopting such a view would allow Pleasant Grove to claim this as government speech. Consequently, they acted within the bounds of the demands of the Constitution.

Conclusion

This case clearly illustrates the clash between a time when traditional religion was closely identified with society and government and the contemporary rise of diversity. When the monument was placed there, Will Herberg's ideas, even if no one on the city council might have read his book, held sway. The broad ecumenism of Judeo-Christian values was simply accepted. Now, though, new religious groups such as Summum are elbowing for a place at the table. Furthermore, public displays of the Ten Commandments have taken on a different meaning to many. They are often seen, by both proponents and opponents, as part of the efforts of conservative Christians to reassert the central place of traditional religion. The Kentucky courthouse case, for instance, is a good example.

Nevertheless, traditional religion won this case hands down. Both liberal and conservative justices sided with the city and turned aside Summum's demands. Critics have been quick to pounce on this decision. Jessie Hill, arguing from a more secularist perspective, has argued that a strict separation calls for a presumption against all monuments of religious theme.[2] It would, in her eyes, be a rebuttable presumption, legally; however, it would be a high wall to climb. In all likelihood, following her approach would necessitate the taking down of almost all monuments with religious messages. Leslie Griffin reaches a similar conclusion by coming at the issue from the diversity standpoint. She contends that the Founders were concerned about tolerance when they laid out the religion clauses.[3] To be sure, in their days, tolerance meant not discriminating against the multitude of minority Protestant sects, Catholics, and Jews. But the principle was still a broad tolerance. Applied today, that same principle would mean granting legitimacy to Buddhists, Muslims, Hindus, and all others that make up American religious diversity. This would mean that cities such as Pleasant Grove would either have to accept all comers or take down the monuments that favor one group over another.

Mary Jean Dolan has proposed a middle ground between Alito's opinion and these critics. She grounds her analysis in "social meaning" theory. This term was discussed by Lawrence Lessig in the 1990s, and defined by Lawrence Sager and Christopher Eisgruber later as "the meaning that a competent participant in the society in question would see in that event or expression."[4] Now, obviously, social meaning can change with time. Lessing offers the examples of the Confederate flag taking on new meaning with its adoption by anti-integration Southerners in the 1950s and 1960s and how the country of Ecuador sought to change its national identity through the incorporation of more of its Indian heritage. Applied to the Ten Commandments, the changes noted above need to be taken into account, Dolan says. Therefore, she proposes that the Court should establish a two-prong test regarding monuments in public places: "(1) requiring a clear disclaimer explaining government's intended secular message and (2) imposing strict neutrality requirements on any future public monuments with religious themes."[5] Thus, she is drawing a line between monuments already in place and future ones. Those erected back when the link between Judeo-Christian and American identity was accepted would largely be given a pass, provided a government could reasonably claim some secular meaning. Ones offered up in our day, however, would be subject to a more stringent test, which realistically few could meet.

For the moment, though, none of these critics would seem to have much standing in the Roberts Court. A unanimous Court held for Pleasant Grove, and given subsequent decisions we will discuss, there would seem to be little appetite for significant change.

CHAPTER 5

Must a Cross from World War I Be Removed from What Was Federal Property?

Salazar v. Buono

We have here yet another case, which, technically, at the Supreme Court in any event, was decided on an issue removed from the establishment clause. Nevertheless, it is clearly an establishment clause case in all but name. Reinforcing the notion that this is at heart an establishment clause case is the fact that the justices split along conservative/liberal lines. Had it been merely a technical issue regarding the law of injunctions, as it is on the surface, such a split would seem unlikely. Justice Kennedy played his role as swing justice, here voting with the conservatives. Chief Justice Roberts selected him to write the opinion for the Court; it only carried a plurality, however. The facts can become a bit tedious, but it is important to keep them in mind as we analyze the decision.

The Facts of the Case

The Mojave National Preserve, administered by the National Park Service, comprises over one and a half million acres within the 25,000 square miles of the Mojave Desert in southern California. In 1934, a local chapter of the Veterans of Foreign Wars erected a simple Latin cross on an outcropping known as Sunrise Rock in the National Preserve. The purpose of the cross was to commemorate American soldiers who had perished in World War I. Over the years, the original cross was repaired and replaced on several occasions, the cost always being borne by private groups or individual citizens. The most recent replacement had taken place in 1998, the work being done this time by a private citizen, Henry Sandoz, who owned a ranch nearby and had been a friend of one of the original VFW members who had been instrumental in having the cross erected. Sandoz had promised his friend he would see that the cross remained and was kept up.[1] At one time, a sign explained the origin and purpose of the cross, but during this litigation the sign was no longer there. Through the years, Easter services had been held by various local churches at the cross. Of some relevance, perhaps, a local Buddhist congregation had asked permission to erect a monument of its own on Sunrise Rock, but their request had been turned down by the Park Service. Finally, the cross is not visible from the nearest highway, but there is a publicly maintained campground nearby.

In 2002, a retired Park Service employee, Frank Buono, represented by the American Civil Liberties Union, filed a suit in a Federal District Court asserting that he was offended by the presence of the cross on public land. He claimed it violated the establishment clause and asked the court to issue an injunction to the Park Service mandating that it remove the cross.

After determining that Mr. Buono had standing to bring the action, the District Court turned to the *Lemon* test to decide the appropriateness of the injunction. Recall that this test requires that a government action (1) have a secular purpose, (2) have a primary effect that "neither advances nor inhibits religion," and (3) not entail "excessive entanglement" between government and religious bodies. The District Court chose to put aside the first and third portions of the test and focus exclusively on the second. In order to address the question raised by the second section of the test, the District Court utilized Justice O'Connor's endorsement test. Would the presence of the cross on federal land be perceived by a "reasonable observer" as a governmental endorsement of religion? The judge answered in the affirmative and consequently issued the injunction requested by Buono, forbidding the government "from permitting the display of the Latin cross in the area of Sunrise Rock in the Mojave National Preserve." The phrase "permitting the display" was purposely drawn to circumvent any contention that the cross was erected and maintained by private parties. Following this decision, the Park Service put a plywood covering around the cross, pending the government's appeal.

The Court of Appeal upheld both Buono's standing and the legitimacy of the injunction. The government did not appeal this decision to the Supreme Court. For this reason, the decision of the Court of Appeals on the establishment clause question became final. That is, when the case did end up at the Supreme Court, it had to take the establishment clause issue as settled. Nonetheless, as we shall see, the Supreme Court successfully waltzed around this issue.

Meanwhile, Congress got involved in the dispute. Even before Buono's suit went before the District Court, Congress inserted a proviso in an appropriations bill that no government funds could be used to remove the cross. It followed up this admonition with a resolution designating the cross "a national memorial commemorating United States participation in World War I and honoring the American veterans of that war." Soon after the District Court issued its injunction, Congress again forbade the use of governments funds to remove the cross. Next, while the case was at the Court of Appeal, Congress passed a "land-transfer statute." The Secretary of the Interior was authorized to transfer to the VFW an acre of land surrounding the cross. Henry Sandoz, in exchange, would hand over five acres of land elsewhere in the Preserve (some of the Preserve is in private hands) to the government. Any difference in value would be equalized by a cash payment. The statute also contained a "reversionary clause," stipulating that if the property was ever not devoted to a memorial to World War I servicemen, it would revert to the government.

In response, Buono went back to the District Court and sought an injunction to stop the land transfer from taking place. The Court was asked to declare that the congressional move was a façade for keeping the cross in place and therefore invalid. The Court found for Buono and the Court of Appeals affirmed. The government appealed this decision to the Supreme Court. Legally, therefore, all that was before the Supreme Court was the validity of the injunction ordering a halt to the land transfer, not whether or not the presence of the cross (before or after the land-transfer statute passed) violated the establishment clause.

The Opinion of the Court

Question one was standing. This was actually two separate questions. The first was whether Buono had standing to bring the original suit. The government argued that he did not, inasmuch as he does not object to crosses in general, if, for example, it was on private land. It was therefore not personal to him; in short, he was not made to feel either coerced or excluded by the cross itself. The Court was able to put this issue to one side, noting that the government had not sought review of this question within the 90-day period required by the rules of federal procedure. Thus,

Buono had standing to pursue the original suit and that holding was held to be unreviewable. However, whether he had standing to request applying the injunction to the land transfer is another question. After a brief discussion of the rules regarding injunctions, the Court ruled for Buono. In Kennedy's view, the current case was closely enough related to the original injunction to establish standing. That is, Buono was merely trying to have the earlier injunction enforced. The government tried to argue that he was seeking an extension of the injunction, not the mere application of a previous injunction. The Court ruled, though, that Buono was entitled to seek enforcement of the original injunction in the current case. "Based on the rights he obtained under the earlier decree—against the same party, regarding the same cross and the same land—his interests in doing so were sufficiently personal and concrete to support his standing…. This is not a case in which a party seeks to import a previous standing determination into a wholly different dispute." Importantly, to stress once again, no decision was made by the District Court on whether or not the land transfer was itself a violation of the establishment clause. Instead, it confined itself to the issue of Buono's request to have the original injunction enforced. At the Supreme Court, the charade that this was not an establishment clause case continued, but the reasoning of the Court is pretty transparent.

Beginning with a brief description of the character of injunctions, Kennedy stresses that injunctions should be "ordered only after taking into account all of the circumstances that bear on the need for prospective relief." This is especially necessary when an injunction "implicates public interests." And, quoting a previous case, a court should "never ignore significant changes in the law or circumstances underlying an injunction lest the decree be turned into an 'instrument of wrong.'" He was building up to saying that here the District Court did not pay enough attention to the changed circumstances, namely the land-transfer statute.

> The court … did not acknowledge the statute's significance. It examined the events that led to the statute's enactment and found an intent to prevent removal of the cross. Deeming this intent illegitimate, the court concluded that nothing of moment had changed…. Even assuming the land-transfer statute was an attempt to prevent removal of the cross, it does not follow that an injunction against its implementation was appropriate.

By resting its conclusion on the "illicit" character of Congress's motives, the District Court had not taken appropriate cognizance of the changed circumstances wrought by the new statute. Congress, Kennedy argued, had much more in mind than merely evading an injunction. While the cross is "certainly a Christian symbol," here the intent was "not an attempt to set the *imprimatur* of the state on a particular creed. Rather those who erected the cross intended simply to honor our Nation's fallen soldiers."

Moreover, as in *Van Orden v. Perry*, time must be considered. The cross stood for nearly 70 years with no complaints. Congress's designation of the cross as an official memorial to soldiers who served in World War I (in fact, this is the only governmentally endorsed memorial to those who fell in that war) was recognition of "the historical meaning that the cross had attained." Congress, therefore, had quite properly sought to balance the various interests involved and had come up with the land transfer as a workable remedy. It was improper of the District Court to dismiss this as mere evasion.

Nevertheless, Buono argued that the government's interest must still give way to the continued establishment clause violation embodied in the continued presence of the cross. At this point Kennedy moves directly into how the District Court applied the endorsement test.

First, he says, the endorsement test (which, recall, is the method the District Court used to assess the second prong of the *Lemon* test) does not require the removal of each and every religious symbol from public property. "The Constitution does not oblige government to avoid any public acknowledgement of religion's role in society." If the land-transfer statute was to be voided, then the District Court should have faced the endorsement test anew, not simply relied on its previous finding of a violation of the establishment clause. It should have "evaluated Buono's modification request in light of the objectives of the 2002 injunction." Specifically, that order was based on a cross on public land, not private land.

Kennedy makes his position rather clear, when he goes one step further and lays out how he thinks the endorsement test should be considered in this case. The endorsement test "requires the hypothetical construct of an objective observer who knows all of the pertinent facts and circumstances surrounding the symbol and its placement." In this case, the cross is more than a straightforward religious symbol. To be sure, while a cross has religious connotations, a

> Latin cross is not merely a reaffirmation of Christian beliefs. It is a symbol often used to honor and respect those whose heroic acts, noble contributions, and patient striving help secure an honored place in history for this Nation and its people. Here one Latin cross in the desert evokes far more than religion. It evokes thousands of small crosses in foreign fields marking the graves of Americans who fell in battles, battles whose tragedies are compounded if the fallen are forgotten.

He is plainly loading the dice in favor of keeping the cross where it is. Even though he then ordered the case remanded to the District Court for further proceedings, in essence he had decided the matter.

The Concurring and Dissenting Opinions

Chief Justice Roberts penned a one-paragraph concurring opinion. He pointed out that if the government took down the cross, sold the land in question to the Veterans of Foreign Wars, gave the cross to the VFW, and they put it back up, there would be no issue. Thus, skipping "that empty ritual" and doing the land transfer is essentially no different.

Justice Alito, in contrast, wrote a much longer concurring opinion. He agreed with Justice Kennedy on all major points save one. He would have settled the establishment clause issue directly and explicitly and not sent it back to the lower courts. "The factual record has been sufficiently developed to permit resolution of these questions, and I would therefore decide them and hold that the statute may be implemented."

Given the cross's placement and history, it conveys two distinct messages. It "is of course the preeminent symbol of Christianity," and, accordingly, "Easter services have long been held on Sunrise Rock." At the same time, the original reason for erecting the cross was to honor American war dead. Echoing Kennedy, he stresses that "the symbol that was selected, a plain white unadorned cross, no doubt evoked the unforgettable image of the white crosses, row on row, that marked the final resting places of so many Americans who fell in that conflict."

When the District Court issued the initial injunction, Congress faced a dilemma. Should the cross be removed after 70 years of standing there unmolested, people might think the government was not being neutral toward religion, even perhaps hostile to it. One possible way out of the dilemma would have, Alito said, been to supplement the cross with a Star of David, recognizing the faith of some 3,500 Jewish soldiers who perished in what was then known as The Great War. (This had been done in the World War I cemeteries in Europe.) However, it is unlikely that Buono would have been satisfied by this gesture, turned off as he was by any religious symbol on public property.

He then takes aim at Justice Stevens' use of the endorsement test in his dissenting opinion. Assume, Alito says, that the endorsement test is the appropriate measuring rod. That test requires the construction of "a hypothetical reasonable observer who is deemed to be aware of the history and all other pertinent facts relating to a challenged display." Concerning the cross on Sunrise Rock,

> this observer would be familiar with the origin and history of the monument and would also know both that the land on which the monument is located is privately owned and that the new owner is under no obligation to preserve the monument's

current design [by the statute it merely had to be a monument commemorating the veterans of World War I]. With this knowledge, a reasonable observer would not view the land exchange as the equivalent of the construction of an official World War I memorial on the National Mall. Rather, a well-informed observer would appreciate that the transfer represents an effort by Congress to address a unique situation and to find a solution that best accommodates conflicting concerns.

This would seem to be a rather high bar for any normal person. It shows how any test, and specifically the endorsement test in this instance, can be calibrated to be stringent or loose, seriously affecting the outcome of a case.

Finally, like Justice Kennedy, Alito criticizes those who see an illicit motive in the passage of the land transfer. "I would not jump to the conclusion that Congress' aim in enacting the land-transfer was to embrace the religious message of the cross." Instead, Congress' claim to be establishing a fitting memorial for American dead from World War I should be taken as legitimate.

Justice Scalia also felt moved to write a concurring opinion, joined by Justice Thomas, in which he concurred in the plurality's nod toward the government but dissented rather vigorously regarding the grounds for decision. Harkening back to some of our earlier cases, he denied that Frank Buono even had standing to bring the case.

Scalia notes at the outset that Buono's standing to bring the original suit is not at issue; neither is the question of whether he can seek an enforcement of the first injunction. Scalia believes (and he thinks Kennedy all but agreed) that what Buono now seeks is a new injunction. The earlier injunction sought to force removal of the cross from federal land; now, though, the cross is on private land, which changes the legal situation.

To secure this new injunction, Buono would have to demonstrate some "actual or imminent injury." During depositions, Buono stated that he had no objection to a cross on private land. Consequently, the absence of some kind of injury should have precluded the District Court from considering his request for the second injunction. To quote Scalia, "The revised injunction is directed at Buono's *new* complaint that the manner of abandoning public ownership and the nature of the new private ownership violate the Establishment Clause." (Emphasis in original.) But it takes a party with standing to bring that issue before the court. Lacking that, the merits need not be discussed.

It is interesting that Scalia here declined to wade into the establishment clause question itself. He could have used this as a platform to attack the endorsement test itself and through it the *Lemon* test, which he had repeatedly said he disliked. (Recall that the endorsement test, as used here, is a method for applying the second prong of the *Lemon* test). However, by reverting to the matter of standing, he is also erecting a barrier against suits even challenging potential establishment clause violations. In a sense, this is a firmer dyke than ruling in favor of government in an establishment clause case.

Justice Stevens authored the principal dissent, running 26 pages, an analysis which was joined by Ginsburg and Sotomayor.[2] Some of his opinion is a technical analysis of the law of injunctions, but mostly it hammers home the point that by acting as it did Congress is still endorsing the cross, which is, to him, patently a primarily religious symbol. Accordingly, he would allow the District Court's follow-up injunction to stand.

Put simply, "the question we confront," he said, "is whether the District Court properly enforced its 2002 judgment by enjoining the transfer." This requires a two-pronged analysis: "In answering that question, we, like the District Court, must first consider whether the transfer would violate the 2002 injunction. We must then consider whether changed circumstances nonetheless rendered enforcement of that judgment inappropriate; or conversely whether they made it necessary for the District Court to bar the transfer, even if the transfer is not expressly prohibited by the prior injunction, in order to achieve the intended objective of the injunction." He believed that the answer to the first question was clearly "yes." The transfer would permit—indeed "encourage"—the cross remaining on Sunrise Rock. As for the second question, the District Court, in his view, properly thought that stopping the transfer was an essential step to end the perceived endorsement of religion that allowing the cross to stay entailed.

Context is important here. It is not the case that the original injunction dealt only with the cross's presence on federal land, as Justice Scalia had proposed. The government did own the land and undertook an "affirmative act" in order to keep the cross in place. The government had "no other purpose" than keeping the cross where it was. Thus, the transfer violated the original 2002 injunction. Furthermore, there is still the perception of endorsement even after the transfer.

> In my view, the transfer ... would not end government endorsement of the cross for two independent reasons. First, after the transfer it would continue to appear to any reasonable observer that the Government has endorsed the cross, notwithstanding that the name has changed on the title to a small patch of underlying land. This is particularly true because the Government has designated the cross as a national memorial, and that endorsement continues regardless of whether the cross sits on public or private land. Second, the transfer continues the existing

government endorsement of the cross because the purpose of the transfer is to preserve its display. Congress' intent to preserve the display of the cross maintains the Government's endorsement of the cross.

Stevens disputes the perceptions the plurality offered regarding the "reasonable observer." Initially, Stevens argues that our "reasonable observer" would have known that, in spite of the cross being erected with private funds, it stood on public land, that Congress had acted to designate it as a war memorial, that a congressional resolution had forbidden using public funds to remove the cross, and that the Park Service had kept Buddhists from adding their own monument. Then, after the transfer, this same observer would have been cognizant of the fact that the cross used to be on public land; that an injunction had ordered its removal; that Congress had undertaken the transfer for the specific purpose of keeping the cross up; and the reversionary interest the federal government retained in the land. "From this chain of events, in addition to the factors that remain the same after the transfer, he would perceive government endorsement of the cross." He then goes through a lengthy analysis of Congress's actions to show that the only reasonable conclusion is that "The Government has expressly adopted the cross as its own," and that it "conveys an inescapably sectarian message."

He then attacks the whole premise that the cross being on private land makes it private speech. One simply must take account of how this private ownership came to be, and in so doing one can only conclude that this does "not change the fact that the cross conveys a message of government endorsement of religion."

Moreover, he believes that it is easy to demonstrate that Congress had an illicit purpose in enacting the land transfer. Therefore, the District Court was not amiss when it ruled that the transfer was a sham, and that did not cure the need for enforcement of the original injunction. But even if we grant Congress some latitude here, the issue of objective endorsement remains. Congress has not done enough, he thinks, to distance "itself from the cross to end government endorsement of it."

He concludes with a jab at Congress for not having a more noteworthy memorial to World War I soldiers. (Stevens, it is perhaps worth noting, was the only veteran on the Court.)

[B]ecause Congress has established no other national monument to the veterans of the Great War, this solitary cross in the middle of the desert is *the* national World War I memorial. The sequence of legislative decisions made to designate and preserve a solitary Latin cross at an isolated location in the desert as a memorial for those who fought and died in World War I not only failed to cure the

Establishment Clause violation but also, in my view, resulted in a dramatically inadequate and inappropriate tribute.

Justice Breyer wrote a much shorter, six-page, dissent. He believed that the question revolved around technical aspects of the law of injunctions. The Supreme Court should not, in his view, have even heard the case, as no substantial federal question was raised, which would have left the Court of Appeals' decision in place.

Conclusion

Doctrinally, this case presents a number of issues, and well illustrates the muddied waters establishment clause cases, especially those dealing with displays on public property, raise. It is hard not to believe that to a large degree, this bending and twisting is tied to the philosophical preferences of the justices. Considering matters from a legal perspective alone, we can see that that two frameworks emerge: this endorsement test and the historical test. The first is used, recall again, as the method for assessing the second prong of the *Lemon* test, whether the primary effect of a given policy inhibits or advances religion. If, as first stated by Justice O'Connor, the display tends to make people feel like second-class citizens, then the display must be dismounted. If one takes the historical approach, then the longevity of the display must be factored in, and a justice must be largely "indifferent to the impact of such displays on observers and outsiders."[3]

The endorsement test, though, must withstand two other challengers: the direct or indirect coercion test. That is, some justices have repeatedly said that in order for a government action to violate the establishment clause there must be some type of coercion. In the area of public displays, of course, such coercion would be very rare, in fact almost nonexistent. It occurs most often when religious exercises at public events is at issue. For example, Justice Kennedy wrote (for the Court) in *Lee v. Wiseman* (the prayer at a middle school graduation case), that nonbelieving students were subjected to indirect coercion through psychological pressure; Justice Scalia vigorously contested that view in a dissent, saying that it was only when coercion was direct, that is by "force of law and threat of penalty," that the line separating the permissible from the impermissible was crossed.

But even if we settle on the endorsement test, the difficulties do not end, as we see in this case. The test comes down to what the "reasonable observer" would perceive. To begin with, it cannot be the "only one person" test. There will always be one person found who will object to any display; consequently, none would be allowed if that is the measure. But who then? Well, it has to be a hypothetical person constructed in a judge's mind, unless we are to take a public opinion survey.[4] But how knowledgeable must this person be about all the surrounding facts and circumstances of a given display? Remember the differing circumstances cited by Justices Alito and Stevens. And when the context contains contradictory facts which ones weigh more heavily? Here, for example, is Congress's rather transparent attempt to keep the cross in place more pertinent than the mere fact that the cross stood on private land after the transfer? Or, consider the role of possible disclaimers posted near the display. Even Justice O'Connor had some difficulty here.

> Justice O'Connor's suggestion that the state might be required to post a disclaimer casts some light on her requirement that the observer be informed. If the observer were fully informed, she would not need to be told by the state that the [display] at issue was private rather than public. Thus, Justice O'Connor suggests that a reasonable person need not be fully informed; else, the (sometimes required) disclaimer would only serve to inform the observer of something she already knows. That said, however, members of the Court have had some difficulty in specifying just what or how much the reasonable observer should know before making a judgment about whether something promotes or undermines religion.[5]

"Some difficulty" is both an understatement and potentially misleading. The plain truth is that the concept is as malleable as a justice—say Alito or Stevens—wants it to be.

A few weeks after this decision was handed down, the cross was mysteriously stolen. Henry Sandoz immediately began work on a new one, but could not put it in place unless and until he was victorious in the litigation. When the case was remanded to the District Court, the VFW and the ACLU began negotiating over a settlement. An agreement was reached in early November 2012, and certified by the District Court judge. The ACLU's attorney explained "The government has agreed that the property will be clearly delineated as private property. There will be fencing around it and signs up to show that it is not government-owned." A California VFW official added his endorsement: "VFW is most pleased that the issue over the cross with the ACLU is now closed, that the property is transferred to the VFW, and we can rededicate a replacement cross on Sunrise Rock."[6] On Veterans Day, 2012, accompanied by a contingent of veterans and onlookers, Henry Sandoz helped erect his cross (made of steel piping and seven feet tall) where the previous one had stood. His wife, Wanda, said, "We are so, so happy that it's going up and staying without opposition, since the Veterans of Foreign Wars owns it now. We are so happy that it all came together and the veterans can have their memorial now."[7] Fittingly, perhaps, the old cross had appeared tied to a fence in San Mateo a few days earlier. No one has ever taken responsibility for stealing it.

As with the *Summum* case, this one has to be scored a victory for traditional religion. Despite what one writer called its "procedural quagmire,"[8] the case provoked a controversy that broke down along predictable lines. The secular-oriented ACLU wanted the Court to flex some neutrality muscle, forcing the government to distance itself from religious symbolism at all costs. Traditionalists felt such notions were an assault on a cherished ideal. Clearly, the cross is a symbol of Christianity, and trying to identify it with war dead in general is disingenuous at best. The central reason it stands is the fact that until recently the association between American identity and a generic brand of Christianity was assumed to be natural and uncontroversial. The emergent America depicted in Chapter 1 lost one here, or two, if you include the denial to Buddhists to erect their own monument.

CHAPTER 6

Public Universities and Religious Student Groups
Christian Legal Society v. Martinez

This case, handed down in 2010, shares some characteristics with the previous ones, but also exhibits some dramatic differences. It is similar in that even though it is clearly a religious liberty case, the Supreme Court once again turned to another area of constitutional law to make, or at least justify, its decision. Here, it was the "limited public forum" line of cases that was used to frame the issue and defend the result. Moreover, it was also another 5–4 split.

However, the differences between this case and the earlier ones are more important. First, it was really a free exercise case rather than an establishment clause controversy. Second, Justice Kennedy played his role as the swing justice, this time siding with the four liberals. This meant that traditional religion lost this time around, the third and key difference.

To the outside observer, the clash between traditional religion and a sensitivity to the concerns of gay and lesbians is what is most evident here. Although the university never said this explicitly, it seems obvious that this was the main question at issue.

The Facts of the Case

The Hastings College of Law at the University of California is one of the nation's premier law schools. As part of its educational mission, it encourages students to form, join, and support all manner of groups. Some have to do with students interested in particular areas of the law (trial lawyers), some are oriented around a cause of some type or another (prolife, prochoice), some are identity based (La Raza, Vietnamese American Law Society), and some are purely recreational (wine lovers, ultimate Frisbee enthusiasts). These groups may apply to the law school to become officially Registered Student Organizations (RSOs), a designation that brings with it certain benefits. From the Court's summary:

> RSOs are eligible to seek financial assistance from the Law School, which subsidizes their events using funds from a mandatory student-activity fee imposed on all students. RSOs may also use Law-School channels to communicate with students: They may place announcements in a weekly Office-of-Student-Services newsletter, advertise events on bulletins boards, send e-mails using a Hastings-organization address, and participate in an annual Student Organizations Fair designed to advance recruitment efforts. In addition, RSOs may apply for permission to use the Law School's facilities for meetings and office space. Finally, Hastings allows officially recognized groups to use its name and logo.

Student organizations, it should be pointed out, are free to organize outside this system. They simply cannot take advantage of any of the listed benefits unless they become RSOs. When this litigation began, there were approximately 60 RSOs, and no application had ever been turned down.

In 2004, a group of conservative-leaning Christian students formed a local chapter of the Christian Legal Society. Organized in 1961, the "Christian Legal Society (CLS) is a nationwide fellowship of Christians committed to acting justly, loving mercy, and walking humbly with their God (Micah 6:8)."[1] Furthermore, it believes that through

> inspiring, encouraging, and equipping Christian lawyers and law students, both individually and in community, to proclaim, love, and serve Jesus Christ through the study and practice of law, the provision of legal assistance to the poor and needy, and the defense of the inalienable rights to life and religious freedom, we are fulfilling the command of Micah 6:8 and ensuring the next generation of Americans has the same opportunities to share their faith in community.

All officers and members are required to sign the organization's Statement of Faith, which reads:

> Trusting in Jesus Christ as my Savior, I believe in:
> One God, eternally existent in three persons, Father, Son and Holy Spirit.
> God the Father Almighty, Maker of heaven and earth.
> The Deity of our Lord, Jesus Christ, God's only son, conceived of the Holy Spirit, born of the virgin Mary; His vicarious death for our sins through which we receive eternal life; His bodily resurrection and personal return.
> The presence and power of the Holy Spirit in the work of regeneration.
> The Bible as the inspired Word of God.

In addition, officers and members must assent to the Community Life Statement. Adherents are to, among other things, "seek to respect the uniqueness of all people," and to cultivate "attitudes and behaviors of love, joy, peace, patience, kindness, goodness, faithfulness, gentleness, and self-control." However, the most controversial part of the Community Life Statement when it came to seeking RSO status says "We renounce unbiblical behaviors, including deception, malicious speech, drunkenness, drug abuse, stealing, cheating, and other immoral conduct such as using pornography and engaging in sexual relations other than within a marriage between one man and one woman."

In 2004, the CLS chapter applied for RSO status, but the application was rejected.

The crux of the rejection was the law school's Nondiscrimination Policy, which was worded as follows:

> [Hastings] is committed to a policy against legally impermissible, arbitrary or unreasonable discriminatory practices. All groups, including administration, faculty, student governments, [Hastings]-owned student residence facilities and programs sponsored by [Hastings], are governed by this policy of nondiscrimination...
>
> [Hastings] shall not discriminate unlawfully on the basis of race, color, religion, national origin, ancestry, disability, age, sex, or sexual orientation. This nondiscrimination policy covers admission, access and treatment in Hastings-sponsored programs and activities.

The aforementioned commitments, the school said, violated the bans on discrimination because of religion and sexual orientation. Somewhat later, when turning down a second application, the school announced that it had an "all-comers" policy regarding RSOs. This policy, it was said, was an interpretive outgrowth of the published Nondiscrimination Policy. Pursuant to this policy, the law school demanded that all RSOs allow any student to participate in its activities, become a member, or serve as an officer.[2] Accordingly, CLS's refusal to agree to this stipulation was the grounds for denying it RSO status. The organization then requested an exemption from the policy, but this was denied also. To become an RSO, "CLS," the law school administration replied, "must open its membership to all students irrespective of their religious beliefs or sexual orientation."

In response, CLS filed a suit claiming that the denial violated their First Amendment rights to free speech, expressive association, and free exercise of religion.[3] The District Court decided in favor of the law school and that holding was endorsed by the Court of Appeal for the Ninth Circuit. CLS then appealed to the Supreme Court.

Legal Precedents

Before turning to the various opinions, it will be helpful to lay out some of the more important precedents that have a bearing on the case.

The landmark case involving freedom of association is *NAACP v. Alabama* (1958). The state of Alabama had ordered the NAACP to provide its membership lists to state authorities. The obvious purpose was to allow economic sanctions (or perhaps worse) to be visited on people who were members. The NAACP refused and appealed a contempt order issued by the state courts to the Supreme Court. A unanimous court found for the organization. In order to do this expeditiously, the justices held that there was a "freedom of association" connected to the First Amendment's right of freedom of speech, made applicable to the states by the Fourteenth Amendment's due process clause. "It is beyond debate that freedom to engage in association for the advancement of beliefs and ideas is an inseparable aspect of the 'liberty' secured by the Due Process Clause of the Fourteenth Amendment, which embraces freedom of speech." In this way, freedom of association was made a First Amendment right even though it is not explicitly mentioned in the Constitution's text.

A 1984 case, *Roberts v. United States Jaycees*, however, stressed that this right was not absolute and had to be measured against a state's interest in equal opportunity, especially if direct expression was not involved. The bylaws of the Jaycees, a civic and business organization, limited membership to males. Minnesota had a law barring gender discrimination in places of "public accommodation." A unanimous Court held that while certainly a right to expressive association exists, here it must give way to Minnesota's statute. On the one hand, the state had demonstrated that it had a compelling interest in ending gender discrimination in semi-public organizations. On the other hand, admitting women to its ranks would not affect the "organization's ability to engage in these protected activities or to disseminate its preferred views."

In 1995, however, the Court seemed to lean the other way in *Hurley v. Irish-American Gay, Lesbian, and Bisexual Group of Boston*, although it was not exactly association that was involved. Massachusetts had a law similar to Minnesota's, except that it included sexual orientation among its protected categories. The South Boston Allied War Veterans Council was given permission by the city to organize the St. Patrick's Day parade. When an Irish-American gay and lesbian group applied to join the parade, the Council refused to give them a spot. Citing the public accommodations law, the gay and lesbian group filed a suit. A unanimous Court ruled against them, however. It held that "The protected expression that inheres in a parade is not limited to its banners and songs ... for the Constitution looks beyond written or spoken words as mediums of expression." The Veterans Council, therefore, had the right to exclude groups that did not share its views.[4]

In 2000, the Court found itself faced with a case more similar to *Roberts*, in *Boy Scouts of America v. Dale*. New Jersey had also passed a public accommodations law that listed sexual orientation as a protected group. An assistant scoutmaster was dismissed from the organization when he revealed that he was gay. The central question was whether the Boy Scouts were more similar to the NAACP or the Jaycees when it came to holding a position on controversial issues. The Court split 5–4, with the majority favoring the former.

> In determining whether a group is protected by the First Amendment's expressive associational right, we must determine whether the group engages in "expressive association." The First Amendment's protection of expressive association is not reserved for advocacy groups. But to come within its ambit, a group must engage in some form of expression, whether it be public or private.

After surveying several pieces of literature from the Boy Scouts, the Court found that the organization indeed had a position "that homosexual conduct is not morally straight," something that is required of scouts by the Scout Oath and Law.[5] Consequently, the Scouts could exclude those who felt they could not endorse or live out this credo.

Perhaps the most directly applicable precedent arose in 1972, *Healy v. James*. A group of students at Central Connecticut State College organized a chapter of the Students for a Democratic Society. When they requested to be an officially recognized student organization, the president turned down their application. His rationale was that

> [I]t is my judgment that the statement of purpose to form a local chapter of the Students for a Democratic Society carries an unmistakable adherence to at least some of the major tenets of the national organization.... The published aims and philosophy of the Students for a Democratic Society, which include disruption and violence, are contrary to the approved policy of Central Connecticut State College.

After finding that the local chapter's links with the national organization were not at all clear, the justices held that mere disagreement with a group's objectives was not enough to deny it the privilege of registration.

We need to enter a note at this point on public forums (recall that this was relevant in *Pleasant Grove City v. Summum*). The Court has demarcated two types of public forums, traditional and limited. The former is a place that by tradition or practice has been used for the gathering of people to discuss the issues of the day, express ideas, and hold assemblies. The classic example is a public park. Government may place reasonable "time, place, and manner" restrictions, but they may not establish any kind of content or viewpoint regulations. A limited public forum, in contrast, is one established by a government entity itself. As such, it may erect certain limitations, such as allowing only certain types of groups to use the forum. For example, a college or university may confine the forum's use to students. Nevertheless, even in a limited public forum, viewpoint discrimination is not allowed. Two important cases illustrate the Court's thinking in this area.

The first is *Widmar v. Vincent*, decided in 1981 by a nearly unanimous Court, 8–1. The University of Missouri at Kansas City, citing establishment clause concerns, denied a Christian organization, whose meetings were to include prayer and Bible reading, the use of university rooms. Notably, other student groups were allowed to use the rooms on request. The university's regulations said that university property could not be used "for purposes of religious worship or religious teaching." The Court made two important holdings. First, since the university had created a limited public forum, any content prohibitions would have to meet strict scrutiny, that is, that the state could only prevail if it could show a compelling interest in the stated policy and that it had utilized the least restrictive means to accomplish its ends. That requirement was not met here. Second, an "equal access policy," granting equal use to all student groups, would not violate the establishment clause.

The other, *Rosenberger v. Regents of the University of Virginia*, came 14 years later and more sharply divided the Court. Students at the university paid into a student activity fund. Proceeds were used in part to fund publications of various student organizations. A Christian organization published a magazine purporting to offer a Christian view of various aspects of the university, and asked to be reimbursed its printing costs. Pointing to a university policy that banned its monies being used for a religious activity, defined as any activity that "primarily promotes or manifests a particular belief in or about a deity or an ultimate reality," the application was turned down. Five justices held, first, that a limited public forum need not be spatial, and, further, that if the university promotes speech, then it must promote all speech equally. The Court stressed that there was a distinction between viewpoint discrimination and subject matter discrimination. The latter would be permissible if doing so would preserve the purposes of the limited public forum, but the former was not allowed. Thus, the university could not legitimately deny student activity funds to the student organization in question.

The Opinion of the Court

Justice Ginsburg wrote the opinion for the five person majority in *Christian Legal Society v. Martinez.* Fundamentally, three constitutional issues are raised here: free exercise of religion, expressive association, and free speech. The District Court dismissed the free exercise claim and the Supreme Court concurred, based on the 1990 *Smith* decision that we discussed earlier. Claims for judicially granted exemptions to generally applicable laws and policies are only legitimate if the law or policy is targeted at a religious group. The situation here seems to make this a debatable question; however, CLS chose to focus its arguments on the latter two issues.[6] CLS did want, however, the Court to consider each argument as free-standing. Ginsburg, though, rejected his position and merged the two concerns into the limited public forum framework. The reason behind this take seems to be that had she considered freedom of association as an issue by itself, it might well have been argued that strict scrutiny would have been appropriate. First Amendment freedoms, that is, normally trigger strict scrutiny, and here she seems to want to climb down from that paradigm. The rationale for moving this case under the limited public forum rests on three propositions, she argued.

"First," she says, "the same considerations that have led us to apply a less restrictive level of scrutiny to speech in limited public forums as compared to other environments apply with equal force to expressive association occurring in limited public forums." It would be "anomalous" if the law school's policy survived constitutional muster under a limited public forum analysis only to falter on the shoals of expressive association." (Exactly why this is so is not spelled out; in fact, the Court often invalidates some measure based on one constitutional provision when it might satisfy another.)

In a similar vein, secondly, applying strict scrutiny in a case such as this one would undermine one of the characteristics of limited public forums—namely, that the government entity may restrict the class of speakers who may use the forum. In this instance, for example, only students at the law school were entitled to use the forum. Thirdly, CLS is in effect seeking a state subsidy. That is, CLS is not being shut down, nor even being denied to right to operate on campus; instead, it is only being denied certain benefits.

Despite the limited public forum framework, the three cases we discussed above involving higher education—*Healy*, *Widmar*, and *Rosenberger*—would seem to point in CLS's favor. Straining a bit, she distinguishes these cases, in spite of language in each that runs counter to her holding. In *Healy* the Court said that a public college cannot "restrict speech or association simply because it finds the views expressed ... to be abhorrent." In a footnote, she attempts to get around this seemingly straightforward statement by saying that it was "dispositive" that the president of the college disagreed with the group's philosophy. In contrast, CLS was merely being denied an exemption to a generally applicable policy. Turning to *Widmar* there is the uncomfortable (for her) fact that the Court there employed strict scrutiny. Her response is that the university in that case was singling out a religious group for differential treatment and in effect practicing viewpoint discrimination. Similarly in *Rosenberger*, the university was singling out a particular viewpoint "which was otherwise within the forum's limitations." Summarizing the holdings of the three cases, and quoting from *Rosenberger*, she argued that "The State may not exclude speech where its distinction is not *reasonable* in light of the purpose served by the forum, ... nor may it *discriminate against speech on the basis of viewpoint* (emphasis added)." Thus, to settle this case, it is necessary to determine (1) Were Hastings' regulations reasonable? and (2) Was viewpoint discrimination involved?

She contends that Hastings' policy is indeed reasonable, and after two boilerplate observations, offers four reasons (drawn from Hastings' pleadings) for this conclusion. The two boilerplate matters are (1) While a substantial amount of deference is owed to the judgment of educational officials the "final arbiter" of constitutional issues remains the judiciary and (2) Extra-curricular activities are an important part of an educational institution's mission.

The first of the four justifications is that the "all-comers" policy "ensures that the leadership, educational, and social opportunities afforded by [RSOS] are available to all students." The nature of the forum is enhanced if all groups in the forum practice equal access to all students. The second is that the policy allows Hastings to make judgments about compliance with the Nondiscrimination Policy based on actions alone rather than having to inquire into motives. That is, how would the law school determine whether a student turned down by an organization was turned away because of belief or status? She offers the rather extreme example of a Male Superiority Club. If it told a female she could not run for its presidency how could school officials know whether it was because of her gender (status) or the fact that she did not share the precepts of the club (belief)?

A third justification centers on the promotion of "tolerance, cooperation, and learning" among the student body. And if the all-comers policy were to lead to conflict? Then, developing "conflict-resolution skills, toleration, and readiness to find common ground" are important aspects of one's legal education. Finally, she notes that the policy is in accord with California law on discrimination.

Consequently, she finds that Hastings has demonstrated that the all-comers policy is "surely reasonable in light of the RSO forum's purposes."

Additionally, she feels the need to stress that CLS is not being denied the right to organize and sometimes use school facilities. In fact, she points out CLS (along with other student organizations at other universities) has been a vibrant organization without RSO status. It is simply being denied a certain official status, which she seems to be saying is not that important anyway. (Students these days, for example, she says, communicate more by social media than through the school's official channels.)

Turning to the question of whether the all-comers policy constitutes viewpoint discrimination, she offers only one rather truncated paragraph.

> Although this aspect of limited-public-forum analysis has been the constitutional sticking point in our prior decisions, ... we need not dwell on it here. It is, after all, hard to imagine a more viewpoint-neutral policy than one requiring *all* student groups to accept *all* comers. In contrast to *Healy*, *Widmar*, and *Rosenberger*, in which universities singled out organizations for disfavored treatment because of their points of view, Hastings' all-comers requirement draws no distinction between groups based on their message or perspective. An all-comers condition on access to RSO status, in short, is textbook viewpoint neutral.

In short, the law school's policy passes both the reasonableness and viewpoint neutrality tests and its rejection of CLS may stand.

Concurring and Dissenting Opinions

Justices Stevens and Kennedy filed concurring opinions to stress various points, even though both joined the opinion of the Court in full. Justice Stevens sought to underline two main issues. First, he defends the religion clause in the Nondiscrimination Policy. By prohibiting discrimination on the basis of religion, the law school is attempting to promote religious liberty, not diminish it. Of course, it can work the other way. That is, religious groups who seek university sanction are thereby barred from discriminating on the basis of religion, but that is not the purpose of the clause. Second, he believes the Court should grant wide deference to university authorities in the construction and operation of their limited public forums. He acknowledges that the way they have chosen to create and administer the program may not the wisest choice, but it is a reasonable one.

Justice Kennedy felt it was important to differentiate this case from *Rosenberger*. "*Rosenberger* is distinguishable from the instant case in various respects. Not least is that here the school policy in question is not content based either in its formulation or evident purpose; and were it shown to be otherwise, the case likely should have a different outcome. Here the policy applies equally to all groups and views." At the same time, he concedes that the all-comers policy can make it difficult for some groups, such as CLS, to express their views. Like the Boy Scouts in *Dale*, it may impede their ability to put forth their message if they are forced to include those who do not share the organization's positions. However, he goes on to say that if such exclusions were allowed at Hastings, the whole purpose of the forum would be impaired. "A vibrant dialogue is not possible if students wall themselves off from opposing points of view." Of course, this evades the question of whether a "vibrant dialogue" is best fostered within or between groups.

Justice Alito wrote a lengthy and sharp-toothed dissent that goes more to the heart of the issues that concern us than does the opinion of the Court. In so doing, he also challenged some factual issues that the majority seemingly brushed aside.

He disputes, for example, Hastings' contention that the all-comers policy is an interpretation of the Nondiscrimination Policy. CLS initial application was turned down based on the Nondiscrimination Policy. Thus, that document should be considered binding on that action. The all-comers policy was only mentioned by the dean of the law school in a deposition some time after the litigation began. Hastings officials claimed the policy had been in effect since 1990 but offered no written documentation to back that up. Furthermore, no "Hastings official has ever stated in a deposition, affidavit, or declaration when this policy took effect." Moreover, until this controversy erupted, several groups had bylaws which contravened the all-comers policy. The Hastings Democratic Caucus, the Vietnamese American Law Society, and La Raza, for example, all had exclusionary membership requirements. When CLS pointed this out to university officials, the groups were then notified that they had to change their policies. Since all these groups had had to file their bylaws with the law school, Hastings officials could not plausibly claim they were unaware of these stipulations.

He also chides the Court for ignoring what happened when CLS tried to take advantage of the school's offer of facilities. On two occasions no reply was forthcoming from the law school until after the date of the proposed event had passed. In the same way, he is critical of the majority's contention that denial of RSO status did not matter much to the organization's vitality. "This Court does not customarily brush aside a claim of unlawful discrimination with the observation that the effects of the discrimination were really not so bad."

Alito believes that the *Healy* case is the most germane precedent. There, he argues, the Court stood up for free speech principles and gave little if any deference to the college's president. From Alito's perspective, there are only two possible differences between that case and this one. One is the funding that was raised here. He dismisses this, though, because the amount involved is minuscule (about $85 per year for each RSO). In any event, most of what CLS desired (the right to set up a table at student events, for example) was cost free. The other is, we should be candid, the "identity of the student group." "The Court pays little attention to *Healy* and instead focuses solely on the question whether Hastings' registration policy represents a permissible regulation in a limited public forum. While I think *Healy* is controlling, I am content to address the constitutionality of Hastings' actions under our limited public forum cases, which lead to exactly the same conclusion."

As stated above, when universities establish limited public forums they are prohibited from engaging in viewpoint discrimination. When Hastings refused to register CLS because of its stances on religion and sexual orientation it did precisely that. Recall he believes that the initial application was only considered under the published Nondiscrimination Policy. According to its terms, RSOs with a secular orientation (say, on environmental issues) should not be able to exclude people on religious grounds, true enough, because religion has nothing to do with the group's ability to advocate certain positions. However, religious groups are not the same. "As our cases have recognized, the right of expressive association permits a group to exclude an applicant for membership only if the admission of that person would 'affect in a significant way the group's ability to advocate public or private viewpoints'" (quoting from *Dale*). For religious groups religious commitment is the sine qua non of the group. As for sexual orientation, Hastings is not allowing CLS to approve only those members who express a certain view. A Free Love Club, he maintains, could allow in only those who abhor traditional sexual mores. "It is hard to see how this can be viewed as anything other than viewpoint discrimination."

However, the Court has chosen to use the all-comers policy as its touchstone. But if that is done, the result should have still been a holding for CLS. Neither Justice Ginsburg's claim that the policy is "reasonable in light of the purpose of the RSO forum" and that it is viewpoint neutral will not stand up to serious analysis.

He dissects each of the four justifications offered by Hastings and endorsed by Justice Ginsburg to buttress the reasonableness claim and refutes each. As for creating as many "leadership, educational, and social opportunities" as possible, it would be better to allow students to form as many groups as they like, no matter how small. Regarding the difficulty of enforcing the difference between status and belief, he thinks this is a red herring. Courts throughout the land work with these differences in federal and state (including California) antidiscrimination laws all the time. On the third issue, encouraging "tolerance, cooperation, learning, and the development of conflict-resolution skills," can anyone seriously say that these laudable skills are not served by a "confident pluralism"? (quoting a brief by a gay and lesbian group). Finally, there is no evidence that California law requires Hastings to deny registration to student groups who limit membership to particular religious adherents.

Turning to the question of viewpoint neutrality, he agrees that the policy can be read as neutral on its face. However, he believes that "there is strong evidence in the record that the policy was announced as a pretext." "The adoption of a facially neutral policy for the purpose of suppressing the expression of a particular viewpoint is viewpoint discrimination." He points to Hastings' shifting policies, the timing of the announcing of new policies, the lack of documentation for certain policies (especially the all-comers policy), and the non-enforcement of the all-comers policy until the litigation began as evidence that the development of these policies was little more than a pretext.

Thus, whether full reliance is placed on *Healy* or whether analysis under the limited public forum rubric is the appropriate route, CLS should be given RSO status.

Conclusion

There is some dispute among legal scholars about the reach of this case. Some contend that it has broad implications for religious freedom. Timothy Tracey feels that the failure of the Court to examine the case from the perspective of "expressive association" opens up many avenues for further doctrinal development.[7] By relying on the "subsidy model" of analysis, it leaves universities free to impose all kinds of restrictions, especially on religious groups that do not conform to the main ideas of the campus culture. Most observers, however, see the case in more narrow terms. Few universities have the comprehensive kinds of policies Hastings did, for example. Furthermore, there are other doctrinal streams that might apply in other, even if roughly similar, kinds of cases.[8] As for the politics of the Supreme Court, Justice Kennedy's role was pivotal, providing the fifth vote for the majority. He has, as often pointed out, been especially sensitive to issues of gay and lesbian rights, and sided with them here.[9]

For our purposes, though, the meaning of the decision is rather clear. It was a loss for traditional religious groups and ideas and an illustration of the power of gay and lesbian groups.[10] It seems obvious that CLS' position on sexual orientation was what got it into trouble with the law school. It is hard not to believe that 40 or 50 years ago that CLS would have been given RSO status without a second thought. Although it only came up indirectly, what would have happened if a Muslim group with similar exclusionary policies and a similar position on homosexuality had applied for RSO status before CLS did? The university would have been presented with a delicate problem: wishing to be sensitive to diversity but needing to adhere to the nondiscrimination policy.

Finally, we can see some of the reaction of traditional groups. Several states passed laws specifically prohibiting their state universities from adopting policies similar to those at Hastings. Ohio's statute is fairly typical:

> (A)No state institution of higher education shall take any action or enforce any policy that would deny a religious student group any benefit available to any other student group based on the religious student group's requirement that its leaders or members adhere to its sincerely held religious beliefs or standards of conduct.
> (B)As used in this section:
>   (1) "Benefits" include, without limitation:
>   (a) Recognition;
>   (b) Registration;
>   (c) The use of facilities of the state institution of higher education for meetings or speaking purposes;
>   (d) The use of channels of communication of the state institution of higher education;
>   (e) Funding sources that are otherwise available to any other student group in the state institution of higher education.[11]

In the end, then, this case might be scored something of a draw. Gay and lesbian groups won at the Court, but the backlash created firm statutory protections for CLS and similar groups in many states. It seems likely that these laws will remain on the books for the foreseeable future. The upshot is that gay and lesbian groups will have policies they prefer in some states but CLS type groups will be able to organize and claim university sanction in others. We shall have, therefore, geographical diversity in this area of the law.

CHAPTER 7

"State Tax Dollars" Going to Private Schools, Including Religious Ones

Arizona Christian School Tuition Organization v. Winn

In a sense, this case harkens back to *Hein v. Freedom from Religion Foundation* (Chapter 3) inasmuch as it was also decided on the grounds of standing, and that it came out the same way. When it was over, that is, the complainants were held to lack standing to bring the case at all.

We have here, again, the familiar liberal-conservative split with a 5–4 decision. Again, too, Justice Kennedy was the swing justice, siding this time with the conservatives, meaning that traditional religion scored another judicial victory, at least for now.

This case presents a particularly interesting political history. Two strands of modern conservatism have coalesced around the idea of channeling some public funds to private schools. One wing consists of those who believe in the sanctity (or near sanctity) of markets as the proper mechanism of social choice. A market is always preferable to government supply of any given service. A private market is inherently, they argue, both morally superior to and more efficient than public provision.[1] In the area of education, with the American commitment to education as a right, restoring a purely private market is unrealistic. Therefore, the remedy is to put public funds in the hands of "consumers," that is, parents, and let them "spend" them as they choose. The other is composed of conservative, including evangelical, Christians who have become disenchanted with the public schools. They believe that liberal secularists are either controlling (in the extreme version) or at least heavily influential in (in the more moderate version) what is taught and practiced in the modern public school system. Taking prayer out of the schools is a marker, they contend, for an assault on traditional values. The public schools have become too secular and too dismissive of religious values. This represents in many ways an inversion of traditional political alliances. When the public schools were for all intents and purposes, as Horace Mann had hoped, a manifestation of a broad ecumenical Protestantism, most Protestants were supportive. They were in most cases strongly opposed to sending any public funds to religious schools, since most of them were Catholic. In fact, responding to anti–Catholic feeling politicians often wrote such prohibitions into state constitutions, so-called "Blaine Amendments" named after the Maine senator who pushed the idea.[2] While it failed at the federal level, a number of states added such provisions to their own constitutions. We will, in fact, come across a case later that revolves around exactly such a provision in the Missouri constitution (see Chapter 12).

The Facts of the Case

Arizona's diversion of public funds to private schools was indirect but real nonetheless. Taxpayers could claim a credit of up to $500 ($1,000 for couples) against their state income tax liability for contributions to a School Tuition Organization (STO). (A "tax credit," unlike a "deduction," is a dollar for dollar reduction in one's taxes. In effect, part of your tax liability is paid to a private organization.) STOs then used the monies to provide scholarships to students attending private schools. All STOs had to meet certain requirements in order to obtain that status. They had, for example, to be designated as charitable organizations under the Internal Revenue Code, had to give at least 90 percent of all income for student scholarships at "qualified schools," and they could not provide funds to only one school. Qualified schools had to agree not to discriminate on the basis of "race, color, handicap, familial status, or national origin" when selecting students. However, significantly for this case, they could discriminate on the basis of religious affiliation. The program's challengers calculated that approximately $50 million annually was directed to private schools. In 1998, 94 percent of the available credits "went to STOs that granted scholarships exclusively to students at religious schools."[3] Furthermore, in 2009, the four largest religiously oriented STOs garnered more than half of all monies given through the tax credit plan.[4]

The challengers first went to the state courts, and in the end the Arizona Supreme Court upheld the program on the merits. Frustrated there, the opponents of the program went to the federal courts. The District

Court denied that, as taxpayers, the challengers had standing. The Court of Appeal reversed and held against the state on both the standing issue and on the merits. When appealed to the United States Supreme Court, a majority of justices confined themselves to the standing issue.

The Opinion of the Court

Kennedy's opinion for the majority in this case is notably short, mostly retracing much of the ground covered in *Hein*. He reiterates the general principles from *Frothingham v. Mellon* and *Doremus v. Board of Education*, that taxpayers do not have standing to challenge specific governmental expenditures, while nodding again to the exception from *Flast v. Cohen*. Only when two conditions are met—that a "logical link" must exist between being a taxpayer and the type of statute at issue and that there must be a "nexus" between taxpayer status and a precise constitutional prohibition (there and probably only elsewhere the establishment clause). He stresses that in a key part of the *Flast* opinion the Court said that government must "extract and spend" monies in order for taxpayers to have standing. What distinguishes this case, then, is that it does not involve a governmental expenditure but rather a tax credit. Kennedy admits that expenditures and tax credits can have "similar economic consequences"; however, he thinks there are significant differences.

If government takes your money through taxes and then spends it on some object, you have contributed to that activity, even if only a minute amount. If, though, government sets up a tax credit, citizens are electing to spend their own money. "When Arizona taxpayers choose to contribute to STOs, they spend their own money, not money the state has collected from ... other taxpayers." This, therefore, distinguishes this case from *Flast*.

At one point, Kennedy turns to James Madison to support his reading of *Flast*. (Madison, it should be recalled, was instrumental in drafting the First Amendment, including its religion clauses.) However, as we will see when we take up Justice Kagan's dissent, it is a curious platform for Kennedy to stand on. In 1785, the Virginia legislature was considering a bill that would have created a tax "to support teachers of the Christian religion." Each taxpayer could designate his portion of the proposed tax to go to the denomination of his choice; if he did not select one, the legislature would give the money to "seminaries of learning," many of which were themselves religious in character. Madison objected, arguing that government should not "force a citizen to contribute three pence only [a trivial sum even then] of his property for the support of any one establishment." The critical point, according to Kennedy, is that it was a tax that was at issue. Thus, to the extent that the Court relied on Madison in *Flast*, he contended, its holding only refers to taxes.

Kennedy does have what seems like a major problem, but he dismisses it out of hand. A number of cases (five to be exact) decided after *Flast* with facts awfully similar to the STO program allowed taxpayer challenges. Kennedy brushes these aside with an odd argument. In none of these cases, he pointed out, did the Court actually discuss the standing issue, moving straight to the merits. "The Court," he says, "would risk error if it relied on assumptions that have gone unstated and unexamined." Kennedy surely knows this is a bogus argument. The Court does not reexamine its assumptions and principles in every case. When something is considered settled law, it is not examined anew in each case that comes up. The reason the Court did not discuss standing in those cases is that it was assumed, following *Flast*, that the taxpayers had standing. Of course, they may not, and often did not, prevail on the merits, but their ability to bring the case was simply assumed.

As an aside, at both the beginning and the end of the opinion, he provides some boilerplate comments about how important judicial restraint is. "Few exercises of the judicial power are more likely to undermine public confidence in the neutrality and integrity of the Judiciary than one which casts the Court in the role of a Council of Revision, conferring on itself the power to invalidate laws at the behest of anyone who disagrees with them." Anyone who has followed Justice Kennedy's career, especially in recent years, would point out that he has been one of the justices least hesitant to overrule legislative enactments in any number of cases.[5]

Concurring and Dissenting Opinions

Justice Scalia, joined by Justice Thomas, wrote a one-paragraph concurrence in which he simply reiterated his view that *Flast* should be overruled rather than sidestepped.

Justice Kagan, joined by her other three liberal colleagues—Ginsburg, Breyer, and Sotomayor—composed a thorough and convincing dissent. In her view, if *Flast* is still considered a viable precedent, then the taxpayers here deserve to have their day in court.

The core of her argument rests on two propositions. First, she contends that there is no essential difference between tax credits (or deductions or exemptions for that matter) and regular expenditures. In fact, most government budgets (including Arizona's) label them "tax expenditures." "Taxpayers experience the same injury for standing purposes whether government subsidization of religion takes the form of a cash grant or a tax measure." She offers several cogent examples, one of which seems especially compelling. "[A]ssume a State wishes to subsidize the ownership of crucifixes. It could purchase the religious symbols in bulk and distribute them to all takers. Or it could mail a reimbursement check to any individual who buys her own and submits a receipt for the purchase. Or it could authorize that person to claim a tax credit equal to the price she paid. Now, really—do taxpayers have less reason to complain if the State selects the last of these three options?"

Her point here is buttressed by the advertising used by some of the STOs. One told parents that by using the tax credit scheme, "you can send children to our community's [religious] day schools and it won't cost you a dime." Another told donors to "imagine giving [to charity] with someone else's money.... Stop Imagining, thanks to Arizona tax laws you can!"

Taking up the five cases in which the Court had granted taxpayer standing to challenge manipulations of the tax system in order to subsidize religious institutions, she points out that "The Court in all five of these cases divided sharply on the merits of the disputes. But in one respect, the Justices were unanimous: Not a single one thought to question the litigant's standing." In short, "they did not discuss what was taken as obvious." In fact, a couple of the cases have been cited as "exemplars of jurisdiction" in other contexts.

Additionally, she says the Court misconstrues James Madison's objections to the Virginia assessment law. What Kennedy neglected to note is that the bill Madison objected to included a provision that allowed conscientious objectors to contribute their money to a fund for constructing and maintaining county schools. She quotes an article by Noah Feldman, a prominent scholar of church-state relations, noting that the proposed law was "designed to avoid any charges of coercion of dissenters to pay taxes to support religious teachings with which they disagreed."[6] Therefore, the Arizona system is very close to the Virginia bill, making Madison's protests a thin reed for the majority. By pointing to him, Kennedy "betrays Madison's vision."

In short, what this decision will do is allow states to avoid having anyone challenge their attempts to direct funds to church-related schools, or also to challenge other establishment clause violations.

Today's decision devastates taxpayer standing in Establishment Clause cases. The government, after all, often uses tax expenditures to subsidize favored persons and activities. Still more, the government almost *always* has this option. Appropriations and tax subsidies are readily interchangeable; what is a cash grant today can be a tax break tomorrow. The Court's opinion thus offers a roadmap—more truly, just a one-step instruction—to any government that wishes to insulate its financing of religious activity from legal challenge. Structure the funding as a tax expenditure, and *Flast* will not stand in the way. No taxpayer will have standing to object. However blatantly the government may violate the Establishment Clause, taxpayers cannot gain access to the federal courts.

Conclusion

Commentators have been sharply divided over the decision in this case. Patrick Gillen supports both the standing aspect of the case and what this might mean for the substantive jurisprudence of the establishment clause.[7] He is critical of *Flast*, but is willing to live with the narrow reading of that case Kennedy trumpeted here. Most importantly, he argues that the establishment clause should be read as prohibiting only governmental spending for "inherently religious activities." Spending for general welfare purposes, such as for education, should not be seen as violating the establishment clause. Thus, even if Arizona had issued checks directly to religious schools, as long as it was for a general welfare purpose (for example, a secular aspect of the school, say, teaching mathematics), then it would pass muster, in his view. Thus, he says, "I believe that *Winn* puts the Supreme Court within reach of a comprehensive reform of its taxpayer standing doctrine that is both principled and consistent with the original understanding of the provision."[8]

Other supporters have gone further. Those who support school choice, for example, have cheered the constitutional doctrine enunciated here. By equating tax credits with private action and holding that the First Amendment only forbids government action, they see this as a "constitutional blueprint" for moving forward in this area.[9] By Bruce Van Buren's account, seven states are already moving in this direction and discussions are going on elsewhere. Going further still, Tim Keller has argued that the holding takes a step toward the idea that any decision an individual makes regarding his or her money is free from governmental restrictions. "It should be common sense that funds that never enter the government's coffers remain private funds."[10]

On the other side, William Marshall and Gene Nicol argue that Kennedy is wrong on the technicalities of the standing issue and, further, that his position leads to a substantive result that is at odds with the very purposes of the establishment clause. They echo Kagan's critique regarding the standing issue, concluding that "The problem with Kennedy's opinion … is that it makes little sense to purport to recognize taxpayer harm as a legitimate Establishment Clause concern while denying standing to those who bring such claims. Yet, *Winn* does exactly that through a hypertechnical account of injury that is so convoluted it strains credibility."[11] More fundamentally, the decision means that large swaths of potential infringements of the establishment clause are now immune from judicial scrutiny. "The Establishment Clause is in large measure aimed at curbing injuries that are, by their very nature, intangible and widely shared,"[12] injuries that Justice Scalia labeled "psychic harm" in his *Hein* concurrence. If a citizen's status as a taxpayer does not allow a challenge to these measures in court, then only the political process is available to those who dissent from any given policy. Their reworded take on Kagan's critique of how a state may proceed is this:

> We mean to provide money to support religious undertakings, but we seek to avoid the annoyance of constitutional accountability and judicial review. Therefore, we will provide tax credits to compensate for various church activities. No one will miss the significance. They will be assured that we have thrown the power of the state behind religious endeavors. (Or, at least behind those religious endeavors that meet our approval.) But no one will be allowed to use the courts to challenge our efforts.[13]

Clearly, this case represents a victory for more traditional religion. Conservative Protestant and Catholic schools will undoubtedly be among the main beneficiaries, for now at least. But the decision could be unsettling for adherents of traditional religion in the long run. If the trends we documented in Chapter 1 continue, other religious groups stand to grow in numbers. Among those who might then choose to wall themselves off from the broader society as much as today's conservative Christians do, the STO program will serve their interests nicely. Will conservative Christians be enthralled with the program should, say, fundamentalist Islamic schools proliferate?

Furthermore, how this program has played out illustrates the problems devout Christians face when they mix their brand of conservatism with the more business-oriented ethic. When public money floats about, there are always those who will seek to make a profit; after all, that is the way business works. And those with ties to the political system often stand to gain handsomely. It has ever been that way (think of land speculators after the American Revolution or Civil War military contractors, just to cite two historical examples) and I imagine always will be. The *New York Times* reported that Steve Yarbrough, president of the Arizona State Senate, for example, and a key supporter of the tax credit program, has done rather well.[14] One STO, the Arizona Christian School Tuition Organization (the party to this case), took in $72.9 million in donations from 2010 to 2014. Recall that 10 percent of this can be used for "overhead." Mr. Yarbrough is the executive director of the group, a job that pays him $125,000 a year. In addition, the STO uses his data processing firm for a variety of tasks, for which it was paid $636,000 in 2014 and several million in total over the last decade. Further, the organization rents office space from Mr. Yarbrough for $52,000 a year. Surely this type of activity has to be worrying to ordinary people in the pews.

Another irony is that the same Justice Kennedy who handed traditional religionists their victory here was the author of the majority opinion in *Obergefel v. Hodges*, the case which mandated the nationwide legalization of same-sex marriage and became such a lightning rod for conservative Christians in the 2016 election. As here, he was the decisive fifth vote for the majority.

In short, this decision has to be scored a win for traditional religion. However, it enunciated a doctrine that may well make adherents of those same traditional religions uncomfortable in the future.

CHAPTER 8

Who Is a "Minister" and Why Does It Matter?

Hosanna-Tabor Lutheran Church and School v. Equal Employment Opportunity Commission

This decision, handed down in January of 2012, was clearly an important one, close perhaps to a landmark case. For example, Richard W. Garnett, a professor of law at the University of Notre Dame and the Director of the University's Program in Church, State, and Society, said while the case was under consideration that "it could prove to be among the most important religious-liberty cases in many years."[1] Going even further, the *Wall Street Journal* believed that it was one of the "most important religious liberty cases in a half century."[2]

What elevated the case to this status? The chief reason was that a major philosophical issue was all but unavoidable: When government's entirely justified desire—reflecting widely held societal preferences—to enforce nondiscrimination in the workplace clashes with the autonomy of churches, how far can the government go in insisting on nondiscrimination?

The Supreme Court handed traditional religion a seemingly resounding victory. The justices voted 9–0 in favor of Hosanna-Tabor Lutheran Church and School, and most religious leaders rejoiced, both in the outcome and in the unanimity. To cite but one example, Bishop William E. Lori, Chairman of the United States Conference of Catholic Bishops' Religious Liberty Committee, contended that it was "a great day for the First Amendment," for the Court had stood up for "the historical and constitutional importance of keeping internal church affairs off limits to the government."[3] The decision was even more important to church leaders in light of an argument the Obama administration had made in its brief to the Court, something we will take up momentarily. It was an argument that stated clearly the secular position many want to see the courts adopt when deciding religious liberty cases, something deeply offensive to most religious leaders. To their delight, the Supreme Court all but ridiculed the administration's position.

However, it is possible that the leaders of traditional religious bodies should temper their enthusiasm. While it is certainly true that in this case a traditional religious group won a clear victory, and by implication other traditional religious groupings shared in the victory, the legal doctrine which the Court established will have to be applied across the board. Other groups, who frankly traditional religious leaders often find antithetical to society's best interest, or downright "un–American," will be able to lay claim to the same protection. In the end, as with other cases, traditional religionists may well have second thoughts about this decision.

Doctrinally, we finally come to a case that took up the religion clauses directly. Interestingly, though, and in contrast to many church-state cases, this decision rested on both the establishment clause and the free exercise clause. Ordinarily, either one or the other of the clauses is at issue, but here both were front and center.

A final reason the case was deemed important by Court watchers is that it would provide a window to the justices' thinking on church-state issues. It was the first time, for example, that Justice Elena Kagan, who had replaced Justice John Paul Stevens, had a chance to vote in a church-state case. Stevens had often been skeptical of religious liberty claims, and observers wondered if, as a fellow liberal, she would follow suit. Furthermore, how would the liberal and conservative blocs on the Court come down on the case?

The Case's Factual Background

The Lutheran Church-Missouri Synod (LCMS) is one of the more traditional, conservative Lutheran bodies in the United States. Theologically, for instance, it insists on the inerrancy of Scripture. Its practices, too, reflect a heavily orthodox conservatism. It only ordains men to the main pastoral role and, in general, restricts communion to LCMS members. It has 2.4 million baptized members worshipping in 6,200 congregations, making it the second largest Lutheran body and the eighth largest Protestant denomination in the United States.

It also maintains the largest Protestant educational system in the country. This includes 1,044 elementary and secondary schools, which enroll over 125,000 students. It also sponsors 10 universities and seminaries. These institutions are all considered to be an integral part of the church's witness to the world. Serving the denomination's churches and schools are approximately 10,000 pastors and teachers. It is worth noting that LCMS schools employ two kinds of teachers. One, called teachers, are commissioned ministers, whose status will be explained more fully later. These individuals are strongly preferred by LCMS schools, but when they are not available, the schools turn to contract teachers. Contract teachers are not "called" in any fashion, and indeed need not even be Lutherans. Normally, they are employed on a year-to-year basis to teach specific subjects.

Beginning in 1999, Cheryl Perich was employed as a teacher in the elementary school operated by Hosanna-Tabor Lutheran Church in Redford, Michigan. During her first year she began as a contract teacher, but she soon completed the requirements for becoming a commissioned minister and her status was converted to a called teacher. From 1999 until the 2003–2004 school year, she taught kindergarten, at which time she was assigned to the fourth grade. In that capacity, she taught both secular and religious subjects. Included in the former were math, language arts, social studies, science, gym, art, and music. Though many of the materials used in these classes were the same as those utilized in public schools, LCMS schools expect that the Christian perspective will always be brought to bear when pertinent. The religion class met four days a week for 30 minutes. In addition, two to three times a year she was in charge of the chapel service, where she chose the liturgy and delivered the message. All told, the time she devoted to directly religious activities made up on average about 45 minutes of a seven-hour school day. From every indication, she was a competent and respected teacher.

In June 2004, Perich became ill and her doctors were initially unsure of the diagnosis. In August, when Perich was no better, the school principal suggested she take disability leave. Perich was assured that she would have her job back when she was able to return to work. The school paid Perich's salary and insurance, and worked around her absence by combining some classes. As the spring semester approached, though, and Perich's return was still uncertain, they employed a temporary teacher to handle her duties. In December 2004, the doctors found that she suffered from narcolepsy, a rare condition that makes one fall into a deep sleep at unexpected intervals. With treatment underway, her doctor felt that she could safely return to work in two or three months; she immediately informed the principal of this fact. In late January 2005, Perich and the principal exchanged a series of emails discussing her disorder and her possible return. The principal was concerned that should her condition recur it might present a safety hazard to the students, or at the least frighten them if she were to collapse in class. In response, Perich insisted, and provided documentation, that her doctor had certified that she would soon be ready to return to work. Several communications between the two ensued, with each hardening their position as time went on. The principal then consulted with the school superintendent and the president of the congregation. Their feeling was that Perich should be offered a "peaceful release" (explained below). Perich refused this offer and on February 8 sent the principal a formal notice that her doctor believed she would be fully capable of returning to work on February 22. On February 13, the school informed her that there was not a position for her until at least the next fall. On February 22, the day her doctor indicated she would be fit to take up her duties, Perich came to the school. She refused to leave until she was given a written statement saying she had reported for work. That same day Perich told the principal that if she were not reinstated she would sue the school. The principal informed her that that would violate LCMS policy, which required settling disputes of this nature within the church's adjudicative system. Negotiations between Perich and the school board followed, but were unsuccessful in settling the matter. In April, the church voted to rescind her call. Perich then filed a claim under the Americans with Disabilities Act (ADA) of 1990, bypassing the internal bodies the LCMS has to hear such disputes.

Perich and the ADA

Title I of the ADA provides that

No covered entity shall discriminate against a qualified individual with a disability because of the disability of such individual in regard to job application procedures, the hiring, advancement, or discharge of employees, employee compensation, job training, and other terms, conditions, and privileges of employment.

As is customary in such statutes, the law contains provision for defenses if the differential treatment of people with disabilities is "job-related and consistent with business necessity." The enforcement of this title falls to the Equal Employment Opportunity Commission (EEOC). The commission was established in 1965 to administer the parts of the early civil rights laws regarding employment discrimination; as subsequent categories of people were added to equal employment opportunity laws, the EEOC's role expanded. The commission has the power to hear complaints, investigate, and, if warranted. to bring suits against employers for violations. Thus, had Perich's complaint been pursued under the normal processes, a hearing would have been held and both sides would have had the opportunity to present their evidence. A ruling would have then followed, which either party could appeal to the courts if they desired.

However, this was not what happened. Another section of the ADA provides:

> No person shall discriminate against any individual because such individual has opposed any act or practices made unlawful by this chapter or because such individual made a charge, testified, assisted, or participated in any manner in an investigation, proceeding, or hearing under this chapter.

Hosanna-Tabor said that Perich was being discharged for bringing the action to the EEOC at all. Instead of taking legal action, the church believed, she should be bound by the rulings of internal LCMS bodies. Her argument was that she had a legal right, established by the ADA, to institute the action and that federal law trumped LCMS procedures. The church's position that she be bound solely by its procedures violated the second section of the ADA quoted above.

To appreciate the stance of the church, it is necessary to clarify the structural role of ministers in the denomination and why it insisted on the sanctity of its internal procedures.

The LCMS has two types of ministers. There is first the "ordained clergy" who "preach the word and administer the sacraments." Alongside them, there are "commissioned ministers," who perform a variety of tasks within the church, such as ministers of music, church youth workers, and teachers in Lutheran schools. The vast majority of commissioned ministers serve in this last capacity. Commissioned ministers may be either graduates of one of the Synod's universities (but if so they must be certified as eligible to become a commissioned minister by the officials of the university) or, if their bachelor's degree is from elsewhere, enroll in a "colloquy" program. This program consists of a series of eight university-level correspondence courses on theology. Following satisfactory completion of these studies, the candidate must obtain an endorsement from the Synod and pass an oral examination. A person may then become a commissioned minister; to emphasize the seriousness of the achieving of this status, a special public ceremony is held to bestow this office on him or her.

Upon commissioning, the new minister is ready to receive a "call" from a local congregation. If a person receives and accepts a call, then the congregation may only dismiss the commissioned minister for malfeasance or by a supermajority vote of the congregation. Given the seriousness of the commitment the commissioned minister, especially a teacher, has made and the reciprocal obligations of the congregation, it is not surprising that although it is not mandatory, "the normal expectancy of the church and teacher candidates is that, unless prevented by personal circumstances, the teaching ministry of an individual will be followed as a lifelong calling."[4]

The LCMS has a long-established procedure for settling disputes between its ministers (both ordained and commissioned) and local congregations. To the LCMS it is an article of faith, based on I Corinthians 6:1–8, that disputes be settled inside the church. Verses 1 and 7(a) form the heart of this belief: "When one of you has a grievance against another, does he dare go to law before the unrighteous instead of the saints?" and "To have lawsuits at all with one another is already a defeat for you." A series of panels, significantly staffed by people called "reconcilers," is maintained by the church.[5] These panels are independent of the hierarchy and are as protective of ministerial rights as congregational rights. It is important to note that the church believes that the hand of God moves within these panels as they try to reconcile the parties, of if the matters cannot be reconciled, to render a decision favoring one party or the other. The Synod claims, and no one seriously disputes, that "In all these processes, the Synod concerns itself with procedural justice."[6] As proof that the cards are not stacked against commissioned ministers in these proceedings, the LCMS points out that congregations have been expelled from the denomination for treating their commissioned ministers unfairly.

To Hosanna-Tabor, therefore, and the LCMS more generally, when Ms. Perich opted to pursue her dispute at the EEOC, it was a serious violation of the canons of the church. To Perich and the EEOC, on the other hand, the church's taking action against her for filing her claim violated the section of the ADA which outlawed retaliation for merely filing such a claim.

The "Ministerial Exception"

We must now examine a key legal doctrine known as the "ministerial exception." The doctrine is rooted in the concept of "church autonomy."

The "exception" had historically been recognized by all the country's Courts of Appeal, but the Supreme Court had never ruled on its validity. True, the Supreme Court had indirectly upheld it by denying several attempted appeals where the doctrine had been applied by the lower courts. Nevertheless, this was far from constituting a specific endorsement.

The doctrine grew from the embryo of church property disputes. The landmark Supreme Court case in this area was *Watson v. Jones*, dating from 1871. In the aftermath of the Civil War, a Presbyterian Church in Louisville, Kentucky, suffered a serious division, the basis of which was interpretation of church doctrine. A series of church bodies heard the dispute and finally awarded the church property to one of the factions. The other appealed to the courts, citing what they believed were erroneous conclusions by the church councils. However, Justice Miller, speaking for the Court, felt that the secular courts must defer to church authorities on matters such as these.

> In this class of cases, we think the rule of action which should govern the civil courts, founded in a broad and sound view of the relations of church and state under our system of laws, and supported by a prepondering weight of judicial authority, is that whenever the questions of discipline or of faith or ecclesiastical rule, custom, or law have been decided by the highest of these church judicatories to which the matter has been carried, the legal tribunals must accept such decisions as final and as binding on them in their application to the case before them.

The courts have continued to apply this doctrine to church property disputes, down to the present day. For example, Justice William Brennan wrote in a 1969 case (*Presbyterian Church v. Mary Elizabeth Blue Hall Memorial Presbyterian Church*), that religious liberty is plainly jeopardized when church property litigation is made to turn on the resolution by civil courts of controversies over religious doctrine and practice. If civil courts undertake to resolve such controversies in order to adjudicate the property dispute, the hazards are ever present of inhibiting the free development of religious doctrine and of implicating secular interests in matters of purely ecclesiastical concern.

In time, especially as the First Amendment was applied to the states via the Fourteenth, the church autonomy doctrine became constitutionalized. This was made explicit in 1952 in *Kedroff v. St. Nicholas Cathedral*. New York State had enacted a statute stripping the Russian Orthodox hierarchy in Moscow of jurisdiction over its properties in the state (alleging that the church was now only an arm of the Soviet government). The

Supreme Court ruled the law unconstitutional under the church autonomy doctrine. As an aside, though it was unnecessary to the decision of this case, the Court alluded to the right of a church to select its own clergy "Freedom to select clergy, where no improper methods of choice are proven, we think, must now be said to have federal constitutional protection as a part of the free exercise of religion against state interference."

Solidifying this conclusion, the Court expressly applied the church autonomy doctrine to personnel cases in 1976 in *Serbian Eastern Orthodox Diocese v. Milivojevich*. Milivojevich was the head of the church's American branch, but was removed from office by the church's hierarchy in Yugoslavia. Whatever the merits of Milivojevich's claims, the Court said they would take a hands-off approach when it came to internal church disputes over who should sit in an ecclesiastical position. The autonomy rule for settling property cases "applies with equal force to church disputes over church polity and administration."

The first case to connect the church autonomy doctrine to employment discrimination law, and the root of the "ministerial exception," was *McClure v. Salvation Army*, a Court of Appeals decision from 1972. Title VII of the Civil Rights Act of 1964 banned, among other things, employers from engaging in gender discrimination in hiring or promotion. No exemption was made for religious organizations or institutions.[7] The act also made retaliation against an employee claiming discrimination illegal. McClure, an ordained female minister in the Salvation Army, alleged that she was fired for complaining that she was paid less than comparably qualified men, in violation of Title VII. The court held, however, that the free exercise clause required a "ministerial exception" to antidiscrimination law. Her suit was therefore barred. The judges laid out their rationale as follows:

> The relationship between an organized church and its ministers is its lifeblood. The minister is the chief instrument by which the church seeks to fulfill its purpose. Matters touching this relationship must necessarily be recognized as of prime ecclesiastical concern.

Over the years that followed, all the Courts of Appeal adopted the ministerial exception as settled doctrine. Two questions lurched in the inevitable gray areas, though. (1) Did the doctrine reach beyond churches and cover religiously affiliated institutions, and if so, how far? (2) Who could be classified as a minister? In general, the Courts of Appeal adopted a broad approach to both questions. Two cases will illustrate this point.

In *Petruska v. Gannon* (2006) a female chaplain appointed at a Catholic university was assured that she would have a job even if a qualified male became available. Later, she complained to the provost and the bishop about sexual harassment by the university's president. The chaplain's office was then restructured and she was demoted. She then filed a gender discrimination suit under Title VII of the Civil Rights Act of 1964. The Court of Appeal held, however, that despite rather clear evidence of her having been the object of gender discrimination her suit had to fail in light of the ministerial exception. Gannon University's decision regarding who to install in these positions and the manner in which their duties were to be divided were spiritual decisions. The university's choices were consequently constitutionally protected from governmental interference by the free exercise clause. In *Tomic v. Catholic Diocese of Peoria* (2006), a dispute between a church organist (who was not ordained) and the priest over Easter music escalated to the point that the priest dismissed the organist. He contended that the real reason for his removal was age discrimination, which is barred by the Age Discrimination in Employment Act (ADEA). The Court of Appeals held that the organist was a minister and therefore could not bring a suit under the ADEA. Leslie Griffin believes that the courts have been too "problematic and excessively deferential to religious institutions" when deciding which institutions can fall under the exception and in defining who is a minister. In the process, they have turned "elementary and secondary school teachers, university and seminary professors, school principals, communications managers, administrative personnel, music directors, organists, and musicians into ministers."[8] Nevertheless, the broad framework has stood.

The chief question as *Hosanna-Tabor* was docketed was whether the Supreme Court would give its imprimatur to the doctrine. But even if so, there were other important questions. For example, which constitutional basis would they select to rest the doctrine on? And, how would they define the guidelines for determining who could be labeled a minister in the future?

As for the constitutional issue, the ministerial exception could rest on any one of three different bases. The free exercise clause is the most oft-cited, the courts finding in it the rationale for church autonomy. Specifically, the right of individuals to exercise their religion as they see fit is generalizable to religious institutions. Part of that autonomy, as the quote from *McClure* explains, is choosing who can be a minister and what their terms of employment are.

A second possibility is the establishment clause. Two different facets of the establishment clause offer themselves. One of these looks back to English practices that were carried over to colonial days. As the Church of England was an officially established church, the governing authorities appointed, paid, and dismissed clergy. Clearly, this is one practice that was forbidden by the establishment clause. This becomes pertinent in employment discrimination cases because the remedy in secular situations is often reinstatement. Consequently, if a court ordered a church to reinstate an unfairly dismissed member of the clergy, the state would be in effect appointing ministers. The other aspect of the establishment clause one could lean on to build the ministerial exception derives from the third prong of the *Lemon* test, that governments must avoid "excessive entanglement" with the church. If the courts were to take up cases involving the dismissal (or demotion, etc.) of ministers, they would have to delve into the details of ministerial working conditions. This would inevitably produce a good bit of entanglement, likely often to be excessive. Better to steer clear of this entirely.

The third rationale comes from what we encountered in *Christian Legal Society*, the right of expressive association. The courts have found in the general thrust of the First Amendment a right of people to gather in groups in order to advance certain causes. Groups are guaranteed the right to choose their own objectives and to select whom they would like to be the spokespersons for the group. (Recall this was the critical factor in *Boy Scouts v. Dale*.) Churches have the same right in this regard as any other group. A major part of this right when it comes to churches is appointing members of the clergy, using whatever means and criteria the church chooses. These decisions, therefore, are outside the realm where courts should tread.

In the written briefs and the oral argument at the Supreme Court, the clashing views on these matters were thrown into sharp relief. Furthermore, this case illustrates the theme of this book in clear fashion. The argument of the Obama administration was rooted in a plainly secular view of religious liberty, stirring the ire of many religious groups.

The brief for Hosanna-Tabor and all the religious groups who filed *amici* briefs (of which there were 18[9]) argued for a strong version of the ministerial exception based on all three emanations from the religion clauses, and, that it should largely be up to individual religious groups to decide who was to be classified as a minister. The LCMS brief, for example, said a minister should be any "employee who performs important religious functions."

The government contended that the right of expressive association was what should be argued here, and that alone. Leondra Krueger, representing the Solicitor General's office, said churches have, in this regard, only the same rights as, say, labor unions. Justice Scalia interrupted to say "That's extraordinary."

The Court should, the government said, not adopt a broad, categorical exemption for ministers. Only in certain narrow cases, such as the always cited one of not applying gender discrimination rules to Catholic churches selecting a priest, should any ministerial exception apply. That is, only when a clear theological imperative is held by the church should the courts grant deference. But these cases should be adjudicated on a case-by-case basis, and not subjected to a categorical rule.

Ready with a fallback position, the government's brief said that "If, however, the Court adopts a categorical exemption, it should be limited to those plaintiffs who perform exclusively religious functions and whose claims concern their entitlement to occupy or retain their ecclesiastical office." Near the end of the brief the government reiterated this position in even stronger words—that any rule should apply only to "those employees whose positions have no secular equivalent." During oral argument, Ms. Peich's attorney was arguing in that vein that she was not a minister: "[T]he principal reason is she carries out such important secular functions in addition to her religious duties." Justice Roberts replied: "That can't—I'm sorry to interrupt you but that can't be the test. The Pope is a head of state carrying out secular functions, right?"

The Opinion of the Court

Chief Justice Roberts wrote the opinion for the Court. The justices unanimously endorsed the ministerial exception as a valid part of constitutional law, and chastised the administration's and the EEOC's position. They had somewhat divergent views, though, on how it should be defined. While holding that Perich was clearly a minister, Roberts was of the view that the Court should not, at this point, lay out detailed guidelines, leaving it to future cases to decide the coverage and scope of the exception. Justice Alito, joined by Justice Kagan, was prepared to assert that determining who is and who is not a minister should itself be left to the various religious bodies.

Roberts begins by nodding to Magna Carta and other early English documents that assert a right of the church to elect its own officials. This right was attenuated by subsequent kings, however (Henry II, for example, sent a letter to the church electoral body in Winchester intoning that they could hold a "free election but [I] forbid you to elect anyone but Richard, my clerk") and abolished altogether by Henry VIII when he made himself supreme head of the Church of England. When the Church of England was transplanted to and became established in several colonies, the right of royal authorities to appoint the clergy continued. Puritan New England and some other colonies (especially Pennsylvania) freed themselves of this tradition, and even where Anglicanism was established, controversy occasionally erupted over the practice. Roberts concludes that the religion clauses of the Constitution "ensured that the new Federal Government— unlike the English Crown—would have no role in filling ecclesiastical offices. The Establishment Clause prevents the Government from appointing ministers, and the Free Exercise Clause prevents it from interfering with the freedom of religious groups to select their own."

To buttress this position, he then recalls two events from James Madison's career, made especially relevant by Madison's key role in drafting and pushing for the First Amendment's religion clauses. The first one came about when Madison was Secretary of State in the Thomas Jefferson administration. After the Louisiana Purchase, a Catholic bishop asked Madison if he had a recommendation on who should be appointed to head the Catholic church in the newly acquired territory. Madison responded that the "scrupulous policy of the Constitution in guarding against political interference with religious affairs" made it improper for him to offer any suggestions whatever in the "selection of ecclesiastical individuals." The second took place while Madison was president. A bill came to his desk that incorporated the Episcopal Church in the District of Columbia (Congress, it should be recalled, has administrative jurisdiction over the District). Madison vetoed the bill on the grounds that it contained details of church organization and polity "comprehending even the election and removal of the Minister."

Having established this background, Roberts reviews the Supreme Court's decisions in *Watson, Kerdoff,* and *Milivojevich.* He then takes up the matter of the ministerial exception, endorsing it and explaining its dual constitutional foundations.

> We agree that there is such a ministerial exception [as the Courts of Appeal have held]. The members of a religious group put their faith in the hands of their ministers. Requiring a church to accept or retain an unwanted minister, or punishing a church for failing to do so, intrudes upon more than a mere employment decision. Such action interferes with the internal governance of the church, depriving the church of control over the selection of those who will personify its beliefs. By imposing an unwanted minister, the state infringes the Free Exercise Clause, which protects a religious group's right to shape its own faith and mission through its appointments. According the state the power to determine which

individuals will minister to the faithful also violates the Establishment Clause, which prohibits government involvement in such ecclesiastical decisions.

He immediately and in no uncertain terms rejects the EEOC's argument that the sole constitutional basis for the ministerial exception is freedom of association. It is simply "untenable." Further," [w]e cannot accept the remarkable view that the Religion Clauses have nothing to say about a religious organization's freedom to select its own ministers."

He then addresses another argument that the EEOC and Perich made, namely that the *Smith* case holding that one cannot use free exercise to justify disobeying a generally applicable law works against Hosanna-Tabor. That is, the provision in the ADA that forbids retaliation against those bringing actions under its provision is a generally applicable law, covering all employers. But, Roberts argued, there is a distinction. "*Smith* involved government regulation of only outward physical acts [in that case the taking of small amounts of a banned drug]. The present case, in contrast, concerns government interference with an internal church decision that affects the faith and mission of the church itself."

Having validated the ministerial exception, it must now be determined whether Perich is a minister. While concluding that she should be classified as a minister, Roberts believed that at the moment the Court should not "adopt a rigid formula for deciding when an employee qualifies as a minister." The District Court had held that was the central consideration, and given the circumstances of Perich's employment and the fact that the church and she both held her out as a minister, she was therefore deemed a minister and her suit barred. The Court of Appeal disagreed and reversed. They based their decision largely on the fact that only a small fraction of Perich's time was spend on religious classes and religious activities.

Roberts marshalled several features of Perich's role and work to justify labeling her a minister. First, the church placed her in "a role distinct from that of most of its members." She bore the formal title of "commissioned minister" and received a "diploma of vocation" from the church. She was deemed "a professional person in the ministry of the Gospel." Second, her becoming a commissioned minister had involved substantial special training followed by a solemn ceremony and endorsement by the Synod. Third, Perich's own actions indicated that she considered herself a minister. For example, she claimed the ministerial housing allowance on her tax return. Moreover, after her termination she had submitted a form to the Synod stating that she felt "God is leading me to serve in the teaching ministry," and that she was "anxious to be in the teaching ministry again soon."

Fourth, the central role of religion in the work of commissioned ministers at the school was underlined by several church documents, of which Perich was well aware. Teachers were to "lead others toward Christian maturity" and to "teach faithfully the Word of God, the Sacred Scriptures in its truth and purity and as set forth in all the symbolical books of the Evangelical Lutheran Church." Thus, the religious activities Perich performed at the school were of far more importance than the mere allocation of 45 minutes of her work day might indicate.

Roberts unhesitatingly overturned the Court of Appeals decision, citing in particular the undue emphasis they gave to the time Perich spent on secular subjects, saying Perich's status should not turn on a "stopwatch" approach. "The amount of time an employee spends on particular activities is relevant in assessing that employee's status, but that factor cannot be considered in isolation, without regard to the nature of the religious functions performed." Roberts also took care to dismiss the EEOC's contention that only employees with "exclusively religious functions" should be considered ministers. "[W]e are unsure whether any such employees exist," he said, further noting, perhaps recalling his statement about the Pope during oral argument, that "[t]he heads of congregations themselves often have a mix of duties, including secular ones such as helping to manage the congregation's finances, supervising purely secular personnel, and overseeing the upkeep of facilities."

Perich was, therefore, a minister and her suit was barred.

Justice Alito wrote a concurring opinion joined by Justice Kagan. The central thrust was only a mild rebuke to the majority opinion. In Alito's view, Roberts' preference for a future case-by-case approach to setting the parameters of the ministerial exception was misguided. Instead, he preferred a functional approach.

What he meant by that was rooted in the observation that the term "minister" is not applicable to all religious groups. Muslims and Jehovah's Witnesses, for example, do not have firm lines between the clergy and the laity. Anyone "who serves in positions of leadership, those who perform important functions in worship services and in the performance of religious ceremonies and rituals, and those who are entrusted with teaching and conveying the tenets of the faith to the next generation," regardless of their title, ought to fall under the ministerial exception. As for Perich, she was clearly a "minister" under any kind of functional definition. "What matters is that [she] played an important role as an instrument of her church's religious message and as a leader of its worship activities."

A secondary point was that Perich's claim that her firing because she went outside the church bodies (that is, to the EEOC and the courts) was a mere pretext cannot stand. If the courts were to take that question up, they would have to decide how important the doctrine of settling disputes internally is to Lutherans. To determine that they would have to inquire into a range of theological issues, which is something the courts are not equipped to do, and ought to be barred by the First Amendment from doing in any case.

Conclusion

Consequently, Hosanna-Tabor won a resounding victory. Even Douglas Laycock, who argued the case for the church, did not expect a unanimous verdict in his favor.[10] When the decision was rendered, the praise from religious bodies, especially traditional ones, was universal. Reverend Matthew Harrison, the president of the LCMS said that he was "delighted" with the decision. The church's statement went further.

> The Court, in upholding the right of churches to select their own ministers without government interference, has confirmed a critical religious liberty in our country. The Lutheran Church-Missouri Synod places great emphasis on the religious education of its children and the important role of commissioned ministers in promoting our faith, so we are thankful that the Court has confirmed our church's right to decide who will be serving as ministers in our churches and schools.[11]

Bishop William E. Lori, the chair of the U.S. Conference of Catholic Bishops Religious Liberty Committee seconded this sentiment, saying that it was "a great day for the First Amendment," adding "This decision makes resoundingly clear the historical and constitutional importance of keeping internal church affairs off limits to the government—because whoever chooses the minister chooses the message."[12] The Baptist Joint Committee on Public Affairs' statement was a bit more restrained, but still strongly supportive: "It is a helpful decision explaining the important and unique way that the Constitution protects religious organizations in matters of internal governance."[13] The Mormon affiliated *Deseret Morning News* announced that "On January 11, the U.S. Supreme Court rang the religious liberty bell loud and clear."[14]

Nevertheless, some groups were dismayed. Reverend Barry Lynn of the Americans United for Separation of Church and State contended the decision meant that "Clergy who are fired for reasons unrelated to theology—no matter how capricious or venal those reasons may be—have just had the courthouse door slammed in their faces." Marci Hamilton, a respected scholar of church-state law, said she was glad the decision was narrowly tailored so that perhaps some future claims might stand.[15]

Moreover, legal doctrines cannot be selectively applied. True, the LCMS is a stalwart manifestation of traditional religion. But, as we stressed in previous chapters, a Supreme Court doctrine will have to be applied across the board. Suppose a radical sect of Islam wants to retain a radical cleric. Will the Lutherans, Catholics, Baptists, and Mormons quoted above be enthusiastic about that? As a weather vane for that possibility, the Muslim-American Public Affairs Council filed an *amici* brief on the behalf of itself and several small minority religious groups arguing how important it is to minority religious groups to have autonomy in their affairs. Lurking behind the seeming generic arguments the brief makes are several important questions about how far a religious group can go in organizing its own affairs. The right is surely not absolute. But if the Alito argument is followed to its logical conclusion, such a group can go a long way. This case could turn out to be a victory for more than traditional religious bodies.

Another sidelight to this case is that most religious groups were outraged at the Obama administration's arguments, seeming to limit religious liberty to a right of expressive association. In addition to the general anger this position generated, the *Deseret Morning News* writer made the explicit connection between what the administration argued here and the abortion drugs mandate in the regulations promulgated under the then recently-passed Affordable Care Act. We will take this issue up momentarily; but first, in order to follow our chronological narrative, we need to examine an establishment clause case revolving around opening city council meetings with a prayer.

CHAPTER 9

Prayers at a Town Council

Town of Greece v. Galloway

Beginning in 1999 the town council of Greece, New York, a Rochester suburb, population 94,000, had opened its monthly sessions with a minister from one of the town's churches giving a brief prayer, after the roll was called and the Pledge of Allegiance recited. Two local residents, Susan Galloway and Linda Stephens, who occasionally attended the council meetings to speak on various matters, challenged the prayers as a violation of the establishment clause. A Federal District Court upheld the town but the Court of Appeals reversed. The town then appealed to the Supreme Court.

To some, perhaps even most, people, this dispute seems trivial. The prayer takes up at most a few minutes of time and would appear to do no harm. In the vernacular, it is "no big deal." If it adds to the solemnity of the council's deliberations, its stated purpose, or even if it doesn't, why should anyone object? However, prayer at any public occasion, especially if done by a religious official, mingles church and state, and that is the rub. If it is proper on some occasions but not others, which ones fall on which side of the line? Who will select the prayer givers? Must the prayers not offend citizens who do not share the religious beliefs or traditions of the person offering the prayer? If so, does a public official need to approve the prayer in advance? Does identifying the institutions of the state with the faith of a majority, even in small governmental units with relatively homogenous populations, inevitably make those outside the dominant religion feel like second-class citizens? We have touched on these issues before in the context of displays on public property, but they stand out with special poignancy when it comes to prayer.

Indeed, we can see here three of the tensions that are our main theme, the changing American religious landscape: the issue of growing diversity,

100

the rise of secularism, and the reaction of conservative Christians to these trends. As an example of the latter, one local clergyman in Greece praised the prayer practice and found it deeply troubling that other towns did not have "God-fearing" leaders. Another said that Galloway, Stephens, and others who objected were "ignorant of the history of our country."

The Supreme Court upheld the town, but split 5–4 along the liberal-conservative lines we have already encountered in several cases. Justice Kennedy wrote the opinion, but only for a plurality, over the forceful dissent of Justice Kagan.

The Case's Factual Background

A new town council member suggested that, given his experience at the county level, beginning monthly meetings with a brief prayer would set an important tone for the council's deliberations. No objections being made, a clerical employee of the town was directed to compile a list of local clergy and invite them in voluntary rotation to offer the prayer. She utilized a local guide to congregations published by the Chamber of Commerce and called the various congregations in the town, asking if each of the clergy would agree to be put on the list to give the invocation. The sequence was apparently set up randomly. All of the ministers who gave the prayers were unpaid volunteers. The minister who was designated each month was given the title of "Chaplain of the Month," thanked for his or her service, and given a plaque. In line with the relative homogeneity of the town, all the congregations in the Chamber's guide were Christian. Not all the residents of Greece, even those who were religious, were affiliated with Christian churches, but adherents of other faiths attended houses of worship in nearby Rochester. (Several Jewish synagogues, for instance, were right over the city boundary line.) The town did not advertise the policy in any way, by putting it on its website, for example.

No effort was made by the council to offer guidance to the clergy on the content of the prayer, nor was any policy in place to approve the prayer in advance. Accordingly, each "chaplain" was free to compose whatever prayer he or she chose. A good many were rather generic, or at least generically Christian, but several dwelled unabashedly on Christian themes. Two examples will suffice. The first:

> Lord we ask you to send your spirit of servanthood upon all of us gathered here this evening to do your work for the benefit of all in our community. We ask you to bless our elected and appointed officials so they may deliberate with wisdom

and act with courage. Bless the members of our community who come here to speak before the board so they may state their cause with honesty and humility.... Lord we ask you to bless us all, that everything we do here tonight will move you to welcome us one day into your kingdom as good and faithful servants. We ask this in the name of our brother Jesus. Amen.

The second:

Lord, God of all creation, we give you thanks and praise for your presence and action in the world. We look with anticipation to the celebration of Holy Week and Easter. It is in the solemn events of next week that we find the very heart and center of our Christian faith. We acknowledge the saving sacrifice of Jesus Christ on the cross. We draw strength, vitality, and confidence from his resurrection at Easter.... We pray for peace in the world, an end to terrorism, violence, conflict, and war. We pray for stability, democracy, and good government in those countries in which our armed forces are now serving, especially in Iraq and Afghanistan.... Praise and glory be yours, O Lord, now and forever more. Amen.

Some observers and critics have felt that the physical aspects of the opening ceremony are pertinent. The clergyman or clergywoman stood at a lectern at the front of the room, facing the audience, with the council seated behind him or her. He or she usually said something like "Let us pray," and sometimes asked the attendees to stand or bow their heads.

Of some significance also was the type of business the council conducted. After the roll call, the Pledge, and the prayer, the first order of business was also largely ceremonial. Passing a resolution thanking the fire department for its service, for example, or congratulating a local Boy Scout troop for winning an award. The second part of the council meeting was given over to what might be called legislative business, discussing and voting on general policy issues: raises for town employees or matters of traffic control. Finally, the council would turn to more adjudicatory matters: individuals or businesses' requests for licenses or permits of various sorts (e.g., building permits) or requests for zoning variances.

In 2008, after Ms. Galloway and Ms. Stephens filed their suit, the council reached out for others to offer the prayer. A Jewish layman who was a friend of one of the council members was twice invited to offer the prayer. The council also announced that anyone could ask to give the invocation. Responding, the chairman of the local Baha'i Temple and a Wiccan priestess applied and were offered the opportunity to open the meeting. Nevertheless, these were the only exceptions to local Christian clergy offering the prayer. Between the initiation of the practice and 2010, 126 out of 130 board meetings were opened with Christian clergy giving the prayer.

Precedents and Legal Framework

Prayer on public occasions touches a deep nerve in American life. This is especially true when the prayer buttresses the once predominantly Christian, or within Christian even, Protestant character of the population. Constitutionally, it throws into stark relief the strict separationist and accommodationist ideas regarding establishment. Must the government at all levels remain strictly secular or can it make a nod to the religious character of our people. If it treats all religions equally (although what counts as a legitimate religion may be a rub for many)?

In chapter two, we briefly surveyed how the Supreme Court has stood on this question of prayer in public spaces, beginning with *Engel v. Vitale* (ending publicly ordained and sponsored prayer in public school classrooms) to *Lee v. Wiseman* (overturning prayers at a public school graduation ceremony). Following these precedents would make Greece's prayers untenable. However, the Court was faced with an important counterprecedent that relied on alternative reasoning.

The logical place to begin in any establishment clause case is with the old standby, the *Lemon* test, with its three-prong requirement that policies have a secular purpose, that their primary effect be neither the advancement nor the inhibition of religion, and that the state avoid excessive entanglement with religion. Despite many criticisms, the Court has left the test standing. In *Lee v. Wiseman*, as we discussed in chapter two, a middle school principal had invited a local rabbi to give an opening and closing prayer at the graduation ceremony, a move challenged by a parent. The Court held, in a 5–4 decision, with the opinion authored by Justice Kennedy, that there was no need to reexamine the *Lemon* test. In this instance, in spite of the fact that the principal had given the rabbi a set of guidelines (given to all clergy who had led the prayers) about keeping the prayer nonsectarian, the very facts that a public institution endorsed the prayer and that we were dealing with young people were controlling. According to Kennedy, there would be subtle pressure on those who did not wish to participate in the prayer. They could stand and give tacit consent. Or they could remain seated; but, if they did, they would be conspicuous. Either option was unacceptable. The central guideline that emerged from the case was this: "It is beyond dispute that, at a minimum, the Constitution guarantees that government may not coerce anyone to support or participate in religion or its exercise, or otherwise act in a way which 'establishes a [state] religion or religious faith, or tends to do so.'" (Internal quotation from *Lynch v. Donnelley*.) After this case, recall, the

Supreme Court also struck down prayers at other public school events, such as football games.

Obviously, though, there are a number of differences between the prayers voided in the school cases and what was being done in Greece. In one sense, the situation at Greece bore more resemblance to the cases on public displays than to cases involving school prayer before young people. Nevertheless, there was a precedent involving prayer that the majority chose to lean on, namely *Marsh v. Chambers*, a 1983 case. For 16 years, a paid Presbyterian minister had given an opening daily prayer to the Nebraska legislature. For many years, the prayer had been grounded in Christian themes. When a Jewish member of the legislature spoke to him about this however, the chaplain made the prayers more ecumenical.

The majority of six cast aside the use of tests of any type and instead turned to history. Prayers at the opening of legislative sessions are "deeply embedded in the history and tradition of this country." The practice was begun in the Continental Congress of 1774 and continued into the first Congress under the Constitution. One of the first orders of business in 1789 was, in fact, the authorization of chaplains for both houses of Congress. Notably, three days after these clergymen were appointed, Congress reached agreement on the wording of the Bill of Rights. Would, any reasonable observer might ask, the members have approved the First Amendment if they had just violated it? However, a more germane question, perhaps, is how much weight should be given to actions of early congresses, all of which contained many men who wrote and voted on constitutional provisions? In one view, dubbed originalism, their action should be all but determinative. The words and phrases of the Constitution should be construed, as far as possible, in light of what they meant at the time. Some adopt a slightly more flexible version of this approach, arguing that modern interpreters should seek the intent of the provisions rather than the narrow dictionary meaning of the words.[1] Furthermore, should any weight be given to social changes that have occurred since the late eighteenth century?

Writing for the six-member majority in the case, Chief Justice Burger gave a strong but not determinative place to history. He wrote that

> Standing alone, historical patterns cannot justify contemporary violations of constitutional guarantees, but there is far more here than simply historical patterns. In this context, historical evidence sheds light not only on what the draftsmen intended the Establishment Clause to mean, but also on how they thought that clause applied to the practice authorized by the First Congress—their actions reveal their intent.

After surveying the long history of prayer in American legislative bodies, he concluded, "In light of the unambiguous and unbroken history of more than 200 years, there can be no doubt that the practice of opening legislative sessions with prayer has become part of the fabric of our society." Thus, the intent of the framers is seconded by long historical practice. In the end, Burger and five of his colleagues felt that neither the fact of the chaplain coming from one denomination, the use of public funds to pay him, nor the nature of the prayers he offered posed constitutional problems. The Court did note, though, that the minister should not use the prayer as an opportunity to "proselytize or advance any one, or to disparage any other, faith or belief."

Justice William Brennan authored a strongly worded dissent. He chastised the majority for not using the *Lemon* test, arguing that any first-year law student who applied this test would vote against the prayer. Further, even if we adopt history as our guidepost, we need to keep the purpose of the establishment clause before us. It was designed, in his view, to guard against church and state becoming entangled with each other, and given the current diversity of the nation, manifesting that purpose would argue against having a clergyman from one denomination give a prayer in this type of formal governmental setting. Brennan's dissent, however, gave way to the majority when both the Court, and the dissenters, used *Marsh* as the key precedent in Greece's case.

The Opinion of the Court

Kennedy begins by saying that while some regard *Marsh* as an exception to the Court's decisions on public prayer, in reality it is compatible with the precedents in this area. His reasoning was that legislative prayer was qualitatively different from prayer in other settings because of its uninterrupted prevalence throughout our history, beginning with the first congress in 1789. The case, does not, though, he was quick to stress, stand for the proposition that any practice with a historical pedigree is constitutionally valid. Nonetheless, historical understanding is important when it comes to evaluating how public institutions conduct their business. Since the town council is not exactly parallel to a national or state legislature and its proceedings are somewhat different, the Court must determine whether the similarities or differences are the most salient. In the legal jargon, the case is "fact intensive." As Kennedy put it, "The Court's inquiry, then, must be to determine whether the prayer practice in the town of Greece fits within the tradition long followed in Congress and the state legislatures."

Galloway and Stephens did not seek to overturn *Marsh*, but instead insisted that what was being done in Greece fell outside the holding in that case. First, they argued that the prayers that opened the Nebraska legislature were generic whereas those offered in Greece were often if not usually deeply sectarian. Second, they contended, looking to *Lee v. Wiseman*, that there was an element of coercion here. While there was certainly no overt coercion, there were subtle pressures on citizens attending the meetings to participate in the ceremonial prayer, especially if one had business coming up before the council (say, an application for a zoning variance).

Kennedy stressed that while the prayers the Nebraska chaplain had offered were often rather generic when the case was heard, that was only because the chaplain had voluntarily responded to the concerns voiced by a Jewish member of the legislature. It was not a policy, and was certainly not prescribed by the legislature. Throughout our history, legislative prayers have been "decidedly Christian" and the Court has not seen this as a constitutional violation. True, the nation has become far more religiously diverse in recent years and Congress (and presumably many state legislatures) has taken this into account. Congress "acknowledges our growing diversity not by proscribing sectarian content but by welcoming ministers of many creeds."

Chad Flanders has called the contrast between having prayers with only generic content versus inviting various religious figures to offer a prayer and letting them sound whatever themes (sectarian or not) they wish as "thin" and "thick" diversity.[2] Thin diversity is inherently appealing, but in many ways it pleases no one. What exactly is a nonsectarian prayer? Further, nonreligious people are likely to still demur from any type of prayer. At the same time, deeply religious people are likely to be offended by the watering down of theological positions. An exchange at oral argument, while the attorney for Galloway was arguing for the need for generic prayers, is instructive. When pressed, he could not come up with satisfactory concrete examples.

Moreover, any rule that mandated generic prayers would face implementation problems. Some public official, either one appointed by the legislature or a judge, if the matter were appealed to the courts, would have to approve the prayer (either before it was given or afterward). These officials would become "censors of religious speech, [involving] government in religious matters to a far greater degree than is the case under the town's current practice of neither editing or approving prayers in advance nor criticizing their content after the fact."

In spite of this rather sweeping opening for legislative bodies to allow chaplains to compose their own prayers and rely on their own religious traditions as they see fit, Kennedy was careful to point out that "the Court does not imply that no constraints remain" on the content of these prayers. What must be kept uppermost in mind is the purpose of the prayers, "to lend gravity to the occasion and reflect values long part of the Nation's heritage." Should these "invocations denigrate nonbelievers or religious minorities, threaten damnation, or preach conversion," a line will have been crossed. "That circumstance would present a different case than the one presently before the Court." In short, the justices might censor prayers if they go too far. This is shaky ground, given the self-abnegating admonition stated above. But, as Michael Perry has said, nothing can substitute for judgment.[3]

Finally, what are we to make of the argument that even if we accept thick diversity, all of the ministers invited to give the opening prayer were Christians, despite the presence of citizens of other faiths in the town? Kennedy responded that what the council had done was reasonable in the circumstances, using a supposedly comprehensive guide to congregations within the town to make inquiries about whether their ministers would be willing to give the opening prayer. The council was not obligated to look beyond the city limits merely because some citizens of the town worshiped in Rochester. Too, there was no evidence that any other religious leaders were unwelcome. "So long as the town maintains a policy of nondiscrimination, the Constitution does not require it to search beyond its borders for non–Christian prayer givers in an effort to achieve religious balancing."

Let us turn now to the proposition that there is subtle pressure bordering on coercion for audience members to at least passively participate in the prayer. This position is underscored by the fact that the minister stood on a raised dais, faced the audience, and often asked them to stand or perhaps bow their heads. Of course, members of the audience could freely leave if they wished or not stand or bow their heads. But did they feel that their concerns might get less attention from the council if they exercised these options, especially since in small towns and cities most of those present would be known personally to the board?

Kennedy says, first, that the real audience for the prayers was the council itself, not the attending citizens. Second, no one on the council asked that the audience participate. Had they done so, or "singled out dissidents for opprobrium, or indicated that their decisions might be influenced by a person's acquiescence in the prayer opportunity," it would be a different matter. Naturally, the prayers might give offense to an atheist or other nonbeliever; "[o]ffense, however, does not equate to coercion."

Near the end of his opinion, Kennedy is at some pains to distinguish this holding from *Lee v. Wiseman.* The chief reason is that in this instance we are dealing with adults, not middle school students. There is no penalty, social or otherwise, for their departure during the prayer or simply not participating. Instead, the prayers offered here are part of the ceremonial opening of a public legislative body and "but a recognition that, since this Nation was founded and until the present day, many Americans deem that their own existence must be understood by precepts far beyond the authority of government to alter or define and that willing participation in civic affairs can be consistent with a brief acknowledgement of their belief in a higher power."

The Concurring and Dissenting Opinions

Justices Alito and Thomas filed concurring opinions, both of which were joined by Justice Scalia. Justice Breyer wrote a brief dissent and Justice Kagan a lengthy one, endorsed by Breyer along with Justices Ginsburg and Sotomayor. Because Alito's concurrence is largely addressed to Kagan's dissent, it will be helpful to take up the dissents first.

Justice Breyer offered a brief dissent in which he advocated upholding the reasoning of the Court of Appeals, which had decided against the town. This was the classic "fact sensitive" case, he agreed. Taken together, the Court of Appeals had said that the facts weighed against Greece, in that it had not done enough to ensure a diversity of invocation givers. Five facts were relevant, they said, and Breyer agreed.

First, despite the fact that Christians predominate in the town, there are several minority faiths represented in the population. Second, "the town made no significant effort to inform the area's non–Christian houses of worship about the possibility of delivering the opening prayer." (Note the word "area's.") These two findings make the third fact, that almost all the prayers were given by Christian clergy, of singular import. Fourth, the presence of the audience as active participants in the proceedings underscores the need to ensure diversity in those giving the prayer. Finally, although government should not write or censure prayers offered at public occasions, something could have been done to encourage the clergy to be inclusive. He quoted with approval the "guidelines" of the U.S. House of Representatives. "The guest chaplain should keep in mind that the House of Representatives is comprised of Members of many different faith traditions.... The prayer must be free from personal political views or partisan politics, from sectarian controversies, and from any intimations pertaining to foreign or domestic policy." The word "must," though seems to make this more than a "guideline."

Setting all these facts together, Breyer felt that the town had overstepped the boundaries of the establishment clause.

Justice Kagan wrote the main dissenting opinion, an effort in which she was joined by Justices Ginsburg, Breyer, and Sotomayor. Her central thesis is that the American version of religious liberty mandates religious equality. Every citizen, regardless of his or her faith or lack of it has to stand on an equal basis when it comes to interacting with public officials, federal, state, or local. She does not believe, she is quick to assert, that there is a "bright separationist line," and endorses *Marsh v. Chambers* as a correctly decided case. However, what transpired in Greece, she feels, makes its practices qualitatively different from the legislative prayer in Nebraska. For one thing, citizens actively participate in town council meetings whereas they are mere passive observers in a state legislature. For another, the prayers were "predominately sectarian in content." For still another, the town made no effort to broaden the reach of those invited to give the prayer to include people from faiths of the non–Christian residents of the town.

She begins her opinion by laying out three hypotheticals: the opening of a trial to which you are a party; a group of citizens waiting in line to vote on election day; and a naturalization ceremony. In each instance, a public official calls on a Christian clergyman to give a prayer. He then offers up a prayer laced with Christian themes. All of these would cross, she believes, "a constitutional line." Further, she has "every confidence the Court would agree." The problem is not the Christian nature of the prayer per se. The problem would exist if a Jewish rabbi or Muslim imam gave the prayer. It is that citizens are not equal before the public officials that makes for the stumbling block. She buttresses this point by writings of George Washington, Thomas Jefferson, and James Madison in which they explicitly reject public prayers tied to one particular religious tradition. Washington, for example, deleted a phrase in his first inaugural address that was based in Christianity. Jefferson struck any reference to Jesus in his draft of Virginia's Bill for Establishing Religious Freedom so that it would encompass "the Jew and the Gentile, the Christian and the Mahometan, the

Hindoo, and infidel of every denomination." Madison thought great precaution must be taken in public proclamations to avoid "the creed of the majority and a single sect." When, Kagan declares, a citizen stands before government, it is imperative that "she faces no particular religion, either by word or by deed."

She wants to make sure that her readers understand that she agrees on the framework the Court established. She endorses the *Marsh* decision and believes it should not be disturbed. Where she disagrees is on how applicable that precedent is to the situation at hand. To her, there are three important differences between the prayers offered at opening sessions of legislatures and what is being done in Greece, and those differences dictate a different outcome here.

First, there is the physical layout, which has important implications. Members of the Nebraska legislature are on the floor and visitors are in the gallery. The two roles are strictly separated. Second, there is the matter of who is being addressed by the giver of the prayer. In the legislature, it is the members only who are the objects of the prayer. Its goal is clearly to bring solemnity to their proceedings. In the town hall, the minister faces the audience and often asks for their participation by standing and/or bowing their heads. The city council sits behind the minister. Moreover, the city council often interacts with members of the public. It is not solely a legislative body. Citizens are there to address a variety of local issues. Third, there is the content of the prayers. While the Nebraska legislative chaplain removed the most explicitly Christian references when concerns were expressed,[4] Greece has done nothing of the sort.[5] They have betrayed "no understanding that the American community is today, as it long has been, a rich mosaic of religious faiths." "The monthly chaplains appear almost always to assume that everyone in the room is Christian." Moreover, none of them "has thought even to assure attending members of the public that they need not participate in the prayer session."

In short, she contends that these "three differences, taken together, remove this case from the protective ambit of *Marsh* and the history on which it relied." Consequently, she believes that "the majority misapprehends the facts of this case" which set it apart from legislative prayer and that they overlook "the essential meaning of the religious worship in Greece's town hall, along with its capacity to exclude and divide."

She concludes with a story from George Washington's presidency. When he was preparing to visit Newport, Rhode Island he received a letter of welcome from a Jewish layman praising the United States for having "a Government, which to bigotry gives no sanction, to persecution no assistance—but generously affording to All liberty of conscience, and immunities of Citizenship: deeming every one, of whatever Nation, tongue, or language equal parts of the great governmental Machine." Washington replied that "It is now no more that toleration is spoken of, as if it was by the indulgence of one class of people" to others because "[a]ll possess ... alike the immunities of citizenship." It is no less important today to uphold that sentiment than it was then, and she believes that Greece has overstepped this "constitutional line."

Turning to the concurring opinions, Justice Alito was not persuaded by Kagan's dissent. He initially bristled at her suggestion that the majority was blind to the facts. He does not think that the town official who compiled the initial list of clergy willing to give the prayers was negligent or was being discriminatory. When complaints were made, the town moved quickly to open the opportunity to give prayers to representatives of other faiths. Further, the prayers were only said before the "legislative" portion of council meetings, not the "adjudicatory" portion. (This seems like a stretch. The prayers were said before any business at all was conducted and logically would seem to be designed to apply to all portions of the meetings.)

He divides Kagan's objections into a narrow one and a broad one. The narrow one is on diversity. The town council did not engage in either thin or thick diversity. It did not encourage generic prayers from its chaplains and it did not invite a broad spectrum of prayer givers. Thin diversity would present problems of its own. Many clergy might not feel they could give a vague and innocuous prayer. And, of course, if the town tried to approve the prayers beforehand, it would entangle the council in religious doctrine, something obviously undesirable. On the other hand, to castigate the town for not reaching out to more faith traditions really means casting aspersion on the clerk who put together the original list. There was no evidence she acted in a discriminatory manner (and Alito pointedly adds, "I would view this case very differently if the omission of these synagogues were intentional"). She simply did things in the usual way that small towns operate. The "municipality should not be held to have violated the Constitution simply because its method of recruiting guest chaplains lacks the demographic exactitude that might be regarded as optimal."

On the broad issue, Alito does not think Kagan draws on the proper historical material. She stresses the differences between the Nebraska legislature and the town council in Greece. But the real place to look should be to the Continental Congress and the First Congress under the Constitution, especially the latter. It was that Congress that approved the First

Amendment and since all Courts have said the original intent of the amendment's drafters, especially regarding the religion clauses, should be determinative that is the appropriate place to look. The fact that the First Congress appointed chaplains and regularly had prayers to open their session puts an important imprimatur of legitimacy on the practice of legislative prayer. "It is virtually inconceivable that the First Congress, having appointed chaplains whose responsibilities prominently included the delivery of prayers at the beginning of each daily session, thought that this practice was inconsistent with the Establishment Clause." Taking a swipe at the Court of Appeals use of the *Lemon* test (though not by name), he says that if any "test" conflicts with historical practice, it is the test that must give way, not the other way round.

He concludes by criticizing Kagan for giving the impression (although he acknowledges inadvertently) through her hypotheticals that there is a move afoot, endorsed by this decision, to establish a regime in which religious minorities feel uncomfortable. He is at pains to say that "Nothing could be further from the truth." All that is being allowed here is the continuation of a practice that Congress and the state legislatures have utilized since the founding.

Justice Thomas also drafted a concurrence in which he elaborated on his oft-repeated position that the establishment clause was a federalism provision. That is, that it applied only to the federal government and was actually designed to protect state establishments (recalling that several states had established churches in the founding period, Massachusetts being the last to abolish its in 1833). Thus, given the jurisdictional character of the establishment clause, the Fourteenth Amendment should not be read to apply it to the states. To do so would be to invert its original purpose.

Conclusion

There are several important implications here.[6] First, the Court clearly put *Marsh v. Chambers* on firmer ground than it had stood before. For a number of years, most commentators (and Justice Brennan had said so explicitly at least once) had considered it an exception to the general line of cases which relied on the *Lemon* test, and especially the way its second prong had put out the seedling of the endorsement test. Although the Court did not mention the *Lemon* test by name, its methodology gave a clear imprint to the importance of historical practice. When "tests" conflict with history, it is the test which must give way. Does this imply that the *Lemon* test's days are numbered in establishment clause jurisprudence generally? Eric Rassbach believes that even without mentioning *Lemon,* the Court was inching away from its application.[7]

Second, in giving a pronounced place to history, we are automatically carving out a special place for traditional religious faiths. If the Court moves to rely on history in other areas of establishment clause jurisprudence, traditional religions are bound to come out ahead.

The most immediate arena where this might assume greater importance is in the realm of public displays. Many of these were put up when no one thought crosses or other symbols of Christianity were controversial. Suits by other religious groups or secular groups challenging these displays will be less likely to succeed if historical practice becomes the compass needle rather than "endorsement."

A related implication is that municipalities and other local governmental bodies that are legislative or quasi-legislative in character will have more flexibility if they choose to have their meetings open with a prayer.[8] In most cases, this will mean that Christian prayers will predominate. But this may be the difficulty with the case in the long run. Yes, in most areas of the country Christian and Jewish sympathies will rule the day. However, with growing religious diversity the contemporary norm, it is not out of the realm of the conceivable that some municipalities will one day have Muslim (or other) majorities. What will traditional religion's adherents say when they are in the minority and imams from the town's mosques regularly offer the opening prayers?

Thus, while we must score this as a win for traditional religions, it too could turn out to be the classic Pyrrhic victory. It might seem to them then, perhaps, that the Baptist position would have been better followed. While Baptists are about as traditional as you can get, their strong commitment to separation of church and state has made them opponents, as here, of any type of prayers at public functions. One never knows who will be able to write the prayer tomorrow.

CHAPTER 10

Who Can Claim Religious Liberty?

Burwell v. Hobby Lobby Stores

We enter into a different legal realm with this case, namely how the Supreme Court interpreted a statute rather than a constitutional provision, although the decision was laden with constitutional overtones. Reflecting our central theme, we witness in the parties a stark confrontation between traditional religion and the political forces of secularism. Two family-owned business firms won the right to be exempt from an important mandate from the Department of Health and Human Services issued under the aegis of the recently passed Affordable Care Act. When the dust had settled, it was clear that traditional religion had won an important victory, one that might, with the stress on "might," well have important ramifications more broadly. The actual legal question at issue in the case was who could claim coverage under the Religious Freedom Restoration Act (RFRA), a 1997 law designed to enhance religious liberty for all. Consequently, the place to begin is with the rationale for the act, a few details on its passage, and precisely how it sought to carry out its objective. This will necessitate recapitulating some material covered in chapter two, but with some amplification.

Why RFRA?

The origins of RFRA can be traced back to 1961 and the Supreme Court case of *Braunfeld v. Brown.*[1] Pennsylvania had passed a law banning the sale of a variety of retail products on Sunday on the grounds that a general day of rest was a public good. A Jewish shopkeeper, who for religious reasons had to close on Saturday, challenged the law as one that infringed on his free exercise in forcing him to close on Sunday also.[2] By

6 to 3, the justices held that the law did not violate the free exercise clause because the state had a legitimate interest in mandating a general day of rest. Significantly, Justice William Brennan dissented. According to his view, the state could only write such a policy into law if it showed that it had a "compelling interest" in doing so. In this instance, Pennsylvania, he thought, failed that test. Two years later, however, Justice Brennan carried the day in *Sherbert v. Verner.* Adell Sherbert had worked in a textile plant in South Carolina, but was laid off through no fault of her own. When she applied for unemployment benefits, as was the practice in every state, she was first offered other jobs. All these would have required, though, that she work on Saturday. Ms. Sherbert was a devout Seventh-Day Adventist (a denomination which celebrates the Sabbath on Saturday), and if she accepted one of these positions it would mean she would be unable to attend her worship services. Therefore, she turned down the job offers; the state responded by denying her unemployment benefits. She brought a suit claiming that by refusing to give her the benefits the state was unconstitutionally interfering with the free exercise of her religion. Brennan wrote the opinion of the Court and, holding in Ms. Sherbert's favor, established his compelling interest test as the framework for future free exercise cases. If a plaintiff produced evidence that the law in question created a "substantial" burden on his or her free exercise, then the state had to show a compelling interest in enforcing the law against the plaintiff. Here, Brennan held, Ms. Sherbert had shown such a substantial burden and South Carolina's alleged determination to protect the integrity of the unemployment fund by preventing fraud was not sufficiently compelling to deny her the benefits.

We need to make a note at this point on some terminological confusion, namely the relationship between the compelling interest test and the strict scrutiny test. Some years after *Sherbert* the Supreme Court developed the strict scrutiny test for use in several areas of constitutional law, chiefly First Amendment rights and equal protection cases. The test has two prongs: the government must demonstrate that it has a compelling interest in enforcing the policy in question *and* that it has selected the least restrictive means of accomplishing its objectives. The confusion arises because many people have argued that the compelling interest test standing alone contains a least restrictive means component, which if so makes the two tests identical. The confusion was not helped by the fact that when Congress passed RFRA it referred to the compelling interest test but then defined it in strict scrutiny terms. That is, government had to show both a compelling interest and that it had utilized the least restrictive means available. Thus, for purposes of RFRA we say compelling interest, as contained in the words of the statute, but really mean strict scrutiny. As we shall see, this becomes crucially important in the instant case.

In any event, between 1963 and 1990 the Supreme Court applied the compelling interest test (as it was invariably called) to a number of free exercise cases involving all three levels of government. In truth, government lawyers did not find the test particularly burdensome, as they won far more cases than they lost.

On the losing side was an important but unique case, *Wisconsin v. Yoder,* handed down in 1972. The Court held that Wisconsin could not force Amish children to continue in school past the eighth grade despite a state law mandating school attendance until age 16. Leaning on the argument that ruling for the state would threaten the continuation of the Amish community and its underlying religious values, the justices did not feel that Wisconsin made a strong enough case to compel the attendance. Reading between the lines, though, the Court seemed to be saying the holding should not be read to apply beyond the facts of this case.

State governments also lost a series of unemployment benefit cases similar in many ways to *Sherbert.* In *Thomas v. Review Board of Indiana Employment Security Division* (1981), the Court held that a pacifist should not have to forfeit unemployment benefits if he turned down a job in an armaments factory. In 1987, the justices expanded this holding in *Hobbie v. Unemployment Appeals Commission of Florida* when they ruled that even if the applicant had a religious conversion experience during his period of employment the compelling interest test should still be applied. Two years later in *Frazee v. Illinois Department of Employment Security* the Court again stood with a person denied benefits. It held that even if the person's faith had no specific doctrine regarding work on the Sabbath, his individual belief was enough to justify using the compelling interest test.

On the other hand, in most areas of the law, the government normally prevailed despite the compelling interest test. These cases generally fell into two categories. First, the Court said that the test did not apply in two important areas of public policy, the operation of special institutions, such as the military and prisons, and the structure of internal governmental administration. For example, in *Goldman v. Weinberger* (1986), the Court held that military regulations were not subject to the test (denying a Jewish Air Force officer's request to wear a yarmulke as part of his uniform). Along the same lines, in *O'Lone v. Estate of Shabazz* (1987) the Court turned aside an appeal to apply the test to prisons (here a request by Muslim prisoners to have Friday free from work). Internal governmental operations were also shielded from the test. For instance, in *Bowen v. Roy* (1986), parents were forced to obtain a social security number for their child despite having religious objections. Similarly, in *Lyng v. Northwest Indian Cemetery Protective Association* (1988), the Forest Service did not have to meet the test when it planned to construct a road that ran close to an Indian cemetery.

In the second category, when the Court did apply the compelling interest case in areas outside unemployment benefits, the government usually carried the day. In *United States v. Lee* (1982), an Amish businessman claimed that since he did not intend to draw social security benefits he should not have to pay social security taxes. The Court said, however, that having a financially sound social security system was a compelling interest and Mr. Lee had to pay the tax. In *Bob Jones University v. United States* (1983), the Internal Revenue Service ended the university's tax-exempt status because it practiced overt racial discrimination. The Supreme Court ruled that ending racial discrimination was a compelling enough interest to justify the removal of the exemption. When members of the Church of Scientology wanted to claim special "deductions" from their income taxes, the move was voided by the IRS. In *Hernandez v. Commissioner of Internal Revenue* (1989), the Court again sided with the IRS by saying that they had met the compelling interest test. In short, aside from unemployment cases and *Yoder*, governments seldom found the compelling interest test much of a barrier.

The Smith Case

Then, in 1990, the Court upended the longstanding use of the test itself in *Employment Division, Department of Human Resources of Oregon v. Smith*. Galen Smith and a colleague were drug counselors in Oregon and members of the Native American Church. During some of the church's rituals small amounts of peyote, a mildly hallucinogenic drug, were ingested. As part of their employment contracts, both men had signed a statement promising to be drug free. When they were discharged after their supervisor found out about the drug use, they applied for unemployment benefits. Significantly, peyote was illegal in Oregon. Consequently, the state denied them the benefits. As with others discussed above, they brought a suit seeking to overturn the decision on free exercise grounds. After a complicated procedural route through both the Oregon and federal courts, the case ended up on the Supreme Court's docket in 1990. The attorneys for both sides approached the case as a standard unemployment claims case; that is, was the burden on Smith and his colleague substantial and if so did Oregon have a compelling interest that would justify the denial? Justice Scalia, however, chose to move to much broader turf and examine the compelling interest test itself. He ruled that the test ran the risk of creating "anarchy" because it raised the possibility of each person becoming a law unto himself or herself. Furthermore, the courts are not qualified to rule on how central particular religious beliefs are to an individual or whether given laws pose a substantial burden on one's religious life. Generally applicable laws, but not those targeting a specific religious group, therefore, are enforceable against all. Exemptions from statutes may be granted, he pointed out, but these must be given by the legislature.[3] Courts, accordingly, would no longer apply the compelling interest test. The central part of Scalia's opinion, part of which touches on one of our major concerns, follows:

> If the "compelling interest" test is to be applied at all then, it must be applied across the board to all actions thought to be religiously commanded. Moreover, if "compelling interest" really means what it says (and watering it down here would subvert its rigor in other fields where it is applied [free speech and equal protection], many laws will not meet the test. Any society adopting such a system would be courting anarchy, but that danger increases in direct proportion to the society's diversity of religious beliefs.... Precisely because "we are a cosmopolitan nation made up of people of almost every conceivable religious preference" ... we cannot afford the luxury of deeming *presumptively invalid,* as applied to the religious objector, every regulation of conduct that does not protect an interest of the highest order [emphasis in original].

Reaction among religious groups, civil rights organizations, and a number of members of Congress was swift. A coalition of groups that seldom worked together—such as conservative evangelicals and the American Civil Liberties Union—formed, under the name Coalition for the Free Exercise of Religion, to seek ways to overturn the *Smith* decision. A working group of legal experts was put together to come up with a way to restore the compelling interest test in the free exercise area. Though it need not detain us but briefly here, the main question was how to make the Courts apply the test against state and local governments (which is the venue for most cases). The bill's drafters assumed that if Justice Scalia said a legislative body could carve out exemptions from its own generally applicable laws, then Congress could surely enact a blanket exemption for its own statutes. For the states, though, the issue is more complicated. The free exercise clause, and the other provisions of the Bill of Rights (amendments one through eight), are, as we have seen before, made applicable to the states by the due process clause of the Fourteenth Amendment. Section 5 of the Fourteenth Amendment says that "The Congress shall have power to enforce, by appropriate legislation, the provisions of this article." Thus, Congress's legal team believed that Congress could rely on its authority to "enforce" the due process clause (found in section 1 of the Fourteenth Amendment). Thus, by its ability to "enforce" the due process clause it could thereby control interpretation of the First Amendment. Animated discussions (covering everything from abortion to prisons) delayed the bill for three years. In the end, though, it passed the House of Representatives unanimously and by a 97–3 vote in the Senate.

The provisions of RFRA are fairly straightforward. "Government shall not substantially burden a person's free exercise of religion" unless it "is in furtherance of a compelling governmental interest" and employs the "least restrictive means of furthering that compelling governmental interest."

RFRA in the Supreme Court

The part of RFRA relying on section 5 of the Fourteenth Amendment, extending its reach to state and local governments, was declared unconstitutional in 1997 in *City of Boerne v. Flores.* Nothing was said there, however, about RFRA's status vis-à-vis the federal government. In 2003, Congress amended RFRA to specify that it only applied to the federal government. This move was upheld by the Supreme Court in 2006 in *Gonzales v. O Centro Espirita Beneficente Uniao do Vegetal.* To be completely accurate, the Court upheld the constitutionally of RFRA's applicability to the federal government without discussing it.

The case involved a small Brazilian-based religious group with only 130 members in the United States. Part of their (long-established) worship involved drinking a tea which contained a substance listed as a Schedule I drug by the federal Controlled Substances Act. Customs agents had confiscated a shipment of the tea from Brazil and banned further imports. Chief Justice Roberts, writing for a unanimous Court (Justice Alito had only been recently appointed and did not participate), weighed the arguments the government advanced to show that it had a compelling interest in enforcing the Controlled Substances Act, but found them wanting as applied to these specific people (as opposed to a general need to enforce the law). Bowing to Congress's dictate under RFRA, he wrote, with some prescience to our case:

We have no cause to pretend that the task assigned by Congress to the courts under RFRA is an easy one. Indeed, the very sort of difficulties highlighted by the Government here were cited by this Court in deciding that the approach later mandated by Congress under RFRA was not required as a matter of constitutional law under the Free Exercise Clause [citing *Smith*]. But Congress has determined that courts should strike sensible balances, pursuant to a compelling interest test that requires the Government to address the particular parties at issue.

The Facts of the Case

The Affordable Care Act, passed in 2010, requires that any employer with 50 or more employees must have a health insurance plan with certain "minimum essential coverages." Not having such a plan will entail large fines. Among the "minimum essential coverages" is "preventive care and screening" for contraception. Such coverage must be available without imposing a cost on women employees. Congress decided to leave it up to the Department of Health and Human Services (HHS) to draw up the list of contraceptive methods that had to be included in the plans. Accordingly, HHS turned to the Institute of Medicine, a group of volunteer advisers, for help. HHS then adopted their recommendations as the mandated contraceptive methods that had to be included in the employer-adopted insurance plans. Most of the methods on the list prevented fertilization of the egg; however, four of them destroyed the already fertilized egg in the early stages of development. These latter four were therefore seen by many people as abortifacients. Importantly, HHS was authorized to grant exemptions from contraceptive coverage for "religious employers," which the agency defined as "churches, their integrated auxiliaries, and conventions or associations of churches." Undoubtedly seeking to tame anticipated fury, HHS further extended the exemption to religious organizations, defined as a nonprofit organization that "holds itself out as a religious organization" and is opposed to the use of contraceptive devices. As a result of these exemptions and two other exemptions in the law—"grandfathered" health plans in existence when the law was passed in 2010 and the exclusion of employers with fewer than 50 employees—"tens of millions" of Americans were not affected by the contraceptive mandate.

The Hahn family of Pennsylvania and the Green family of Oklahoma both ran family-owned and -operated businesses—a woodworking firm for the Hahns and a chain of retail stores for the Greens—which had well over 50 employees. Both operated, as do most businesses of any size, as corporations. Both the Hahns and the Greens were members of religious denominations that are strongly opposed to abortion. Consequently, they objected to including the four abortifacients in their insurance policies and challenged the HHS mandate on both RFRA and constitutional grounds.

The central question, therefore, was whether the corporations could claim free exercise rights, especially under RFRA. Can a for-profit corporation, that is, "exercise religion" and thereby shield itself from government action? The Court of Appeals thought that it could not.

> General business corporations do not, separate and apart from the actions or belief systems of their individual owners or employees, exercise religion. They do not pray, worship, observe sacraments or take other religiously-motivated actions separate and apart from the intention and direction of their individual actors.

The Opinion of the Court

Justice Alito wrote the opinion for a majority of five, which reversed this holding. He begins by stressing something that happened after RFRA's passage. In 2000, following the Court's decision in *City of Boerne v. Flores*, Congress reacted by passing the Religious Land Use and Institutionalized Persons Act (more on which in a later chapter). In this act, Congress defined "exercise of religion" more broadly than before. RFRA had referred to the First Amendment, but in an attempt to steer clear of any possibility that the Court would again see a congressional attempt to alter the justices' reading of the meaning of free exercise under the First Amendment (as they had in ruling on RFRA's constitutionality), new wording was put in place. In RLUIPA, as it was called, Congress said that "exercise of religion" would include "any exercise of religion, whether or not compelled by, or central to, a system of religious belief," and that these terms were to "be construed in favor of a broad protection of religious belief."

For those without legal training, we might enter a note here on corporations as legal persons. Under American law, there are two kinds of "persons," natural persons (human beings) and corporate persons. Corporations are organized ordinarily under the laws of a state and granted a charter. The practice goes back to the colonial period when the common law was borrowed from England. Corporations were developed under English common law to allow individuals to pool their resources for a business purpose but have their liability limited to the amount of their investment. In other types of business organization, such as sole proprietorships and partnerships, the owners must stand good for any debts of the business. Thus, a corporation offers enormous advantages.[4] (Significantly, corporations can also be organized for nonprofit purposes.) Corporations, as "persons" under the law can therefore engage in a wide variety of legal acts, such as owning property and suing (and being sued) in court. But, crucially, are they "persons" under the meaning of the Constitution? In 1888, the Supreme Court held in *Pembina Consolidated Silver Mining Co. v. Pennsylvania* that corporations were persons within the meaning of the Fourteenth Amendment. This holding was expanded recently in *Citizens United v. Federal Election Commission* (2010), when the Court held that business corporations had free speech rights under the First Amendment (even though the First Amendment, unlike the fourteenth, does not use the word "person").

We might think of the issue in this case as one of a continuum on who can claim free exercise rights (whether constitutional or statutory). Clearly, free exercise applies to individuals. Further, because many religions require group participation (in rituals and rites, such as Christian communion, for example), no one argues against churches and similar organizations (temples, synagogues, mosques, etc.) enjoying free exercise rights. A little further along the continuum are other types of organizations that while not churches per se, are organized for purely religious purposes (schools and colleges, for instance). Almost everyone would agree that these bodies too are entitled to free exercise. (There might be disputes about how closely such organizations need to be tied to religious principles, but that becomes merely a classic gray area question.) Then, a little further along the continuum would be religiously oriented organizations (usually organized it can be noted as corporations, but nonprofit ones) whose operations are indistinguishable from their commercial counterparts (such as bookstores, for example). Next would come "closely held corporations" in which the shares are all owned by one person or at most one family which are for-profit but have religious principles as part of their day-to-day operating code (such as the ones at issue here). Then, there would be for-profit corporations which adhere to religious principles but which have a more diffuse ownership. Finally, there would be large corporations with many unrelated shareholders, such as those traded on public exchanges. Here, the government claimed that the line should be drawn at the nonprofit/for-profit line, while the Greens and Hahns wanted free exercise to be stretched to cover their closely held corporations.

Though Alito wanders into a number of technical arguments, his main contentions are two. First, he notes that even for-profit corporations often pursue other objectives. For example, they may donate to charities or adopt environmental policies or worker safety practices that exceed what the law (either U.S. or foreign) requires. "If for-profit corporations may purse such worthy objectives, there is no apparent reason why they may not further religious objectives as well." Second, he argues that since RFRA does not define "person," the appropriate approach is to turn to the Dictionary Act, which courts normally do when statutory terms are not explicitly defined. The Dictionary Act says that the term "person" includes "corporations, companies, associations, firms, partnerships, societies, and joint stock companies, as well as individuals." Not challenging the use of the Dictionary Act, the government conceded that nonprofit corporations could be covered by RFRA. To Alito, this is a fatal admission:

> This concession effectively dispatches any argument that the term "person" as used in RFRA does not reach the closely held corporations involved in these cases. No known understanding of the term "person" includes *some* but not all corporations. The term "person" sometimes encompasses artificial persons (as the Dictionary Act instructs), and it sometimes is limited to natural persons. But no conceivable definition of the term includes natural persons and nonprofit corporations, but not for-profit corporations [emphasis in original].

At several points Alito was careful to point out that it was doubtful large, publicly held corporations would be able to assert similar free exercise claims.

Having found that RFRA applies to the business firms here and that they can "exercise religion," the next question is whether HHS's mandate imposes a "substantial burden" on the Green's and Hahn's free exercise. Because the fines for not including the contraceptive methods in the companies' insurance policies were rather punitive, that aspect of substantial burden was easy to show. But HHS had another argument. They contended that the connection between the firm's providing the insurance and any use of the four abortifacients was too attenuated to be a substantial burden to the Greens and Hahns. Any use of the methods in question would result from the choice of an employee, not the business. But Alito responded that to the families involved it was immoral for them to furnish the opportunity to use these contraceptive methods. Courts, several previous cases had held, should not question the sincerity of someone's religious beliefs or their applicability to specific situations. Therefore, if the owners felt it imposed a substantial burden, the court had to accept that conclusion. He cited with approval *Thomas v. Review Board of Indiana Employment Security Division* (1982) which we encountered earlier. There, a Jehovah Witness had worked in a steel mill, with some of the output going to weapons. When he was transferred to a section of the mill making tank parts, though, he objected. Dismissed, he was denied unemployment benefits because the authorities thought his distinction was illegitimate. The Supreme Court disagreed, however, saying that "it is not for us to say that the line he drew was an unreasonable one." In a similar vein, if the Greens and Hahns believe they would be acting contrary to their religious beliefs, that must be respected.

Having established that the corporations qualified for coverage under RFRA and that a substantial burden existed on their free exercise, it remained to apply the compelling interest test. Alito only gave the barest attention to the first part, agreeing with the government that "guaranteeing cost-free access to the four challenged contraceptive methods is compelling within the meaning of RFRA."

The least restrictive means component, though, was where the government's argument faltered. The "least-restrictive-means standard," he said at the outset "is exceptionally demanding."

One way that would be much less intrusive on the companies would be for the government simply to provide the insurance, or assume the cost directly, itself. HHS has not shown, he said, that this was not a feasible alternative. True, this would require the government to increase its expenditures on the health care program, but the requirement that the least restrictive means be utilized might well do this in any number of cases. HHS argued that RFRA should not require the setting up of a new program, but Alito disagreed. "HHS's view that RFRA can never require the Government to spend even a small amount reflects a judgment about the importance of religious liberty that was not shared by the Congress that enacted that law."[5]

However, the place where HHS really lost the least-restrictive-means argument was in its own policy toward other organizations. As noted above, in order to accommodate a wide variety of "nonprofit organizations with religious objections" to the abortifacients, HHS had provided them with a waiver. If they adopted the waiver, then the organization's insurance carrier would provide separate payments to the women choosing the contraceptive method without imposing any cost on the organization or the organization's employees. Thus, a less restrictive means of accomplishing the government's objectives was readily at hand.

Alito spends the final section of his opinion addressing some of the issues Justice Ginsburg raises in her dissent, and simultaneously seeks to narrow the applicability of this holding to closely held corporations. He does not believe, for instance, that the decision will open the floodgates to other claims. Racial discrimination in hiring, for example (should an employer harbor racial prejudice on religious grounds), will not be an issue, as providing equal opportunity will easily be shown to be a compelling governmental interest. Or, objections to paying taxes would also fail, as collecting taxes by general rules is surely compelling, as granting exemptions would mean the system could hardly function. The conclusion is that "The contraceptive mandate, as applied to closely held corporations, violates RFRA."

The Concurring and Dissenting Opinions

Justice Kennedy wrote a brief concurring opinion in which he elaborated further on the point that the government already had a less restrictive method in place, namely the one used for nonprofit organizations with religious qualms about the abortifacients. It would be simple, therefore, to allow the same exemption for closely held corporations.

Justice Ginsburg, with full support from Justice Sotomayor and almost full support from Justices Breyer and Kagan, wrote a vigorous dissent. In it, she disagreed with each one of Alito's arguments.

To begin, she points to two items in the legislative history of the ACA that Alito ignored. The initial draft did not contain any requirement that the policies include any contraceptive methods whatever. Senator Barbara Mikulski sponsored an amendment, called the Women's Health Amendment, which put such a requirement in the law and directed HHS to draw up the list of items to be included. It was adopted and it was this provision that led to the mandate in question in this case. The other matter was that a "conscience amendment" was offered that would have let "any employer or insurance provider" opt out of this requirement. This amendment, however, was voted down. Reading these two moves together, it would seem, she said, that Congress was content to allow HHS to develop the list of acceptable contraceptive methods and did not believe employers should be able to evade the requirements because of "conscience."

Ginsburg does agree that the two firm's claims must rest on RFRA alone. The reason is that the *Smith* case removed the compelling interest test for laws of general applicability. RFRA, though, sought to reinstate the pre–*Smith* standard, and, because it applies to the federal government, making that standard the appropriate framework.

Turning to statements made in congressional reports accompanying RFRA and floor statements by its sponsors, she contends that it is clear that it had a narrow purpose. It was only designed to overturn the *Smith* holding but leave previous precedents in place. Furthermore, she believes that Alito's claim that RLUIPA's change in the definition of "exercise of religion" broadened RFRA's reach on who could be said to exercise religion "is not plausible." She points out that a congressional report said the opposite: "There is no doubt that RLUIPA's drafters, in changing the definition of 'exercise of religion,' wanted to broaden the scope of the kinds of practices protected by RFRA, not increase the universe of individuals protected by RFRA."[6]

Another technical point that we broached earlier: Did the Supreme Court's pre–*Smith* jurisprudence put a least restrictive means prong into what it continually called the compelling interest test? Alito argued that by explicitly including a least restrictive means component in its definition of the compelling interest test, Congress was broadening the pre–*Smith* holdings of the Court. Ginsburg disagreed, arguing that in both *Sherbert* itself and the cases decided in its wake, the Court had included a least restrictive means component. The importance of these different readings was whether RFRA wanted the Court to confine itself to pre–*Smith* frameworks or not. If Alito was correct, then a broader reading of RFRA was justified; on the other hand, if Ginsburg was correct, a more narrow approach should be taken.

"With RFRA's restorative purpose in mind," she turned to this case. Four questions need to be addressed in this order: (1) Does a for-profit corporation exercise religion within the meaning of RFRA? (2) Even if so, does the HHS mandate substantially burden this exercise? (3) If it does, can the requirement be seen as satisfying a compelling governmental interest? (4) Assuming that hurdle is cleared, has the government used the least restrictive means to accomplish its objectives? Her answers are No, No, Yes, and Yes.

Taking the Dictionary Act as a starting point to discuss coverage, she quotes the same definition as Alito. But then she points out that the Dictionary Act itself says it "controls only where 'context' does not 'indicate otherwise.'" For context, she feels we must turn to the pre–*Smith* rulings of the Court. "Until this litigation, no decision of this Court recognized a for-profit corporation's qualifications for a religious exemption from a generally applicable law whether under the Free Exercise Clause or RFRA. The absence of such precedent is just what one would expect, for the exercise of religion is characteristic of natural persons, not artificial legal entities." She quotes from opinions by both former Chief Justice John Marshall and former Justice John Paul Stevens to buttress her contention that corporations are dramatically different from natural persons. Further, religious organizations, even when organized as corporations, are not the same as ones put together to earn a profit. The former "exist to foster the interests of persons subscribing to the same religious faith." The latter, in contrast, are qualitatively different. Moreover, had RFRA's drafters wanted to include for-profit corporations within its ambit, they could have easily said so.

She all but mocks the Court's point that for-profit corporations often engage in charitable activities. This is irrelevant, she argues. "[T]he Court forgets that religious organizations exist to serve a community of believers," whereas for-profit corporations are set up to make money. As far back as Blackstone, she notes, the differences between "ecclesiastical and lay" corporations has been recognized. All of this is to sound a warning.

> The Court's determination that RFRA extends to for-profit corporations is bound to have untoward effects. Although the Court attempts to cabin its language to closely held corporations, its logic extends to corporations of any size, public or private. Little doubt that RFRA claims will proliferate, for the Court's expansive reading of corporate personhood—combined with its other errors in construing RFRA—invites for-profit entities to seek religion-based exemptions from regulations they deem offensive to their faith.

She next takes up the substantial burden question. She first gives a nod to the sincerity of the Green's and Hahn's religious beliefs, affirming that no one questions that. But the Court misses an important distinction: between justices granting the sincerity of a litigant's religious beliefs and determining whether in a given instance someone's religious exercise is substantially burdened. While deference must be given the former, establishing the latter is something the Court must undertake for itself. To support this point, she cites a number of pre–*Smith* cases which turned on that exact question. For her, "the connection between the families' religious objections and the contraceptive coverage requirement is too attenuated to rank as substantial." This is because the use of the abortifacients results not from the choice of the companies' owners but from decisions made by individual women and their "health counselors." With two steps, therefore, between the businesses and the objectionable action, we are at too far a remove to make this a substantial burden on the Greens and the Hahns.

Although it is not necessary, given that the Court granted that the government had a compelling interest in enforcing the mandate, she provides a number of details to explain why a compelling interest is served by the policy.

Finally, what about the least restrictive means failure that the Court rests its conclusion on? Recall that Alito said that the government had two less restrictive alternatives: paying for the service itself or allowing closely held corporations to take advantage of the exemption extended to nonprofit religious organizations. Ginsburg rejects both. As for the government shouldering the burden, how far should such an alternative go, she asks? "Suppose an employer's sincerely held religious belief is offended by health coverage of vaccines, or paying the minimum wage, or according women equal pay for substantially similar work." Would the government have to subsidize these employers as a least restrictive means before policies requiring these actions pass muster? The comments she offered earlier on the differences between religious organizations and for-profit corporations make the second alternative equally flawed.

In concluding, she turns to a quotation from *United States v. Lee* (1982), the case in which the Amish businessman sought to be exempt from social security taxes because he did not intend to take advantage of the old age pensions funded by the tax. Making a general point, the Court said "When followers of a particular sect enter into commercial activity as a matter of choice, the limits they accept on their own conduct as a matter of conscience and faith are not to be superimposed on statutory schemes which are binding on others in that activity." Adopting this rule here would settle the case—in favor of the government.

Justices Breyer and Kagan thought that since the Green's and Hahn's claim failed on the merits (that is, that the government had satisfied both the compelling interest and least restrictive means requirements), there was no need to address whether or not RFRA applied to for-profit corporations. Accordingly, they only joined a portion of Ginsburg's dissent.

Conclusion

On the most basic level, this decision was clearly a victory for traditional religion, and, in a sense, for religious liberty more generally. Accordingly, the immediate reaction was predictable. Lori Windham of the Beckett Fund said, "This is a landmark decision for religious freedom. The Supreme Court recognized that Americans do not lose their religious freedom when they run a family business. The ruling will protect people of all faiths."[7] Kim Colby, the Director of the Center for Law and Religious Freedom felt that the Court's interpretation of "RFRA makes religious liberty the default position in any conflict between religious conscience and federal regulation. And that is as it should be for a country founded on religious liberty."[8] White House press secretary Josh Earnest, though, contended that the decision "jeopardizes the health of women employed by the companies.... [W]omen should make personal health decisions for themselves, rather than their bosses deciding for them."[9] This sentiment was echoed by Cecile Richards of Planned Parenthood. "Today, the Supreme Court ruled against American women and families, giving bosses the right to discriminate against women and deny their employees access to birth control coverage. This is a deeply disappointing and troubling ruling that will prevent some women, especially those working hourly-wage jobs and struggling to make ends meet, from getting birth control."[10] However, despite the worries of Justice Ginsburg, the White House, and Planned Parenthood, there did not seem to be a rush of companies wanting to follow Hobby Lobby's lead. Two years after the decision, only 52 corporations had requested a waiver from the contraceptive mandate, and 30 of those were nonprofits.[11]

On the broader political front, however, there was a significant impact. Gay and lesbian groups worried that their efforts, and a scattering of hard-won victories, in adding sexual orientation to anti-discrimination laws, in such areas as employment and housing, might well be in jeopardy. For example, only days after the decision was handed down, five gay rights groups withdrew their support for the Federal Employment Non-Discrimination Act (EDNA), a measure they had been pushing for years.[12] The reason was that it contained an exemption for religious employers, and they feared the courts might read that broadly and weaken the protections. Some gay rights activists have gone so far as to label any exemptions "lawlessness." Thus, for them the demand for exemptions and even religious liberty more generally, are illegitimate. Douglas Laycock quotes a Colorado state senator who was speaking in support of a bill allowing civil unions before the Supreme Court established a right for gay marriage:

> So, what to say to those who say religion requires them to discriminate? I'll tell you what I'd say. Get thee to a nunnery and live there then. Go have a monastic life away from modern society, away from people you can't see as equal to yourself, away from the stream of commerce where you may have to serve them."[13]

This view of religious liberty became immediately evident as states were considering mini-RFRAs, especially in Kansas, Arizona, Mississippi, and Indiana.[14] LGBT organizations' opposition to a proposed state RFRA in Kansas killed the measure. In Arizona, similar pressure resulted in a gubernatorial veto. Meanwhile, in Mississippi the legislature watered down the proposed statute. A proposed change in Indiana's RFRA to add corporations to the covered entities triggered an intense debate and a deluge of boycotts. In response, the legislature amended the law to add protections for gays and lesbians and most of the controversy died down. Realistically, the conflict between a state antidiscrimination law covering LGBT people and a state RFRA can only occur in states with both types of statutes. Now, only four states have both: Connecticut, Illinois, New Mexico, and Rhode Island. However, the symbolism of creating or expanding coverage of a state RFRA in light of *Hobby Lobby* was compelling to both sides.

Thus, this case was a win for traditional religion, certainly. However, in the political arena, gay and lesbian groups took up the fight more concretely, and with more success, than did the advocates of women's reproductive rights. It must be scored, consequently, a legal victory, but only a limited one when the contest turned to politics. Moreover, Frank Ravitch has argued that the case might actually weaken religious liberty in the legal realm as well.[15] He notes, and cites examples to back up his argument, that when the Court broadens a legal category, as they did here, they often retreat in subsequent cases and in effect narrow the definition. The more broadly rights are applied, in short, often the more restrictive the courts become. This view can also become embedded in public perceptions, and erode support for religious liberty. "The less the public views RFRA [and state RFRAs] as being about protecting the rights of religious people, and the more it views RFRA as being a license for those making money to harm third parties, the greater the risk to religious freedom for those traditionally protected by RFRA-religious individuals and entities—will be." In the long run, "*Hobby Lobby* may very well be a case of winning the battle, but losing the war."[16]

Paul Horwitz has argued that *Hobby Lobby* might be seen as a "moment" in the history of religious liberty.[17] Specifically, religious liberty has normally been seen by almost all observers as an important protection for minorities. However, with the injection of gay rights issues into the area, liberals and their allies no longer view it that way. It has become a contested concept itself. "The church-state consensus, drawn into the gravitational pull of this contest [LGBT rights], has been put up for grabs as a result."[18]

Addendum

This case was followed by several others that ended up being consolidated, and were another victory for those opposed to the HHS mandate.

There were several complex procedural moves surrounding these cases, which we can avoid and concentrate on the main religious liberty issues involved.[19] Under rules initially promulgated by the HHS, in order to qualify for the exemption from having to include the complete list of contraceptive drugs in their insurance plans, religious nonprofits had to file a special form with the federal government. The Little Sisters of the Poor and Wheaton College led a parade of religiously affiliated entities from various denominations and traditions to court to challenge the requirement. The former is an order of Catholic nuns that operate homes for the impoverished elderly in several locations in the United States; the latter is a nondenominational evangelical college outside Chicago. Their central concern was that even by filing the form (for which the failure to do so encountered heavy fines) they would be complicit in providing abortifacients. This was because they felt that filing the form would trigger some other entity's responsibility for providing the contested contraceptives. Under RFRA, the argument went, there were other, less restrictive, means, available to the government. (This was assuming they could meet the substantial burden threshold.)

The District Courts and the various Courts of Appeal split on the issue, and it consequently headed to the Supreme Court. In 2016, the Supreme Court consolidated the cases under the name of *Zubik v. Burwell.* Meanwhile, the organizations and their counsel had been negotiating with the government to find a solution. After oral argument, the Court asked the parties to file supplemental briefs on "whether contraceptive coverage could be provided to petitioners' employees, through petitioner's insurance companies, without any such notice from petitioners." In other words, the government was being asked to back off. A plan was put together to accomplish just that, and all parties agreed "that such an option is feasible."

The Court therefore issued a *Per Curiam*[20] opinion that endorsed this approach and remanded the cases to the lower courts to ratify the details. The justices did want to stress, however, that they were not deciding the merits of either side's arguments. "The Court expresses no view on the merits of the cases. In particular, the Court does not decide whether petitioner's religious exercise has been substantially burdened, whether the Government has a compelling interest, or whether the current regulations are the least restrictive means of serving that interest." Justice Sotomayor, joined by Justice Ginsburg, felt she had to file a concurring opinion. Her assent to the opinion of the Court was only obtained, she stressed, for two reasons. First, because it expressed "no view on 'the merits of the cases.'"

Second, because it allowed the lower courts a good bit of flexibility in crafting their orders.

Then, in May 2017 President Trump issued an Executive Order requiring HHS to suspend their actions against the Little Sisters of the Poor and the other groups involved in the suits. Accordingly, on October 6, 2017, the government issued the new regulations. In light of both the Supreme Court opinion and the changed attitude of the government, on February 22, 2018, the District Court for the Northern District of Illinois granted a permanent injunction and declaratory relief to Wheaton[21]; presumably, the Federal District Courts where the other organizations are located will follow suit.

CHAPTER 11

A Prisoner's Beard

Holt v. Hobbs

This case was decided under the terms of the Religious Land Use and Institutionalized Persons Act of 2000 (RLUIPA), a follow up statute to the Supreme Court's decision in *City of Boerne v. Flores.* Recall that that decision held the Religious Freedom Restoration Act (RFRA) unconstitutional as applied to state and local governments. It was assumed, and the Supreme Court later agreed, as noted in the last chapter, that it still applied to the federal government.[1]

Since most contests over religious liberty come as a result of state laws, however, there was widespread concern that the *Boerne* ruling would seriously undermine religious liberty. One response was that a number of states passed so-called "mini-RFRAs" of their own. However, the fact that not all states passed such laws and that the provisions varied by state meant that the result was a patchwork of religious liberty protections. That being the case, there was a good bit of sentiment in Congress that some kind of federal response was called for.[2]

The problem was what exactly to do. After hashing through several suggestions (some of which were far more extreme than others), it was decided to enact a new statute but place it on other, hopefully more secure, constitutional footings. The foundations they chose were the commerce power, the spending clause, and a renewed emphasis on Section 5 of the Fourteenth Amendment.

Background and Facts of the Case

While the ins and outs of RLUIPA's path through the House and Senate need not detain us here, it is pertinent to pause briefly and essay how the main aspect of the politics played out, because it is reflective of our theme. The initial draft of the new statute was called the Religious Liberty Protection Act (RLPA). It contained the same terms as RFRA, but merely claimed to draw on the three new constitutional powers. At first, all the interest groups that had supported RFRA—the broad coalition of religious bodies and civil rights organizations—backed the measure. There was a scattering of opposition, but nothing serious. Prison officials spoke against the proposal, but then they had opposed RFRA as well. Some religious groups, on the right especially, were bothered by using the commerce clause, feeling it denigrated religion to work within this provision. Then, too, some legal scholars doubted whether the courts would look any more sympathetically on RLPA than they had RFRA, inasmuch as Congress was still trying to define a constitutional phrase ("free exercise") differently from how the Supreme Court had defined it (in the *Smith* case). None of this had much impact on the House committee (the House Subcommittee on the Constitution, a subcommittee of the House Judiciary Committee) that was drawing up the bill.

However, as the hearings continued, opposition from civil rights groups began to surface. Gay and lesbian groups and those advocating for the unmarried were the first to voice concerns. They worried that landlords and business firms would try to use free exercise claims to gain exemptions from anti-discrimination laws in housing and employment. The Human Rights Campaign, a gay rights organization, was the first to publicly oppose the bill, saying that "we've always had a problem with this legislation, because, in our view, it would create an environment where people could discriminate" even in jurisdictions that had included sexual orientation in their protected categories under civil rights laws. After years spent working to have sexual orientation added to civil rights laws, they now feared that RLPA might undermine those hard-won efforts. This perception was not unrealistic. One conservative Christian group said they planned to do exactly that. The legal director of the Family Research Council told an interviewer that

> We would support a landlord who holds certain religious beliefs and wants to exclude not only same-sex people but also unmarried couples from living in a residence. We believe in the right of a church or a religious school or a business to hire employees who hold the same viewpoint as the owner of the business or school. I don't think B'nai B'rith ought to be forced to hire David Duke [a former leader of the Ku Klux Klan] any more than someone can be forced to hire someone whose sexual practices are abhorrent to their religious beliefs.

When the full House Judiciary Committee reported the bill out favorably, some members dissented, saying they would support the bill only if there was a "carve out" for civil rights laws. The liberal group People for the American Way, who had been a staunch supporter of RFRA and RLPA early, began to waver, announcing that they hoped that "as the legislative process concerning RLPA continues, civil rights and other concerns can be resolved." Within a month, the Legal Defense Fund of the NAACP announced it was changing its position and now opposed the bill. When the bill came to the House floor, a group of representatives tried to allay these fears by offering an amendment that only individuals and religious organizations could claim coverage under RLPA. Sponsors argued that if this carve out were allowed, naturally, others would be sought and then the whole purpose of the bill, a general prohibition on violating religious liberty, would be undermined. The amendment failed on a vote of 190–234. The whole bill then passed on a 306–118 tally.[3]

Despite this lopsided victory, as the Senate Judiciary Committee convened its hearings, it was evident RLPA was in trouble. Liberal Senators warned that in their view the bill was "dangerously broad." Meanwhile, liberal religious denominations and many civil rights groups withdrew their support, some joining gay and lesbian groups in active opposition. These included the ACLU (which moved from hesitant supporter to outright opponent), People for the American Way, the NAACP, the Religious Action Center of Reform Judaism, the Anti-Defamation League, the National Council of Jewish Women, the National Council of Churches, Americans United for Separation of Church and State, the Presbyterian Church (U.S.A.), and the United Church of Christ. The Child Welfare League and the American Academy of Pediatrics also voiced concerns about how the law might be used to make stopping child abuse more difficult. Before long, it was evident to Senate leaders that the bill could not pass.

Negotiations opened, though, on a scaled-back bill. It took a year, but finally what became RLUIPA, protecting only land use and prisoners, passed, unanimously in both chambers and with the approval of almost all the original RFRA coalition.

Would the Supreme Court sustain its constitutionality, though?[4] It did, in *Cutter v. Wilkinson,* handed down in 2005. The case involved claims by a purported witch and followers of a white supremacy religious group in Ohio's prisons that their free exercise rights were being violated. Ohio replied that RLUIPA was unconstitutional. Justice Ginsburg spoke for a unanimous court in upholding the act. (They did not reach the merits of the prisoners' claims, though.)

Somewhat surprisingly, Ginsburg based her decision on the establishment clause. She stresses at the outset that the Constitution's two religion clauses can sometimes be in conflict; that is, granting an accommodation to one religion can lead it to have a seal of approval that others lack. Consequently, justices have had to struggle "to find a neutral course between the two Religion Clauses, both of which are cast in absolute terms, and either of which, if expanded to a logical extreme, would tend to clash with the other." Given this fact, there must be a space for legislative action "neither compelled by the Free Exercise Clause nor prohibited by the Establishment Clause." The prison portion, at least, "fits within the corridor between the Religion Clauses." RLUIPA therefore "qualifies as a permissible legislative accommodation of religion that is not barred by the Establishment Clause." Ginsburg wanted to stress that the Court was not ruling on these particular claims and warned that the Court might well be skeptical of claims pushed too far. "Should inmate requests for religious accommodations become excessive, impose unjustified burdens on other institutionalized persons, or jeopardize the functioning of an institution, the facility would be free to resist the imposition."

This sentiment was tested when Gregory Holt challenged the policy of the Arkansas Department of Correction (DOC) regarding beards. The Department allowed quarter-inch-long beards for any prisoner with a dermatological problem but required all other inmates to be clean-shaven. Mr. Holt had converted to Islam while in prison (for assaulting his girlfriend). He subsequently requested to grow a half-inch beard as he deemed required by his religion. When denied permission to do so by prison officials, he brought this suit.

The Opinion of the Court

Justice Alito again wrote the majority opinion, but this time for a unanimous Court. Justices Sotomayor and Ginsburg filed concurring opinions. Decided right after *Hobby Lobby*, that case was on everyone's mind, and Alito cited it a number of times in his opinion. Did the decision in *Hobby Lobby* make the conservatives at least more likely to vote in favor of Mr. Holt? It is impossible to say, but had they voted with the prison officials, commentators would have immediately pointed out the inconsistency: Since RFRA's and RLUIPA's wording on religious liberty is nearly identical, how can a business win and a prisoner lose?

The pertinent sections of RLUIPA read as follows:

No government shall impose a substantial burden on the religious exercise of a person residing in or confined to an institution ... even if the burden results from a rule of general applicability, unless the government demonstrates that imposition of the burden on that person (1) is in furtherance of a compelling governmental interest; and (2) is the least restrictive means of furthering the compelling governmental interest.

For good measure, as we found in the last chapter, Congress defined "religious exercise" broadly, as "any exercise of religion, whether or not compelled by, or central to, a system of religious belief." Taking it even another step, the law said this concept "shall be construed in favor of a broad protection of religious exercise, to the maximum extent permitted by the terms of this chapter and the Constitution."

Taking the legal questions, one by one, Alito first says Holt must demonstrate that what he wants to do constitutes "religious exercise." Given the breadth of the statute's definition, this was easily shown. While not all branches of Islam mandate beards for men, many do, and in any event, Holt believed it was part of his religious faith, which, given the discussion in *Hobby Lobby*, was sufficient. In any event, the DOC did not contest his sincerity. Second, Alito points out that Holt must also satisfy the Court that banning the beard places a substantial burden on his religious exercise. Again, the single fact that he was threatened with punishment if he contravened the policy showed that the burden was substantial. Recall, too, that the law, as quoted above, said the test of the substantial burden was measured regarding "that person." Establishing those two thresholds, the burden now shifted to the DOC to prove a compelling interest lay behind the policy and that it had employed the least restrictive means in carrying it out.

The DOC offered two compelling interests: the need to control contraband and the need to secure the identity of all prisoners at all times. Concerning the first, the Department alleged "that prisoners may use their beards to conceal all manner of prohibited items, including razors, needles, drugs, and cellular phone subscriber identity module (SIM) cards." Alito appeared almost incredulous at this position. "We readily agree that the Department has a compelling interest in staunching the flow of contraband into and within its facilities, but the argument that this interest would be seriously compromised by allowing an inmate to grow a ½ inch beard is hard to take seriously." How could he keep it from falling out, for one thing? More basically, why would an inmate hide contraband in a beard when he could better hide it in his hair, the length of which the Department was somewhat lax about?[5] Moreover, even if it were granted that this compelling interest prong of the test were met, what about the least restrictive means component? It is, Alito said, an "exceptionally demanding" standard, again quoting *Hobby Lobby.* Here the answer seems simple: just search the inmate's beard. His clothing and hair are currently searched, so why not do the same with a beard?

As for the identity problem, the DOC argued that both escapes and prisoners entering unauthorized segments of the prison could be aided by prisoners having beards. That is, they could shave them off and change their appearance, thus fooling guards as to who they actually are. Again, Alito agreed that rapid identification was important, but why not just take two photos, one before an inmate began growing a beard and one after?

To hammer home the holding, Alito had two more points to make. First, the policy seems under-inclusive. What difference can another quarter of an inch make when quarter-inch-long beards are already allowed for medical reasons? The evidence does not show that allowing this extra quarter of an inch "poses a meaningful increase in security risk." Second, the federal prison system and 42 states allow half-inch-long beards, often for reasons other than religious ones. Alito does add that just because others have different policies, that does not mean RLUPA automatically requires every prison to follow the same procedures. "But when so many prisons offer an accommodation, a prison must, at a minimum, offer persuasive reasons why it believes that it must take a different course, and the Department failed to make that showing here."

Seemingly worried that this opinion might seem too generous to prisoners, Alito ended on a paean to prison administrators.

> We emphasize that although RLUIPA provides substantial protection for the religious exercise of institutionalized persons, it also affords prison officials ample ability to maintain security. We highlight three ways in which this is so. First, in applying RLUIPA's statutory standard, courts should not blind themselves to the fact that the analysis is conducted in the prison setting. Second, if an institution suspects that an inmate is using religious activity to cloak illicit conduct "prison officials may appropriately question whether a prisoner's religiosity, asserted as the basis for a requested accommodation, is authentic." Third, even if a claimant's religious belief is sincere, an institution might be entitled to withdraw an accommodation if the claimant abuses the exemption in a manner that undermines the prison's compelling interests.[6]

The Concurring Opinions

Justices Sotomayor and Ginsburg both wrote brief, in Ginsburg's case very brief, concurring opinions. Sotomayor wanted to stress that her understanding of the legal standard includes a bit more deference to prison officials. That is, while a policy promulgated by prison administrators cannot rest on mere "unsupported assertions," neither should the prison officials have to refute every conceivable alternative. Nor does it force those officers to prove they considered "less restrictive alternatives at a particular time." Here, she says, the DOC made an inadequate effort to adopt reasonable alternatives presented to them throughout the course of the litigation; but in other circumstances a bit more flexibility could well be warranted. This was rather clearly a swipe at the opinion in *Hobby Lobby*, which said the government could merely pay for the contraceptives at issue themselves, a politically impossible solution. Ginsburg simply noted that in contrast to *Hobby Lobby*, granting Holt's right to wear a beard did not affect anyone but him. Both seem to be echoing the sentiment of Andrew Koppleman and Frederick Gaddis when, soon after *Hobby Lobby* was handed down, they wrote:

> Until *Hobby Lobby*, it appeared that a new regime was coming into existence in which courts would accommodate religious liberty when that could reasonably be done without impairing legitimate state purposes. The Court has now abruptly lurched into an entirely different regime, one Congress never intended, even if the consequence is serious injury to no adherents, so long as there is some *imaginable* less restrictive means for protecting these adherents—and regardless of whether that means is likely to materialize or not[7] [emphasis in original].

Conclusion

In order to essay how our four factors—growing religious diversity, the increase of secularism, the rise of gay and lesbian groups, and the conservative Christian reaction to these trends—play out in this case, it is necessary to probe a bit. On the surface, it is a unanimous verdict, with liberals and conservatives joining together to chastise a prison system. But in a way each saw the case fitting into different strains of church-state relations.

For the conservatives, it was to a large degree a reaffirmation of *Hobby Lobby*. Kim Colby of the Christian Legal Society was explicit about this. "The Court's unanimous decision in *Holt v. Hobbs* is significant on several levels. Most importantly, *Holt* provided timely reinforcement for the *Hobby Lobby* decision."[8] This was true, she said, because the Court stuck to the same standard in both. Many conservative Christians may well be suspicious of Islam, but more thoughtful conservatives see religious liberty as something valuable in and of itself, no matter which faith is on trial. Paul Horwitz has said that "In public discussion and in the scholarly community, the very notion of religious liberty—its terms and its value—has become an increasingly contested subject."⁹ And for more intellectually minded conservatives, a defense of religious liberty in general is the best way to protect religious liberty for all, including what is now seen as a minority, conservative Christians.

What about liberals? If liberal values include a sensitivity to diversity, an opposition to castigating Muslims as unworthy of society's protection, and a sympathy for society's most vulnerable, then this case is easily classified as endorsing liberal values. Thus, each justice "won" for his or her team, but for different reasons.

One has only to look at the *amici* briefs filed in this case to see this stand out in stark relief. Supporting the DOC were a number of other states, standing alone. On the other side, liberal stalwarts such as the American Civil Liberties Union and Americans United for Separation of Church and State were accompanied by the International Mission Board of the Southern Baptist Convention and the Rutherford Institute.

In short, there was something for everyone in the outcome of this case.

CHAPTER 12

Of Recycled Tires and Playgrounds
Trinity Lutheran Church v. Comer

At one level, this case seems like an odd dispute to have taken up time at the Supreme Court, involving whether a church playground qualified to participate in a state-sponsored program providing recycled tires for playground safety. As Chief Justice Roberts said in his opinion, the only likely result of ruling against the church would be "a few extra scraped knees." Yet the case had an outsized importance not for what was directly at stake but what the ruling might portend for future cases. A ruling for either the state agency or the church would provide a notable weathervane about how the contemporary Court might view state aid for church-related institutions, and even churches themselves, in the days to come. Given the political pressures that continue to be mounted by various religious groups, but conservative Christians especially, as they fight the rearguard action we have continually pointed to, how far will the Court go in allowing the channeling of public monies to churches and religious institutions? Justice Sotomayor's strident dissent is largely addressed to this worry, as we shall see.

Background and the Facts of the Case

We have mentioned the Blaine amendments before, but let's elaborate a bit. In 1875, Senator James G. Blaine of Maine was preparing to make a run for the presidency and was casting about for an issue to launch his candidacy. The previous decades had seen a dramatic growth in the public schools throughout the country. By and large, as our Horace Mann quote in chapter one showed, they reflected the then-dominant Protestant majority's ideas of what constituted a proper education, including moral instruction. At the same time, increased Catholic immigration was adding to social stress in many places, and anti–Catholic sentiment sprouted in a number of states. As interest in education grew, Catholics began pushing to include their schools in the distribution of public monies. Blaine believed showing strong support for the public school system would be an ideal platform for his presidential bid. Accordingly, he introduced the following proposed constitutional amendment[1]:

> No State shall make any law respecting an establishment of religion, or prohibit- ing the free exercise thereof; and no money raised by taxation in any State for the support of public schools, or derived from any public fund therefor, nor any pub- lic lands devoted thereto, shall ever be under the control of any religious sect; nor shall any money so raised or lands so devoted be divided between religious sects or denominations.[2]

Historians are divided on whether Blaine was motivated chiefly by anti–Catholic feelings or a desire to protect the public schools (or more prosaically whether he didn't really care about either, and that it was naked political calculation). In any event, the amendment passed the House over- whelmingly, 180–7, but fell a few votes short of the needed two-thirds in the Senate.

After the proposal's defeat in Congress, a number of states added Blaine-type amendments to their own constitutions. Missouri was one of those in 1875, and its terms were repeated in the constitution of 1945.[3] Article I, Section 7 of the state constitution provides:

> That no money shall ever be taken from the public treasury, directly or indirectly, in aid of any church, sect, or denomination of religion, or in aid of any priest, preacher, minister or teacher thereof, as such; and that no preference shall be given to nor any discrimination made against any church, sect or creed of reli- gion, or any form of religious faith or worship.

Missouri instituted a scrap tire program back in 1990 and has reau- thorized it periodically since. A 50-cent charge is added to tire purchases in the state and allocated to the Department of Natural Resources. The Department uses the funds to operate a program whereby it recycles tires and offers grants to various nonprofit organizations that want to use the materials to resurface playgrounds and similar facilities. Because there are more applicants than the Department can fund, it has developed a competitive system of ranking the applications. Adhering to its interpre- tation of the state constitutional provision cited above, however, the Department declared that churches and religiously affiliated organizations were ineligible for the program.[4]

Trinity Lutheran Church of Columbia, Missouri, operates a Child

Learning Center. The Learning Center serves about 90 children, who come from a variety of religious backgrounds. The church, affiliated with the Missouri Synod, one of the more conservative Lutheran bodies, as we noted in chapter eight, is clear that it views the Center as part its mission, to carry out "the commission of.... Jesus Christ as directed to His church on earth" and to "make disciples." Accordingly, it says that the Center is "a ministry of the Church and incorporates daily religion and developmentally appropriate activities" into the curriculum. Therefore, the church affirms that it is its "sincere religious belief "that the Learning Center should "teach the Gospel to children of its members as well as bring the Gospel message to non-members."[5]

In 2012, the church applied to the Department of Natural Resources to replace the pea gravel it had on its playground with the recycled tire material. The Center's application ranked fifth among 44 applications on its merits. Subsequently, 14 grants were awarded that year, but Trinity Lutheran's was put aside because it was a church. The church then brought this suit.

Precedents

Two previous Supreme Court cases constituted important precedents. The first was *McDaniel v. Paty* (1978). Reverend McDaniel, a Baptist minister, sought to run as a candidate for the state's constitutional convention. However, a provision of the Tennessee constitution prohibited members of the clergy from seeking such an office. A ban on clergy being members of legislative bodies was common in the colonies, and had been copied from English practice. The justification was the feeling that "if elected to public office, they [members of the clergy] will necessarily exercise their powers and influence to promote the interests of one sect or thwart the interests of another, thus pitting one against the others, contrary to the anti-establishment principle with its command of neutrality." In short, Tennessee was carrying the non-establishment idea one-step further than the federal constitution does. The Court held nonetheless that the prohibition violated the federal free exercise clause and could not stand.[6] "By its terms, the Tennessee disqualification operates against McDaniel because of his *status* as a 'minister' or 'priest.'" In order to run for public office, he would have to give up his role as a member of the clergy, a choice that government cannot force upon him because of the free exercise clause.

The other, *Locke v. Davey* (2004), was more directly pertinent. Washington's state constitution too goes further toward banning establishment than does the federal one. The relevant provision is Article I, Section 11 (including the "free exercise" portions):

> Absolute freedom of conscience in all matters of religious sentiment, belief and worship, shall be guaranteed to every individual, and no one shall be molested or disturbed in person or property on account of religion; but the liberty of conscience hereby secured shall not be so construed as to excuse acts of licentiousness or justify practices inconsistent with the peace and safety of the state. No public money or property shall be appropriated for or applied to any religious worship, exercise or instruction, or the support of any religious establishment.[7]

The state created a special scholarship program for gifted college students. Davey was awarded one of the scholarships, but when he tried to use it to major in devotional theology (with the aim of becoming a pastor) at a religiously based college, it was withdrawn.[8] Davey brought a suit alleging that this move violated his free exercise. The Court held, however, that Washington had a substantial interest at stake and that removed the program from being constitutionally suspect. Without that presumption, the state must prevail, since the burden on scholarship recipients was "relatively minor." The Court noted that this case presented a classic instance of the necessity for having some "play in the joints" between the two religion clauses. There is a need, that is, to steer "between what the Establishment Clause permits and the Free Exercise Clause compels."

The Opinion of the Court

After laying out the facts of the case, and noting that the parties agree that the federal establishment clause should be set aside here (that is, the focus should be on the conflict between the federal free exercise clause and the state constitutional provision), Chief Justice Roberts sets out the general principles he believes should frame the case. First, the free exercise clause comes into play any time "religious observers" face "unequal treatment." Strict scrutiny (recall that this entails proof of both a compelling governmental interest and the employing of the least restrictive means to meet that interest) will be called forth when any policies "target the religious for special disabilities based on their 'religious status.'" Therefore, "Applying that basic principle, this Court has repeatedly confirmed that denying a generally available benefit solely on account of religious identity imposes a penalty on the free exercise of religion that can be justified only" under strict scrutiny.

He then surveys what he considers the most pertinent precedents. First, he turns back to *Everson v. Board of Education*, pointing to its holding that no one can be denied a public welfare benefit "because of their faith or lack of it." Then he discusses *McDaniel v. Paty* and quotes the sentence that said McDaniel was denied a benefit because of his "*status.*" But, he says, the decisions have not been all one-sided; the Court has turned aside free exercise claims in a number of cases. Nevertheless, lest the reader get the wrong impression, "We have been careful to distinguish such laws from those that single out the religious for disfavored treatment." He cites *Lyng v. Northwest Indian Cemetery Protective Association* (1988), in which the Court granted the Forest Service the right to construct a road even though it disrupted an Indian burial ground as one example. No one was being coerced to act contrary to her religion and everyone, Indians as well as others, could share in the public benefit at issue, namely the road. *Employment Division v. Smith* is his next example, which here stands for the proposition that the Court did not approve people violating a criminal law (ingesting peyote) even if it was done for religious reasons. Nevertheless, he says the Court made it "clear that the Free Exercise Clause *did* guard against the government's imposition of 'special disabilities on the basis of religious views or religious status'" (citing *McDaniel*). Finally, he unearths *Church of Lukumi Babalu Aye v. Hialeah* (1993), which overturned several city ordinances banning animal sacrifices for religious purposes. The ordinances, although facially neutral, were obviously aimed only at one church. The general rule to be gleaned from that case is, he stresses, that government may not discriminate against individuals or religious entities because of their religious beliefs or their religious status.

Turning to the case at hand, he says forthrightly that "The Department's policy expressly discriminates against otherwise eligible recipients by disqualifying them from a public benefit solely because of their religious character." Citing his previous discussions, he says that if "one thing [is] clear, it is that such a policy imposes a penalty on the free exercise of religion that triggers the most exacting scrutiny."

Applying the strict scrutiny test, he then addresses the Department's defenses of its position. In the first place, the Department contends that nothing it is doing impedes Trinity Lutheran from practicing its religion however it chooses. Contrary to what happened in *Lukumi*, government is not prohibiting any kind of religious activity. It is simply not sending a monetary payment it was under no obligation to provide to anyone. Roberts' answer is that Trinity Lutheran Church is not claiming that it has a right to a subsidy. It is merely claiming that it should not have to give up its religious ideals in order to participate in a generally available government program. It has been put in a position that to receive the generally available benefit it would be forced to give up its First Amendment rights.

More troublesome for Roberts' position is *Locke v. Davey*. Missouri contends that it is doing nothing more than what the Court upheld in that case. Washington State was allowed to follow the dictates of the anti-establishment strictures of its own constitution instead of having the free exercise clause force it to modify its scholarship program. But Roberts argued that there was a distinction. "Davey was not denied a scholarship because of who he *was*; he was denied a scholarship because of what he proposed *to do*—use the funds to prepare for the ministry." Not allowing the use of public funds to support the clergy, in fact, Roberts says, is "at the historic core" of the First Amendment's religion clauses. In contrast, Missouri is denying funds to Trinity "simply because of what is is—a church." Moreover, Washington did not put Davey in the position of having to choose between his religious beliefs and receiving the benefit. In short, he could use the scholarship to attend a religious college; he simply could not use it to major in devotional theology (although he could take classes in devotional theology). To most people, this seems like a classic lawyer's "distinction without a difference." Davey did, in fact, have to choose between majoring in devotional theology and receiving the benefit. In Missouri's case, Roberts says, though, "The rule is simple: No churches need apply."

This last sentence is followed by footnote three, from which two of the justices in the majority disassociated themselves. The footnote reads: "This case involves express discrimination based on religious identity with respect to playground resurfacing. We do not address religious uses of funding or other forms of discrimination." The obvious intent of the footnote is to qualify and narrow the ruling. It would seem to be designed to stave off state attempts to read more into the decision than a narrow holding regarding playgrounds (and to retain future flexibility for the Court). Two of the concurrences took the view that the principle should be seen in a broader light.

Roberts continues the body of the opinion by asking what justifications the state can marshal for its policy. His answer is not much. It "offers nothing more than Missouri's policy preference for skating as far as possible from religious establishment concerns." Admirable as this may be, it is restricted by the free exercise clause of the federal constitution. It simply goes too far. Though the "few extra scraped knees" he referred to earlier may be trivial compared to even the exclusion from office found in *McDaniel*, denying the church "a public benefit for which it is otherwise qualified, solely because it is a church, is odious to our Constitution all the same, and cannot stand."

Concurring and Dissenting Opinions

There were three concurring opinions, by Breyer, Thomas, and Gorsuch, with the latter two joining each other's opinions. Breyer wants to make sure that it is understood that he thinks only the particular benefit at issue here is being decided. He feared, apparently, that too much would be read into the decision. "Public benefits come in many shapes and sizes. I would leave the application of the Free Exercise Clause to other kinds of public benefits for another day." It seems likely that Roberts included footnote three to allay some of this concern.

In contrast, Justices Thomas and Gorsuch urge that the ruling should apply more broadly. Thomas felt the Court "appropriately" put a narrow twist on *Locke*. Nevertheless, it remains for him a "troubling" case. The implication is clear that he thinks free exercise should be read more expansively than the majority has been willing to do, and perhaps that *Locke* should be reconsidered. Gorsuch stresses two main points. First, he has doubts about the status versus use distinction. However, even if the distinction makes sense, he does not think it matters in terms of the free exercise clause. It is the "free *exercise* of religion" (emphasis in original) that the clause covers. Accordingly, he thinks that only the historic tradition of avoiding public funds supporting the clergy can justify the decision in *Locke*. In other areas, such as in this case, there is no such tradition. Second, he wants to categorically dissociate himself from footnote three (a position with which Thomas said he agreed), even though it "is entirely correct." What bothers him is that it implies too narrow a reading of the holding. In his view, more general principles should be enunciated by the Court in this area. "And the general principles here do not permit discrimination against religious exercise—whether on the playground or anywhere else."

Justice Sotomayor's dissenting opinion, in which Justice Ginsburg joined, is critical of virtually every aspect of Robert's opinion and sounds a forceful warning regarding what may be in store for the future. Tellingly, at the end of her opinion, she does not add the usual "I respectfully dissent"; instead, she merely says, "I dissent."

To hear the Court tell it, this is a simple case about recycling tires to resurface a playground. The stakes are higher. This case is about nothing less than the relationship between religious institutions and the civil government—that is, between church and state. The Court today profoundly changes that relationship by holding, for the first time, that the Constitution requires the government to provide funds directly to a church. Its decision slights both our precedents and our history, and weakens this country's longstanding commitment to a separation of church and state beneficial to both.

She begins by quoting from several documents showing that Trinity Lutheran maintains a certain theological position and that it views the Learning Center as a key instrument in sustaining and propagating that position. As for the legal framework to be applied, she believes that both the establishment clause and the free exercise clause, and not the free exercise clause standing alone, as asserted by the Court, should be brought to bear on the case.

She reviews several cases that she concludes stand for the proposition that under the establishment clause it is impermissible for funds to go from the public treasury directly to a "house of worship." "Within its walls, worshippers gather to practice and reaffirm their faith. And from its base, the faithful reach out to those not yet convinced of the group's beliefs. When a government funds a house of worship, it underwrites this religious exercise." She admits that the Court has on occasion allowed government funds to be sent to religious institutions. However, she insists that "the funding in those cases came with assurances that public funds would not be used for religious activity, despite the religious nature of the institution." In contrast, the Court's decision here "permits direct subsidies for religious indoctrination," a policy which raises "all the attendant concerns that led to the Establishment Clause."

Even if we confine ourselves to the free exercise clause, though, she believes "the Court errs." Her initial thrust is that historically it was the controversy over religious "assessments" that laid the background for the religion clauses, and that free exercise was as much involved as establishment issues. James Madison's argument that forcing people to pay for the teaching of beliefs they do not share is a violation of one's liberty is adduced for support. Then, she spends several pages marching through the way the battle played out in other states. Her conclusion is that "The course of this history shows that those who lived under the laws and practices that formed religious establishments made a considered decision that civil government should not fund ministers and their houses of worship."

The next arrow in her quiver is the *Locke* case. Unlike the Court, she thinks the parallels between Washington's and Missouri's programs are similar enough to give Missouri the nod also. "Like the use of public dollars for ministers at issue in *Locke*, turning over public funds to houses of worship implicates serious anti-establishment and free exercise interests." States should have some latitude in how they draw lines in this delicate area; the "play in the joints" can be read to allow states to withhold public funds from religious entities if they so choose.[9] "As was true in *Locke*, a prophylactic rule against the use of public funds for houses of worship is a permissible accommodation of these weighty interests. The rule has a historical pedigree identical to that of the provision in *Locke*."[10]

Next, she takes the Court to task for saying that Trinity Lutheran was denied participation in the program because of its status, and that amounted to discrimination, which triggered strict scrutiny. In fact, she says, religious status matters and laws do have to treat religious entities differently for that very reason in some instances and may do so in others. For example, in *Hosanna-Tabor*, it was religious status that forced the government to allow the church to treat certain employees differently. "In all cases," she argues, "the dispositive issue is not whether religious 'status' matters—it does, or the Religion Clauses would not be at issue—but whether the government must, or may, act on that basis." Because of this, a balancing test is more appropriate than strict scrutiny. Missouri meets the demands of such a test easily, since what it is doing is in line with history and the Court's precedents, properly read.

Sounding an alarm, she links this case to what she fears will now come. "The Court today dismantles a core protection for religious freedom…. It holds not just that a government may support houses of worship with taxpayer funds, but that—at least in this case and perhaps others—it must do so whenever it decides to create a funding program." The Court has turned "separation of church and state" into a "constitutional slogan" rather than a "constitutional commitment," meaning far more than a "few extra scraped knees" is at issue.

Conclusion

On the plainest view of the facts, conservative Christians clearly scored a victory in this case. Trinity Lutheran's Learning Center will be able to resurface their playground. At the same time, there are implications for other government programs, but it is unclear how far the decision will stand as a precedent in future cases. Nor is it clear that conservative Christians will always be the winners even if the decision is construed broadly in the future, following Justices Thomas and Gorsuch.

Does footnote three, which it must be stressed only four justices supported, mean that the plurality wanted to explicitly warn observers that this case should not be taken to imply that other government programs that channel public monies to religious institutions will automatically be approved? If so, then these four, coupled with the two dissenters could erect a barrier to other programs. (Justice Breyer would seem to be a shaky vote for approving more programs.) Or, alternatively, were the justices, or at least some of them, hedging their bets, and merely not willing to commit themselves in advance to what they might or might not approve regarding other programs? But, at the very least, the Court did come down on leaving the door open. It moved further along the line from strict separation to accommodation, even if it did not directly address the establishment clause. Kim Colby of the Christian Legal Society said that she believes churches will be motivated to begin applying to participate in "security-related programs, such as anti-terrorism security programs, FEMA programs after natural disasters or government programs to replace lead in their water or asbestos in their ceilings."[11] This possibility clearly worried liberal groups, many of whom had filed *amici* briefs in support of the state. Daniel Mach of the American Civil Liberties Union's Program on Freedom of Religion and Belief was typical, for example saying, "We're disappointed in today's decision. Religious freedom should protect unwilling taxpayers from funding church property, not force them to foot the bill."[12] In light of this, Melissa Rogers of the Brookings Institution, a widely respected church-state scholar, said we should "Expect further litigation over issues involving other forms of discrimination, religious uses of government aid and cases where there isn't express discrimination based on religious identity or character."[13] This case was the first time, it is worth noting, that the Court sanctioned the direct dispersal of public funds to a church. In all other cases, the monies had either been doled out to individuals and they then spent them for services from religious institutions or the grants were to organizations affiliated with churches (such as a charitable arm of a local church). The implications were quickly felt on the ground. For example, the town of Acton, Massachusetts, decided to include churches in bodies eligible for historic preservation funds, a move challenged by Americans United for Separation of Church and State. FEMA's denial of funds to churches in Houston damaged by Hurricane Harvey was challenged from the other side of the coin (the decision has since been rescinded by congressional action).[14]

Nevertheless, the biggest element regarding the future was not that churches might begin applying to participate in other public programs.[15] It was that certain groups would begin pushing for more programs that would allow taxpayer's money to be directed to religious institutions. By far the most controversial of these, and the one with the largest financial implication, is so-called "school choice," an issue we encountered earlier in the Arizona school tuition case. Conservative Christian advocates of school choice have teamed up with other conservative political groups to push for school choice. However, in a number of states the Blaine amendments were seen as a barrier, even if they could maneuver past the federal establishment clause. This decision elated many in the school choice movement, despite its ambiguous footnote three. Michael Bindas, a leading attorney for the Institute for Justice, a strong pro-choice organization, hailed the decision.

> This decision has implications beyond scrap tires and church playgrounds. The Court's reasoning sends a strong signal that, just as the Court would not tolerate the use of a Blaine Amendment to exclude a religious preschool from a playground resurfacing program, it will not tolerate the use of Blaine Amendments to exclude religious options from school choice programs.[16]

Education Secretary Betsy DeVos, an ardent backer of school choice, echoed these sentiments.

> This decision marks a great day for the Constitution and sends a clear message that religious discrimination in any form cannot be tolerated in a society that values the First Amendment. We should all celebrate the fact that programs designed to help students will no longer be discriminated against by the government based solely on religious affiliation.[17]

Voucher opponents, on the other hand, took some heart from the purported narrowness of the Court's holding. Lily Garcia, president of the National Education Association, was buoyed by the Justices "refusal to accept the invitation of voucher proponents to issue a broad ruling that could place in jeopardy the ability of states to protect their public education system." Randi Weingarten, head of the American Federation of Teachers, offered a similar assessment: The opinion "cannot be read as opening the door for states to promote religion or expand vouchers."[18] Even the ACLU's Mach saw a silver lining. "[T]he court went out of its way to clarify that today's decision addressed only grants for playground resurfacing. The court expressly left questions about other funding schemes for another day."[19] Of some note nevertheless is the fact that on the day following the decision, the Supreme Court sent back two state Supreme Court holdings, one from Colorado and one from New Mexico, that had held school voucher programs adopted in their states to be violations of their Blaine amendments. The Court asked the state Supreme Courts to review their decisions in light of *Trinity Lutheran.*

Finally, we should ask: Is this what conservative Christians really want? Some say "no" up front. The Baptist Joint Committee for Religious Liberty (joined by the liberal United Church of Christ) had filed a brief supporting the state and was dismayed by the decision. The ruling was "deeply troubling," they said.[20] Their reasoning harkens back to the Baptist tradition which holds that government aid ultimately undermines the vitality of the church.

> While claiming to stand up for churches, the Court ignores their distinct nature as centers of religious exercise. "No aid" provisions reflect the hard-fought battles of Baptists and other religious dissenters that abolished government controls over religion and secured church autonomy. The decision does not create a free exercise right to government funding of religion, but it unnecessarily blurs the line that ensures religion flourishes on its own.[21]

Further, in line with what we have said about some of the previous decisions, while many conservative Christians believe in school choice because it will help fund their own schools, any proposals will have to include other faiths. If, again, conservative Muslim parents, for example, wish to establish a madrasa, will their support remain unequivocal? In any event, it is almost certain that more cases raising these issues will end up on the Supreme Court's docket.

Conclusion

Table 2 presents a summary of the cases we have examined. The tilt is easy to see: conservative Christians won all but one of the cases, carrying the day 90 percent of the time. Their dominance is evident whether conservative Christians were parties to the case, directly affected by the case, or merely interested in the outcome. Certainly the one they lost, the denial of the Christian Legal Society's application for official status at the University of California law school, was significant. But this should not detract from the overwhelming success they enjoyed. The Court in these years could hardly be said to be a bastion of anti-religious feeling.

Table 2: Case Summary

Cases	Conservative Christians a Party	Issue directly Affects Conservative Christians	Issue important to Conservative Christians	Ruling favorable to or favored by conservative Christians	Vote
Hein v. Freedom from Religion Foundation		X		Y	5–4
Pleasant Grove City v. Summum			X	Y	9–0
Salazar v. Buono			X	Y	5–4
Christian Legal Society v. Martinez	X			N	5–4
Arizona Christian School Tuition Organization v. Winn	X			Y	5–4
Hosanna—Tabor Lutheran Church v. EEOC	X			Y	9–0
Town of Greece v. Galloway		X		Y	5–4

153

Cases	Conservative Christians a Party	Issue directly Affects Conservative Christians	Issue important to Conservative Christians	Ruling favorable to or favored by conservative Christians	Vote
Burwell v. Hobby Lobby	X			Y	5–4
Holt v. Hobbs			X	Y	9–0
Trinity Lutheran Church v. Comer	X			Y	5–4

The votes present an interesting pattern. They are all either unanimous (three cases) or 5–4 (seven cases). We found the unanimity in two free exercise cases and one public display case. Otherwise, there was only a one-vote margin throughout. Moreover, the 5–4 splits were right down predictable ideological lines, with conservatives and liberals lining up with and against each other. Justice Kennedy, as in other current areas of Supreme Court jurisprudence, was the pivotal player. In fact, the one case conservative Christians lost may well have been tied to his proclivity to support LGBT rights. Had the University of California case not been so deeply tied to this issue, would he have voted the other way, given what most analysts say is his preference for liberty?[1] It is impossible to say, of course, but there is at least a little smoke here.

The prevalence of 5–4 votes also shows how precarious the victories of conservative Christians could be. Much in the near-term future will depend, of course, on how Neil Gorsuch views these questions. Although he does not have a lengthy record of votes or many written opinions on church-state issues, in general he has lined up with the conservatives. Richard W. Garnett says, consequently, that his appointment will probably not make much difference because he is in general accord with how Justice Scalia voted.[2] So far, we have only the case *Trinity Lutheran Church v. Comer* to go by, and his vote and concurring opinion were solidly with the conservatives. In fact, his concurring opinion argued for a wider application of the free exercise clause than Roberts' opinion for the Court. Nevertheless, it is simply too early to offer more than a tentative answer. In the longer run, it depends on who might leave the Court and who the appointing president will be. President Trump's appointment of Justice Brett Kavanaugh, to replace the retiring Justice Kennedy—who we can consider a conservative for our purposes here—solidifies the tilt to the right of the present Court. However, church-state issues are seldom of much importance to a president when choosing a nominee, and any future appointment could be a wild card.

Probing another dimension, why did the two public display cases come out differently, as far as the vote was concerned? The only logical explanation seems to be twofold: First, it seems that a cross is a much more directly religious symbol and also more emotive than the Ten Commandments. Second, the cross stood alone but the Ten Commandments stood among other monuments and displays. This gave the cross more prominence and would naturally lead people to read more into its presence.

When we turn to questions of jurisprudence, the trends are rather clear. Take the two approaches to the establishment clause first, the "strict separation" versus the "accommodationist" framework. The former does just what its name says while the latter allows government more leeway as long as it treats all religious groups equally. For many years, the strict separationist blueprint was largely followed by the Court. In our cases, though, there is a marked shift toward the accommodationist stance. This is most evident in the funding cases, even though two were technically decided on standing grounds and the other on free exercise grounds, the result is the same. *Arizona Christian School Tuition Organization v. Winn* allowed government to direct a portion of its tax revenue, although finessed by the sleight of hand of a tax credit, to church related schools. Both the number of people affected and the sums involved are anything but inconsequential. *Hein v. Freedom From Religion Foundation* adds a few small sticks to this fire, since the amounts involved are rather trivial; nevertheless government was allowed more flexibility in its allocation of public monies. Under a strict separation regime, both cases would have gone the other way (assuming standing would have been granted to the challengers). Then, in *Trinity Lutheran Church v. Comer,* the government was compelled against its will to provide public funds for a church. Clearly, to turn the situation around, if Missouri had made the funds available to Trinity Lutheran and a citizen had challenged the action (presuming he or she could get over the standing barrier imposed in *Hein* and *Winn*) the Court would have allowed the expenditure. To see the impact of this holding, recall the Massachusetts case we mentioned in the concluding section of that chapter in which a town government spent public funds for restoring a church. It won the endorsement of the Federal District Court. Critics charge that the *Trinity Lutheran Church* decision has meant that there are virtually now no limits to what a government—state, local, or federal—can do to aid churches financially. Edward Correia has put it bluntly, contending that, given current political realities, the decision "will lead to direct state financial assistance to religious organizations, including churches, far beyond any period in recent history."[3]

Moreover, the presence of religious monuments on public land seems safe, for the time being at least. Even though both *Pleasant Grove City v. Summum* and *Salazar v. Buono* skirted around facing the establishment clause directly, both seem animated by a spirit of allowing governments a good bit of discretion. However, both involved displays that had been around a good while; it is not clear what might happen should a government attempt to erect a new monument of some type with a religious theme. Whatever the tea leaves say in this area, the militant wing of atheism has not been shy about challenging other monuments. As of this writing, a case is being litigated involving a cross on public land in Pensacola, Florida.[4] The cross was erected by private community groups as the United States inched toward entering World War II, and it is one of any number of other displays in the city's parks.

Perhaps even more telling as indicative of the accommodationist stance is *Town of Greece v. Galloway.* Even though one could draw a line between this case and the school prayer decisions—inasmuch as adults are the audience not school age young people—the Court painted with a rather broad brush here. Previously, more often than not *Marsh v. Chambers* (the Nebraska legislative prayer case) was considered an outlier in religious practices jurisprudence. That is, it was not in the mainstream of precedents that guided the Courts in this area. However, in *Town of Greece* the majority inserted it directly into church-state jurisprudence. It seems incontrovertible that local governments (and presumably the states and the federal government) now have more flexibility when it comes to adopting religious rituals into their activities.

All these holdings regarding the establishment clause are reinforced by the two standing decisions, *Hein v. Freedom from Religion Foundation* and *Arizona Christian School Tuition Organization v. Winn.* By making it harder for people and organizations to bring actions against government practices they believe violate the establishment clause, the Court has given governments more freedom to fashion their policies in this area. Fewer challenges automatically means fewer overturns.

Two of the three 9–0 cases involved free exercise issues, *Hosanna-Tabor Lutheran Church v. EEOC* and *Holt v. Hobbs.* But both of these involved pretty low-profile issues that affect only a few people. Almost everyone agrees that prisoners should enjoy some religious freedoms, and wearing a slightly longer beard, as long as reasonable security steps can be taken, hardly seems controversial. Plus, the number of prisoners this decision might affect is minute.[5] As for *Hosanna-Tabor*, the ability of a church to select and retain its ministers is likewise noncontroversial. Here, too, the number of people affected is tiny. Many people might think Ms. Perich was treated badly by her congregation, but the general principle would probably garner near unanimous assent.

Two more cases, though, *Christian Legal Society v. Martinez* and *Burwell v. Hobby Lobby*, were deeply controversial and split the Court down the middle. The former represented the only case that went against the position of conservative Christians and could be read as denizens of political correctness ostracizing conservative Christians. The actual number of people affected, of course, was very small, but the reaction of state legislatures, such as that of Ohio, demonstrates the powerful symbolism the case carried. As for the latter, it was one of the most hotly debated and deeply divisive cases decided by the Roberts Court. Granting standing under RFRA (and presumably by implication under the free exercise clause itself) to for-profit businesses was a huge step. While many advocates of religious liberty cheered, Frank Ravitch soberly warned that the decision was actually a step back for religious liberty.[6] On the one hand, historically when courts have broadened the reach of rights, they have narrowed them in practice for everyone. More importantly, though, is the backlash the case caused. It has led to the very concept of religious liberty becoming a target for advocates of sexual freedom and others, to everyone's detriment. The evidence from state conflicts over their "mini-RFRAs" seem to point clearly to Ravitch's conclusion that this may be one of the worst decisions for religious liberty handed down by the Supreme Court ever. By equating for-profit corporations, even closely held ones, with religious institutions, it has denigrated the value of the latter. One can sympathize with the Green and Hahn families, faced with a choice to participate in an activity they believe is sinful or curtail or even close their businesses. However, as the Alaska Supreme Court pointed out in an opinion in a similar case that predated *Hobby Lobby*, no one is compelled "to enter into a commercial activity that is regulated by antidiscrimination laws."[7] Or any other laws, one might add. That is, when you voluntarily enter the commercial world, you must abide by the rules of the marketplace as set by government.

Nonetheless, taking the decisions as givens, at the end of the day, both the entities and the doctrines of religious liberty have been expanded. *Hobby Lobby* clearly enlarged the range of possible religious liberty claimants. So far, not many for-profit corporations have sought to avail themselves of this opportunity, but the potential is certainly there. Doctrinally, the Supreme Court explicitly endorsed the ministerial exception, which it had not done up until *Hosanna-Tabor*.

From one perspective, the cases in the free exercise area (except *Christian Legal Society v. Martinez)* stand in contrast to those in the establishment sphere. That is, the ones in the latter allow more scope for government action whereas those in the former restrict government action. If we view both sets of cases as coming down on the side of conservatism, they present something of a dilemma. Libertarian conservatives can easily endorse the free exercise cases without qualification. But what about the establishment holdings? Traditional conservatives see these as positive, no doubt, but libertarians? Should government be in the business at all of encouraging one set of beliefs over others? Or, should each individual start from a zero-base line when it comes to developing his or her worldview? Likewise, should traditional conservatives applaud free exercise, even when it deals with other faiths (such as Muslims)? Many traditional conservatives did indeed support Gregory Holt's desire to wear his beard. Some did so out of genuine sympathy for Holt and some because they saw it as the consistent thing to do. But what if it were not isolated Muslim prisoners but a substantial number of Muslim citizens of a local community? Would the support among traditionalists evaporate, or at least diminish?

Regarding the Roberts Court's jurisprudence in the church-state area then, we can safely label it conservative. Nevertheless, there are various streams and counter currents at work that will bear watching as further cases develop.

If we accept the hypothesis that the Court is affected by social change, then the direction of social change in America will be a vital factor for the future of constitutional law regarding the religion clauses. The eminent political scientist Robert Dahl wrote long ago that the philosophical leanings of the justices over the long run fall into line with the dominant political coalition of the time.[8] Retirements and death inevitably produce a new set of justices. There is, he also stressed, often a lag, as holdover justices bearing old ideas come into conflict with presidents and members of Congress who represent the emerging majority. Within a few years, though, according to this model, new ideas find their way into the Court via the appointment process and the conflict abates. Writing in the 1950s, Dahl chiefly had in mind the way the New Deal came to dominate the Court in the long Democratic ascendancy of Franklin D. Roosevelt and Harry Truman. But we might offer a corollary: The 5–4 (and often bitter) splits we have witnessed in so many cases we reviewed may reflect the partisanship of our times. In recent history, Republicans and Democrats have alternated in office, putting in turn different kinds of justices on the

Court (think Roberts and Alito versus Sotomayor and Kagan, for instance). In this way, the current Court reflects our own political times. One political coalition has not replaced another; rather there is a contest between political coalitions. And, as is often the case, political coalitions tend to be guided by their most philosophically rigid elements.

Paul Horwitz has used the term "Liberal treaty" to describe how American society worked up until the last few years.[9] Others have called it a "Post-Reformation settlement."[10] This is the method by which Western societies have maintained religious peace for the last two to three centuries. Fundamentally, it consists of two elements. (1) We may each maintain our own religion, and we may even believe in it intensely. However, we will not coerce others to join our faith. Persuade them if we can, certainly, but no form of coercion will be utilized, or really even mentioned. (2) We agree that, despite our differences, we can cooperate willingly in civic obligations and civil endeavors. Put colloquially, I may think my neighbor is a fool and that he is going to hell to boot, but we can still work together to get street lights installed and build a new public library. It seems incontestable that this paradigm has largely kept the peace and allowed Western societies to prosper. The United States might even be said to have invented the model and served as its prototype.

If we ponder this model a bit further, though, it becomes evident that three conditions have to be met for it to work successfully. (1) There must be nearly universal agreement on the maintenance of a secular state. There are really two options here. In countries with a long history of established churches (say England or Sweden), there must now be a "mild" establishment.[11] That is, the form of establishment may remain but the church needs to either become a (often, very) broad church and/or downplay its role as sole guardian of the nation's religious life. Both England and Sweden exhibit this situation. The other exists where there is no establishment and a corresponding diversity of religious groups with no one being overwhelmingly dominant. In this instance, as in the United States, a separation of church and state becomes the workable arrangement norm. The most trying time for this model in the United States was the position of the Catholic Church in the nineteenth century. The official position of the papacy was that where Catholicism was in the driver's seat, Catholic establishment was to be desired. Where the Church was in a minority, toleration could be endorsed, at least temporarily; but toleration was an expedient, not a central theological principle. In time, of course, the Church, largely led by American Catholic thinkers, took up the idea of toleration and made it their own. (2) The major religious groups in the society (if there is diversity) must not be too far apart. The further apart they are theologically and in their religious rites and practices, the harder it will be to endorse living alongside each other. Again, Protestant fear of Catholicism in the nineteenth century strained the treaty in the United States. But in reality Protestants and Catholics are in the same religious family, and in time as the Catholic Church became more "Americanized," the distrust eroded. Judaism, too, was not that far from other American religious groups. The only other major challenge to the treaty was Mormonism. The ostracism and violence visited upon Mormons is a major scar on nineteenth-century American religious history. In time, too, though, this gave way to acceptance within the American fabric. (3) The dominant religious factions must strongly support the Liberal treaty. In the United States, this function has been played well for the most part by the mainline Protestant denominations. This means that their own theologies (or at least those advocated by the leaders) have to be somewhat "soft" at the edges, and they must see other dominant groups as more or less like themselves. We might put churches in the National Council of Churches in this category. If any of these three conditions no longer hold, the Liberal treaty is unsustainable.

The four trends we identified in the first chapter—growing religious diversity, the rise of secularism (both mild and strong versions), the growth in the political power of gay and lesbian groups, and the "state of siege" mentality among conservative Christians—have led to all three conditions dissolving. The Liberal treaty and its accompanying Supreme Court doctrines about church-state relations consequently no longer characterize American society.

The growth in religious diversity has undermined the second condition above. Whatever distances separated Protestants, Catholics, and Jews, they pale in comparison to the differences now prevailing both among the new groups making up the American religious mosaic and the gulf between almost all the new groupings and the three traditional strands of American religious life. There are no common religious texts and no common religious vocabulary to which a divided citizenry can refer.

The declining influence of mainline Protestant denominations, in many ways the keystone of the Liberal treaty, has eroded number three. Many of the religious "nones" uncovered by the Pew survey were those who had drifted away from these denominations. Attend the regional or national meetings of any of these groups and much of the discussion centers on managing decline. Moreover, if we believe, as I argued at the outset, that we were able to maintain a healthy secular state because we had an informal religious establishment—which was centered on the broad ecumenical Christianity embodied in the mainline denominations and their allies in Catholicism and the more moderate elements of groups such as the Southern Baptist Convention—then the erosion of the influence of this establishment has taken an important prop away from the American version of the secular state as well.

Nevertheless, it is the attack on the Liberal treaty by militant secularists, leaders of the gay and lesbian community, and the equally intense attack by more militant conservative Christians that has spelled the most trouble for the Liberal treaty. The most militant secularists want to see religion erased from society, and are not shy about saying so. More moderate secularists think that if we could all agree that religion is a purely private matter, then we could all get along. Gay and lesbian groups, citing their newly won antidiscrimination laws, think everyone should have to "obey the law." All of these positions call for a militantly secular state, not one that is secular in form but tied to an informal establishment that is in reality a "mild" one in practice. Conservative Christians find this position an anathema. They hover under the banner of a "Christian nation," and at a minimum believe open acknowledgment of the historical place of Christianity in the nation's development is called for. Many go further than that, and often much further, and want public symbols and substantive government policy to openly reflect conservative Christian values. All these positions challenge the legitimacy of the Liberal treaty and likewise the traditional American version of the secular state.

Peering into the future is always a fraught enterprise, but in the short run it is hard to see any of these trends abating much. Religious diversity is here to stay, even if immigration were completely closed off. The emptying of the mainline pews, especially of young people, shows no sign of slowing. At the same time, hardline atheists have found their public breath, and seem determined to continue using the courts in an attempt to make the state more purely secular (for example, in challenging the presence of the cross in Pensacola, Florida). Likewise with gay and lesbian groups. Having largely won the cultural wars, and the large-scale judicial ones with the nationwide legalization of gay marriage in *Obergefell v. Hodges*, they seek to push the victory into every corner of society (in the wedding cake controversy in Colorado, for example). As one of the few sectors of American religion that is holding its own, conservative Christians have the numbers and the wherewithal to strike back. Exhibit A is their overwhelming vote for Donald Trump in 2016.

None of this portends well for compromise in the political realm.

Moreover, we can probably safely predict that more, and more difficult, cases will come to the Supreme Court. But if what we saw in the cases covered in this book is any indication, the Court will be no better equipped to find compromise positions than legislatures. Therefore, given the splits on the Court, we can expect a steady stream of 5–4 decisions. Accompanying those holdings, however they come out, will likely also be strident dissents reflecting the very divisions discussed above.

Chapter Notes

Preface

1. Benjamin Cardozo, *The Nature of the Judicial Process* (New Haven, CT: Yale University Press, 1921), 168.

Chapter 1

1. See Curtis D. Johnson, "Sectarian Nation: Religious Diversity in Antebellum America," *OAH Magazine of History*, 22 (2008), 14–18.

2. Quoted in Andrew Koppelman, *Defending American Religious Neutrality* (Cambridge, MA: Harvard University Press, 2013), 29.

3. Koppelman, *Religious Neutrality*, 38

4. A somewhat dated but still valuable study is Edward Wakin and Joseph F. Scheuer, *The De-Romanization of the American Catholic Church* (New York: Macmillan, 1966).

5. Will Herberg: *Protestant, Catholic, Jew: An Essay in American Religious Sociology* (Garden City, NY: Doubleday, 1955), 260.

6. Kevin Schultz, *Tri-Faith America: How Catholics and Jews Held Postwar America to Its Protestant Promise* (New York: Oxford University Press, 2011).

7. Joseph Bottum, "The Death of Protestant America: A Political Theory of the Protestant Mainline," *First Things*, August 2008.

8. Margaret Sands Orchowski, *The Law that Changed the Face of America: The Immigration and Nationality Act of 1965* (Lanham, MD: Rowman and Littlefield, 2015) provides a thorough summary.

9. Paul Numrich, *The Faith Next Door: American Christians and their New Religious Neighbors* (New York: Oxford University Press, 2009).

10. Ihsan Bagby, *The American Mosque, 2011, Report No. 1, Basic Characteristics of the American Mosque; Attitudes of Mosque Leaders.* (Washington: Council on American-Islamic Relations, 2012), 5, 6 and 9.

11. Data are available at http://www.pluralism.org.

12. The most reliable data on both Buddhists and Hindus can be found in Gurinder Singh Mann, et al., *Buddhists, Hindus, and Sikhs in America: A Short History* (New York: Oxford University Press, 2007).

13. Koppelman, *Religious Neutrality*, 38.

14. The figures in this paragraph are taken from Pew Research Center, *America's Changing Religious Landscape*, May 12, 2015.

15. *New York Times*, March 4, 2015.

16. Koppelman, *Religious Neutrality*, 39.

17. Pew Research Center, *Changing Landscape*, 12.

18. Richard Dawkins, *The God Delusion* (Boston: Houghton Mifflin, 2006).

19. Steven Smith, *The Rise and Decline of American Religious Freedom* (Cambridge, MA: Harvard University Press, 2014).

20. See, most pointedly, Christopher Eisgruber and Lawrence Sager, *Religious Freedom and the Constitution* (Cambridge, MA: Harvard University Press, 2007.)

21. Further information can be gleaned from the websites of these two organizations.

22. In 2014 Representative Jared Polis of Colorado introduced such a measure, which garnered 150 votes in the House.

23. Roosevelt, incidentally, was a practicing Episcopalian.

24. National Opinion Research Center, September, 2011.

25. Pew Research Center, *Religion and Public Life Survey*, July 29, 2015.

26. The lowest rise has been among African-Americans. The support for gay marriage has risen from 32 percent to only 39 percent. Thus, while the trend line is the same, significant numbers of African-Americans still oppose gay marriage.

27. *United States v. Windsor*, 570 U.S. 744 (2013).

28. *Obergefess v. Hodges*, 576 U.S. ___ (2015).

29. Public Religion Research Institute Poll, March 15, 2012.

30. Barna Group Poll, October 1, 2015.

31. Public Religion Research Institute Poll, June 11, 2014.

32. Fox News Poll, July 21, 2015.

33. The controversy is discussed in Bob Smietana, "Murfreesboro Mosque Fight Laid to Rest after Supreme Court Ruling," *Religion News Service*, June 3, 2014.

Chapter 2

1. Burke's most famous treatise is *Reflections on the Revolution in France*, first published in 1790. A well-known summary of his ideas is C.B. Macpherson, *Burke* (New York: Oxford University Press, 1980). Russel Kirk's major work was *The Conservative Mind: From Burke to Elliot* (Washington: Regnery, 1978; originally published in 1953 under the title *The Conservative Mind: From Burke to Santayana*). A penetrating recent analysis of Kirk's life and influence is Bradley J. Birzer, *Russel Kirk: American Conservative* (Lexington: University Press of Kentucky, 2015).

2. Hayek's most well-known work is *The Road to Serfdom* (Chicago: University of Chicago Press, 1944). A more complete analysis is *The Constitution of Liberty* (Chicago: University of Chicago Press, 1960.)

3. This phrase was first popularized by Alexander Bickel in his *The Least Dangerous Branch: The Supreme Court at the Bar of Politics* (Indianapolis: Bobbs-Merrill, 1962). A thorough review can be found in Barry Friedman, "The Birth of an Academic Obsession: The History of the Countermajoritarian Difficulty," *Yale Law Journal*, Vol. 112 (2002), 153–259.

4. Donald Drakeman, *Church, State, and Original Intent* (New York: Cambridge University Press, 2010).

5. Steven D. Smith, *Foreordained Failure: The Quest for a Constitutional Principle of Religious Freedom* (New York: Oxford University Press, 1995).

6. This is convincingly argued in Garrett Epps, *Democracy Reborn: The Fourteenth Amendment and the Fight for Equal Rights in Post-Civil War America* (New York: Henry Holt, 2007).

7. One prominent scholar maintains that there were actually some non-worship exemptions in the colonial and early national periods. Michael McConnell, "The Origins and Historical Understanding of the Free Exercise of Religion," *Harvard Law Review*, 103 (1990), 1409–1517. However, see the critique of McConnell in Victor Munoz, "Two Concepts of Religious Liberty: The Natural Rights and Moral Autonomy Approaches to the Free Exercise of Religion," *American Political Science Review*, 110 (2016), 369–381.

8. There were two cases in the 1940s involving Jehovah's Witnesses children refusing to salute the flag in school opening exercises. *Minersville School District v. Gobitis* (1940) and *West Virginia State Board of Education v. Barnette* (1943). The first upheld the school district demand but it was overruled in the second.

9. Any law targeting a specific religion would still be invalid, however.

10. Technically, this case belongs in the Roberts Court era. However, since it dealt largely with a qualification to *Boerne*, I left it out.

Chapter 3

1. "The powers not delegated to the United States by the Constitution, nor prohibited by it to the States, are reserved to the States respectively, or to the people."

2. The initiative would seem to have had its intended effect. From 2003 to 2006 there was a 38 percent increase in the number of federal grants going to faith-based organizations, which represented an increase of $239 million in funds, a 21 percent increase. Laura Michaels, "*Hein v. FFRF*: Sitting This One Out," *Harvard Civil Rights and Civil Liberties Review*, 43 (2008), 213–237, fn. 5, citing a White House Press Release.

3. Article I, Section 8 contains this clause: "The Congress shall have Power To lay and collect Taxes, Duties, Imposts, and Excises, to pay the Debts and provide for the common Defence and general Welfare of the United States."

4. Its exact wording, found in Article I, Section 6, is "No Senator or Representative shall during the Time for which he was elected, be appointed to any civil Office under the Authority of the United States. .. and no Person holding any Office under the United States, shall be a Member of either House."

5. This position is cogently argued by Cass Sunstein in *One Case at a Time: Judicial Minimalism on the Supreme Court* (Cambridge, MA: Harvard University Press, 1999).

6. Parenthetically it might be noted that

he took exactly the opposite view in his majority opinion in *City of Boerne v. Flores*, telling Congress to stay out of the business of constitutional interpretation.

7. See Michael Perry, *Constitutional Rights, Moral Controversy and the Supreme Court* (New York: Cambridge University Press, 2008).

Chapter 4

1. There were some slight differences in the facts considered determinative by then-Chief Justice Rehnquist, who authored the majority opinion, and the critical concurrence by Justice Breyer. Rehnquist stressed the historical meaning of the Ten Commandments for the development of Western law while Breyer felt that the presence of the surrounding monuments and plaques celebrating various aspects of Texas history, the private funding, and the fact that the monument had stood without controversy for four decades were more important.

2. B. Jessie Hill, "Putting Religious Symbolism in Context: A Linguistic Critique of the Endorsement Test," *Michigan Law Review*, 104 (2005), 491–545.

3. Leslie Griffin, "Fighting the New Wars of Religion: The Need for a Tolerant First Amendment," *Maine Law Review*, 62 (2010), 23–74.

4. Lawrence Lessig, "The Regulation of Social Meaning," *University of Chicago Law Review*, 62 (1995), 943–1044. Christopher Eisgruber and Lawrence Sager, *Religious Freedom and the Constitution* (Cambridge, MA: Harvard University Press), 291.

5. Mary Jean Dolan, "Government Identity Speech and Religion: Establishment Clause Limits after *Summum*," *William and Mary Bill of Rights Journal*,19 (2010), 50.

Chapter 5

1. Details are in an Associated Press release, April 30, 2012 by Robert Jablon.

2. It is perhaps worth noting that Justice Stevens was the only veteran on the Court, having served in the Navy during World War II. He did not serve in a combat zone, however, being posted as an intelligence officer in Washington. Nonetheless, he earned a Bronze Star.

3. Mary Jean Dolan, "*Salazar v. Buono:* The Cross between Endorsement and History," *Northwestern University Law Review*, 105 (2010), 45.

4. Even then we would probably know little about intensity.

5. Mark Strasser, "The Endorsement Test is Alive and Well: A Cause for Celebration and Sorrow," *Pepperdine Law Review*, 39 (2013), 1275.

6. Adelle M. Banks, Religion News Service, November 7, 2012.

7. Angela Lu, "War Memorial Cross in Mojave Desert Resurrected on Veterans Day after Long Legal Battle," *Christian Headlines. com*, November 12, 2012.

8. Christopher Linas, "*Salazar v. Buono:* A Blow against the Endorsement Test's Core Principle," *Denver University Law Review*, 88 (2011), 603.

Chapter 6

1. All the following material is taken from the organization's website, www.clsnet. org. Accessed April 21, 2017.

2. There is some dispute about when the all-comers policy was adopted. See the discussion of Justice Alito's dissenting opinion below.

3. These provisions of the first amendment are made applicable to the states, recall, by the due process clause of the fourteenth amendment.

4. In later years, the Council agreed to include gay and lesbian groups in the parade.

5. The Boy Scouts, too, has recently modified its position on gay scouts and leaders.

6. See Rene Reyes, "The Fading Free Exercise Clause," *William and Mary Bill of Rights Journal*, 19 (2011), 725–750.

7. Timothy J. Tracey, "*Christian Legal Society v. Martinez* in Hindsight," *University of Hawai'i Law Review*, 34 (2012), 71–123.

8. See, for example, William E. Thro, "The Limits of *Christian Legal Society*," *Cardozo Law Review*, 2014 (2014), 124–128. A more thorough analysis of what happens when governments apply conditions to subsidies is Toni M. Massaro, "*Christian Legal Society v. Martinez*: Six Frames," *Hastings Constitutional Law Quarterly*, 38 (2011), 569–629.

9. He wrote the opinions in all three key cases involving the rights of homosexuals: *Lawrence v. Texas*, 539 U.S. (2003); *United States v. Windsor*, 570 U.S. ___ (2013); and *Obergefell v. Hodges*, 576 U.S. ___ (2015).

10. Gay and lesbian groups were quick to see the case as an important victory. See Max Kanin, "*Christian Legal Society v. Martinez*: How an Obscure First Amendment Case Inadvertently and Unexpectedly Created a Sig-

nificant Fourteenth Amendment Advance for LGBT Rights Advocates," *American University Journal of Gender, Social Policy and the Law*, 19 (2011), 1317–1326.

11. Ohio Revised Statutes 3345.023 (A and B).

Chapter 7

1. The classic exposition of this position is Milton Friedman, *Free to Choose* (Chicago: University of Chicago Press, 1962).

2. An in-depth analysis of the Blaine amendment at the federal level and its surrounding politics is Ward McAfee, *Religion, Race and Reconstruction: The Public School and the Politics of the 1870s* (Albany: State University of New York Press, 1998), especially chapter 8. The original federal Blaine amendment read:

> No state shall make any law respecting an establishment of religion or prohibiting the free exercise thereof, and no money raised by taxation in any state for the support of public schools or derived from any public fund therefor, nor any public lands devoted thereto, shall ever be under the control of any religious sect, nor shall any money so raised or land so devoted be divided between sects or denominations.

When the amendment failed to gather enough support to pass both houses of Congress by the required two-thirds vote, a number of states enacted their own versions. See James Cauthen, "State Constitutions and Challenges to Nonpublic School Transportation Programs," *Journal of Church and State*, 55 (2013), 498–526.

3. William Marshall and Gene Nicol, "Not a *Winn*-Win: Misconstruing Standing and the Establishment Clause," *Supreme Court Review*, 2011 (2011), 218.

4. Marshall and Nicol, "Not a *Winn*-Win," 218.

5. Aside from his opinion in *City of Boerne v. Flores* invalidating the Religious Freedom Restoration Act, he has voted to overturn major congressional legislation on health care, voting rights, and restrictions on federal benefits to same sex couples, along with state laws on same-sex marriage and local ordinances on gun control.

6. Noah Feldman, "The Intellectual Origins of the Establishment Clause," *New York University Law Review*, 77 (2002), 383.

7. Patrick Gillen, "A *Winn* for Originalism Puts Establishment Clause Reform Within Reach," *William and Mary Bill of Rights Journal*, 21 (2013), 1107–1152.

8. Gillen, "*Winn* for Originalism," 1108.

9. Bruce Van Buren, "Tuition Tax Credits and *Winn*: A Constitutional Blueprint for School Choice," *Regent University Law Review*, 24 (2011–2012)), 515–528. A more balanced review of the pros and cons of school choice can be found in Adam Sloustcher, "*Arizona v. Winn*: Negative Implications for First Amendment Proponents and Possibly for Our Nation's School Children," *Hastings Constitutional Law Quarterly*, 40 (2013), 983–987.

10. Tim Keller, "*Arizona Christian School Tuition Organization v. Winn*: Does the Government Own the Money in Your Pocket?" *Cato Supreme Court Review*, 2011–2012 (2011–2012), 182.

11. Marshall and Nicol, "Not a *Winn*-Win," 237.

12. Marshall and Nicol, "Not a *Winn*-Win," 231.

13. Marshall and Nicol, "Not a *Winn*-Win," 225.

14. Kevin Carey, "Arizona's Shady Tale of Tax Credit Vouchers," *New York Times*, March 3, 2017.

Chapter 8

1. Richard W. Garnett, "A Case in Point About Our Church-State Divide," *USA Today*, April 25, 2011.

2. Quoted on website of the Beckett Fund for Religious Liberty. www.becketlaw.org/case/eeoc-v-hosanna-tabor-evangelical-lutheran-church-school/ Accessed July 18, 2017.

3. Quoted in Adam Liptak, "Religious Groups Given 'Exception' to Work Bias Law," *New York Times*, January 2012.

4. LCMS Commission on Theology, as quoted in *Amicus Curiae* Brief for the LCMS, 15.

5. The details of these panels can be found in the Brief for the LCMS, 18–22. As they relate specifically to commissioned ministers, see pp. 23–25.

6. Brief for the LCMS, 21.

7. There was a "religious" exception for religious bodies. As part of the act, discrimination against people because of their religion was made illegal, but religious institutions were exempted from this requirement. They were not, however, exempted from the other prohibitions under the act, such as gender discrimination.

8. Leslie C. Griffin, "The Sins of *Hosanna-Tabor*," *Indiana Law Journal*, 88 (2013), 1006 and 1007.

9. There were two other *amici* briefs, one by a law professor and one by eight states including Michigan. Ten *amici* briefs were filed in support of Perich and the EEOC.

10. Douglas Laycock, *"Hosanna-Tabor* and the Ministerial Exception," *Harvard Journal of Law and Public Policy*, 35 (2012), 859. For a more complete analysis of the unanimous character of the decision, see Ira C. Lupu and Robert W. Tuttle, "The Mystery of Unanimity in *Hosanna-Tabor Lutheran School v. EEOC." Lewis and Clark Law Review* (2016–2017), 1265–1315.

11. St. Louis *Post-Dispatch,* January 12, 2012.

12. Quoted in Adam Liptak, "Religious Groups Given 'Exception' to Work Bias Law," *New York Times,* January 11, 2012.

13. Baptist Joint Committee on Public Affairs website. bjconline.org/hosanna-tabor-reaction-roundup/ Accessed August 20, 2017.

14. Hannah C. Smith, "Supreme Court Sends Clear Message on Religion," *Deseret Morning News* (Salt Lake Coity), January 17, 2012.

15. Quoted in John H., Cushman, "Religious Groups Greet Ruling with Satisfaction," *New York Times,* January 11, 2012.

Chapter 9

1. Originalism's two strongest proponents were Robert Bork and Justice Scalia. Bork's views are presented in *The Tempting of America* (New York: Free Press, 1990). Scalia's position is laid out most succinctly in "Originalism: The Lesser Evil," *University of Cincinnati Law Review,* 57 (1989), 849–865. For a careful and thoughtful analysis of how originalism has come to be the guiding principle in establishment clause cases, see Donald Drakeman, *Church, State, and Original Intent* (New York: Cambridge University Press, 2009).

2. Chad Flanders, "Religious Diversity: Thick and Thin," *Scotus Blog,* Posted May 6, 2014. Accessed September 18, 2017.

3. Michael Perry, *Constitutional Rights, Moral Controversy, and the Supreme Court* (New York: Cambridge University Press, 2008).

4. As Justice Alito points out in his opinion, the constitutional legitimacy of the prayer did not hinge on this fact.

5. In an important footnote, she points out that Baptists oppose prayer on public occasions even if they agree with its content. Their heritage is for a strict separation between church and state. The Baptist Joint Committee for Religious Liberty filed an *amicus* brief urging decision for Galloway.

6. For useful summaries, see Lisa Shaw Roy, "The Unexplored Implications of *Town of Greece v. Galloway," Albany Law Review,* 80 (2016–2017), 877–891; Alan Brownstein, "Constitutional Myopia: The Supreme Court's Blindness to Religious Liberty and Religious Equality in *Town of Greece v. Galloway," Loyola of Los Angeles Law Review,* 48 (2014), 371–438; and Paul Horwitz, "The Religious Geography of *Town of Greece v. Galloway," Supreme Court Review* (2014), 243–295

7. Eric Rassbach, "*Town of Greece v. Galloway:* The Establishment Clause and the Rediscovery of History," *Cato Supreme Court Review* (2013), 71–93.

8. Christopher Lund has argued that it is better to leave these matters to the political process. "Leaving Disestablishment to the Political Process," *Duke Journal of Constitutional Law and Public Policy,* 10 (2014), 45–57.

Chapter 10

1. I have laid out the background and passage of RFRA in more detail in *Congress, the Supreme Court, and Religious Liberty:* The Case of *City of Boerne v. Flores* (New York: Palgrave, 2015), especially chapter 2.

2. The law was also challenged on establishment clause and equal protection grounds. These challenges also failed.

3. Unless, that is, they target a specific religious group.

4. There are some disadvantages too, especially in the tax realm.

5. That would assume Justice Alito can read the mind of the Congress that enacted the law, surely quite a leap. Moreover, this was a political nonstarter.

6. It is not at all clear who, Alito or Ginsburg, is right about congressional intent. The public record is inconclusive at best but law professor Douglas Laycock, who helped draft the statute, said that "corporations are clearly persons protected by the statutory text and Congress understood RFRA to protect persons engaged in for-profit activities." Douglas Laycock, "Religious Liberty and the Culture Wars," *University of Illinois Law Review,* 2014 (2014), 854.

7. Quoted on the Beckett Fund's website.

8. Kim Colby, "After *Hobby Lobby,*" *The Christian Lawyer,* December 2014, 30.

9. Quoted in Adam Liptak, "Supreme Court Rejects Contraceptive Mandate for

Some Corporations," *New York Times,* June 30, 2014.

10. Quoted in Laura Bassett and Ryan J. Reilly, "Supreme Court Rules in Hobby Lobby Case, Dealing blow to Birth Control Coverage," *Huffington Post,* June 30, 2014.

11. Jennifer Haberkorn, "Two Years Later, Few Hobby Lobby Copycats Emerge," *Politico,* October 11, 2016.

12. The Senate had actually passed the measure in November of 2013 by a 64–32 vote. See Lyle Denniston, "New Fallout from *Hobby Lobby*," *Scotus Blog,* July 8, 2014.

13. Laycock, "Religious Liberty and the Culture Wars," 871.

14. See Ira C. Lupu, "*Hobby Lobby* and the Dubious Enterprise of Religious Exemptions," *Harvard Journal of Law and Gender,* 38 (2015), 35–203, esp. 45ff.

15. Frank Ravitch, "Be Careful What You Wish For: Why *Hobby Lobby* Weakens Religious Freedom," *Brigham Young University Law Review,* 2016 (2016), 55–116.

16. Ravitch, "Be Careful," 88–89 and 89–90.

17. Paul Horwitz, "The *Hobby Lobby* Moment," *Harvard Law Review,* 128 (2014), 154–190.

18. Horwitz, "Moment," 160.

19. Most of these are detailed in Samantha T. Ford, "*Little Sisters of the Poor Home for the Aged v. Sibelius:* Ramifications for Church Plans and Religious Nonprofits," *University of Colorado Law Review,* 87 (2016), 581–620. Further details can be found on the website of the Beckett Fund for Religious Liberty.

20. The phrase translates to "Opinion of the Court," and they are unsigned.

21. The case is 1:13-cv-08910. February 22, 2018.

Chapter 11

1. The case, as we saw earlier, was *Gonzales v. O Centro Esprita Beneficente Uniao do Vegetal,* 546 U.S. 418 (2006).

2. I have covered the passage of RLUIPA more thoroughly elsewhere. *Religious Free Exercise and Contemporary American Politics: The Saga of the Religious Land Use and Institutionalized Persons Act of 2000* (New York: Continuum, 2011). All subsequent quotations may be found there.

3. It is interesting that Justice Alito did not mention this episode in *Hobby Lobby.* It would have strengthened his argument that corporations were covered under the law.

4. Actually, these were two separate

questions. The prison part was the easiest, as most prisons take federal funds of one sort or another. Thus, attaching conditions to these grants, as Congress often does with many federal programs, seemed acceptable under the spending clause. There were some technical issues, but they did not seem insurmountable. Land use decisions, though, are normally made by local government bodies that seldom take federal grants. Thus, the commerce clause and the renewed emphasis on evidence on which to base a Section 5 claim had to do more of the heavy lifting (although the spending clause could be invoked if acceptance by any branch of a local government obligated all of its parts to be subject to a federal condition). As noted in the text, the prison portion of RLUIPA received the Supreme Court's imprimatur. It has, however, not ruled directly on the land use section. Nevertheless, several lower courts have upheld the land use part and the Supreme Court has left those decisions undisturbed.

5. Hair had to be worn "above the ear" and "no longer in the back than the middle of the nape of the neck."

6. The internal quotation is from *Cutter v. Wilkinson.*

7. Andrew Koppleman and Frederick Gaddis, "Is *Hobby Lobby* Worse for Religious Liberty than *Smith*?" *University of St. Thomas Journal of Law and Public Policy,* 9 (2015), 224.

8. Kim Colby, "*Holt v. Hobbs:* Reinforcing *Hobby Lobby*," *Journal of Christian Legal Thought,* 4 (2014), 16.

9. Paul Horwitz, "The *Hobby Lobby* Moment," *Harvard Law Review,* 128 (2014), 155.

Chapter 12

1. A good study of Blaine and his amendment is Steven K. Green, "The Blaine Amendment Reconsidered," *American Journal of Legal History,* 36 (1992), 38–69.

2. Not only would this amendment have made it illegal for states to siphon money to parochial schools. It would also have cleared up any doubts about whether the fourteenth amendment made the first amendment's religion clauses applicable to the states.

3. See Aaron E. Schwartz, "Dusting off the Blaine Amendment: Two Challenges to Missouri's Anti-Establishment Tradition," *Missouri Law Review,* 73 (2008), 129–176. The focus in this piece is on how a general voucher system might fare under the state constitution. Schwartz contends that there

is little evidence of anti-Catholic sentiment in Missouri in 1875 and none in 1945.

4. In April 2017, the governor ordered the Department to reverse its policy. Both sides agreed, though, that this did not make the case moot, since a future governor might change course again.

5. These statements are from the church's website and are quoted in Justice Sotomayor's dissenting opinion.

6. Article VI of the U.S. Constitution says that all state constitutions (and laws) are inferior to the federal constitution. It is known, consequently, as the Supremacy Clause.

7. This, incidentally, was not a Blaine amendment, having been adopted much later, in 1889.

8. It was not, it should be stressed, the nature of the college that led to the withdrawal of the scholarship, but his chosen major. Other students at the school in question, a devoted Bible-based institution, received the scholarship. It was only the major he chose to pursue that led the state to terminate the funding.

9. She notes that Missouri's Supreme Court has allowed the state to aid religious institutions in certain circumstances. Thus, it has hardly been rigid on this score.

10. This is somewhat debatable, as Washington's constitution, as noted above, was drafted long after the movement to adopt Blaine-type amendments in state constitutions had died out.

11. Quoted in Sarah Pulliam Bailey, "The Supreme Court Sided with Trinity Lutheran Church. Here's Why That Matters," *Washington Post*, June 26, 2017. In the immediate aftermath of Hurricane Harvey, FEMA ruled that churches would be ineligible for disaster grants, citing establishment clause concerns. Congress, however, reversed this decision, a direct result it seems of this decision. See the Becket Fund for Religious Liberty's press release of February 9, 2018 describing the congressional action.

12. Quoted in Valerie Strauss, "Will the Supreme Court's Trinity Decision Lead to the Spread of School Voucher Programs?" *Washington Post*, June 26, 2017.

13. Quoted in Bailey, "Spread of School Voucher Programs?"

14. These two cases (*Caplan v. Town of Acton* and *Harvest Family Church v. FEMA*) are explained in Becket Fund press releases of September 7, 2017 and October 13, 2017.

15. Richard Garnett and Jackson Blais called it the "elephant in the room." "Religious Freedom and Recycled Tires: The Meaning and Implications of *Trinity Lutheran*," *Cato*

Supreme Court Review, 2016 (2016), 123–125.

16. Quoted in Strauss, "Spread of School Voucher Programs?"

17. Quoted in Straus, "Spread of School Voucher Programs?"

18. Both quotations are from Erica L Green, "Supreme Court Ruling Could Shape the Future of School Choice," *New York Times*, June 27, 2017.

19. Quoted in Bailey, "Why That Matters."

20. Holly Hollman, the General Counsel for the BJC, "Hollman Report," August 16, 2017.

21. Press release, Baptist Joint Committee for Religious Liberty, June 26, 2017.

Conclusion

1. See Helen J. Knowles, *The Tie Goes to Freedom: Justice Anthony Kennedy on Liberty* (Lanham, MD: Rowman and Littlefield, 2009) and Frank Colucci, *Justice Kennedy's Jurisprudence: The Full and Necessary Meaning of Liberty* (Lawrence: University Press of Kansas, 2009).

2. Richard W. Garnett, "Neil Gorsuch, the Supreme Court, and Religious Freedom," *Religion and Politics*, the John C. Danforth Center on Religion and Politics, Washington University of St. Louis, March 22, 2017.

3. Edward Correia, "*Trinity Lutheran Church v. Comer:* An Unfortunate New Anti-Discrimination Principle," *Rutgers Journal of Law and Religion*, 18 (2017), 280.

4. *Kondrat'yev, et al. v. City of Pensacola*. Currently at the Court of Appeals for the Eleventh Circuit. See the website of the Becket Fund. See their press release of May 16, 2018. A Federal District Court ordered the cross removed.

5. It is interesting that the other half of RLUIPA, the restrictions on land use, has not reached the Supreme Court, even though it affects many more people and many more locations throughout the country. Several Court of Appeals decisions have upheld the constitutionality of the law and the Supreme Court has not intervened. Thus, indirectly, its constitutionality seems on firm ground. The lower courts, though, are awash in RLUIPA cases, and many observers feel that churches still suffer discrimination when it comes to zoning decisions. Douglas Laycock and Luke W. Goodrich have written that "RLUIPA was and is needed. Churches continue to be a disfavored use in the zoning context and fundamental First Amendment rights continue to be subject to highly dis-

cretionary decisions by local officials."
"RLUIPA: Necessary, Modest, and Underenforced," *Fordham Urban Law Journal*, 39
(2013), 1071. See also the heart-wrenching
story of the zoning fight encountered by a
multiethnic church in Bergen County, New
Jersey in Emma Green, "The Quiet Religious-
Freedom Fight that is Remaking America,"
The Atlantic, November 5, 2017.

6. See Frank Ravitch, *Freedom's Edge: Re-
ligious Freedom, Sexual Freedom, and the
Future of America* (New York: Cambridge
University Press, 2016), chap. 5.

7. Quoted in Ravitch, *Freedom's Edge*, 130.

8. Robert Dahl, "Decision-Making in a
Democracy: The Supreme Court as a National Policy-Maker," *Journal of Public Law*,
6 (1957), 279–295.

9. Paul Horwitz, *The Agnostic Age: Law,
Religion, and the Constitution* (New York:
Oxford University Press, 2011), chap. 1. To
try to keep clarity, I am using upper case
"Liberal" when referring to the general political philosophy, say enunciated by John
Locke and his followers, and keeping the
lower case "liberal" for the political position
commonly associated with the American
left.

10. William Galston, *The Practice of Liberal Pluralism* (New York: Cambridge University Press, 2004).

11. I'm borrowing this term from Rex
Ahdar and Ian Leigh, *Religious Freedom in
the Liberal State*, 2nd ed. (Oxford, UK: Oxford University Press, 2013), chap. 4.

Bibliography

Ahdar, Rex, and Ian Leigh. *Religious Freedom in the Liberal State*. 2nd ed. Oxford, UK: Oxford University Press, 2013.

Bagby, Ihsan. *The American Mosque, 2011, Report No. 1. Basic Characteristics of the American Mosque: Attitudes of Mosque Leaders*. Washington: Council on American-Islamic Relations, 2012.

Bagenstos, Samuel R. "The Unrelenting Libertarian Challenge to Public Accommodations Law." *Stanford Law Review*, 66 (2014): 1205–1240.

Bailey, Sarah Pulliam. "The Supreme Court Sided with Trinity Lutheran Church. Here's Why That Matters." *Washington Post*, June 26, 2017.

Banks, Adelle M. Religion News Service, November 7, 2012.

Barna Group Poll, October 1, 2015.

Bassett, Laura, and Ryan J. Reilly. "Supreme Court Rules in Hobby Lobby Case, Dealing Blow to Birth Control Coverage." *Huffington Post*, June 30, 2014.

Becket Fund for Religious Liberty. Various press releases.

Bickel, Alexander. *The Least Dangerous Branch: The Supreme Court at the Bar of Politics*. Indianapolis: Bobbs-Merrill, 1962.

Birzer, Bradley J. *Russell Kirk: American Conservative*. Lexington: University Press of Kentucky, 2015.

Blackford, Russell. *Freedom of Religion and the Secular State*. Oxford, UK: John Wiley, 2012.

Bork, Robert. *The Tempting of America*. New York: Free Press, 1990.

Bottum, Joseph. "The Death of Protestant America: A Political Theory of the Protestant Mainline." *First Things*, August 2008.

Brownstein, Alan. "Constitutional Myopia: The Supreme Court's Blindness to Religious Liberty and Religious Equality in *Town of Greece v. Galloway*." *Loyola of Los Angeles Law Review*, 48 (2014), 371–438.

Cardozo, Benjamin. *The Nature of the Judicial Process*. New Haven, CT: Yale University Press, 1921.

Carey, Kevin. "Arizona's Shady Tale of Tax Credit Vouchers." *New York Times*, March 3, 2017.

Cauthen, James. "State Constitutions and Challenges to Nonpublic School Transportation Programs." *Journal of Church and State*, 55 (2013), 498–526.

Cohen, Jean L., and Cecile Laborde, eds. *Religion, Secularism, and Constitutional Democracy*. New York: Columbia University Press, 2016.

Colby, Kim. "After *Hobby Lobby*." *The Christian Lawyer*, December 2014.

_____. "*Holt v. Hobbs*: Reinforcing *Hobby Lobby*." *Journal of Christian Legal Thought*, 4 (2014), 15–18.

Colluci, Frank. *Justice Kennedy's Jurisprudence: The Full and Necessary Meaning of Liberty*. Lawrence: University Press of Kansas, 2009.

Correia, Edward. "*Trinity Lutheran Church v. Comer*: An Unfortunate New Anti-Discrimination Principle." *Rutgers Journal of Law and Religion*, 18 (2017): 280–297.

Cushman, John H. "Religious Groups Greet Ruling with Satisfaction." *New York Times*, January 11, 2012.

Dahl, Robert. "Decision-Making in a

Democracy: The Supreme Court as a National Policy-Maker." *Journal of Public Law*, 6 (1957), 279–295.

Dawkins, Richard. *The God Delusion.* Boston: Houghton Mifflin, 2006.

Denniston, Lyle. "New Fallout from *Hobby Lobby. Scotus Blog,* July 8, 2014.

Dolan, Mary Jean. "Government Identity Speech and Religion: Establishment Clause Limits after *Summum.*" *William and Mary Bill of Rights Journal,* 19 (2010): 1–74.

_____. "*Salazar v. Buono:* The Cross between Endorsement and History." *Northwestern University Law Review,* 105 (2010): 42–59.

Drakeman, Donald. *Church, State, and Original Intent.* New York: Cambridge University Press, 2010.

Eberstadt, Mary. *It is Dangerous to Believe: Religious Freedom and Its Enemies.* New York: HarperCollins, 2016.

Eisgruber, Christopher, and Lawrence Sager. *Religious Freedom and the Constitution.* Cambridge, MA: Harvard University Press, 2007.

Epps, Garrett. *Democracy Reborn: The Fourteenth Amendment and the Fight for Equal Rights in Post-Civil War America.* New York: Henry Holt, 2007.

Feldman, Noah. "The Intellectual Origins of the Establishment Clause." *New York University Law Review,* 77 (2002): 346–428.

Fish, Stanley. "Mission Impossible: Setting the Just Bounds between Church and State." *Columbia Law Review,* 97 (1997): 2255–2333.

Flanders, Chad. "Religious Diversity: Thick and Thin." *Scotus Blog.* May 6, 2014.

Ford, Samantha T. "*Little Sisters of the Poor Home for the Aged v. Sebelius:* Ramifications for Church Plans and Religious Nonprofits." *University of Colorado Law Review,* 87 (2016), 581–620.

Fox News Poll, July 21, 2015.

Friedman, Barry. "The Birth of an Academic Obsession: The History of the Countermajoritarian Difficulty." *Yale Law Journal,* 112 (2002): 153–259.

Friedman, Milton. *Free to Choose.* Chicago: University of Chicago Press, 1962.

Galston, William. *The Practice of Liberal Pluralism.* New York: Cambridge University Press, 2004.

Garnett, Richard W. "A Case in Point About Our Church-State Divide." *USA Today,* April 25, 2011.

_____. "Neil Gorsuch, the Supreme Court, and Religious Freedom." *Religion and Politics.* St. Louis: Washington University, John C. Danforth Center on Religion and Politics, March 22, 2017.

_____, and Jackson Blais. "Religious Freedom and Recycled Tires: The Meaning and Implications of *Trinity Lutheran.*" *Cato Supreme Court Review,* 2016 (206): 105–130.

Gillen, Patrick. "A *Winn* for Originalism Puts Establishment Clause Reform Within Reach." *William and Mary Bill of Rights Journal,* 21 (2013): 1107–1152.

Gillman, Howard. "Party Politics and Constitutional Change: The Political Origins of Liberal Judicial Activism." Ronald Kahn and Ken I. Kersch, eds. *The Supreme Court and American Political Development.* Lawrence: University Press of Kansas, 2006.

Green, Emma. "The Quiet Religious Freedom Fight that is Remaking America." *The Atlantic,* November 5, 2017.

Green, Erica L. "Supreme Court Ruling Could Shape the Future of School Choice." *New York Times,* June 27, 2017.

Green, Steven K. "The Blaine Amendment Reconsidered." *American Journal of Legal History,* 36 (1992), 38–69.

Griffin, Leslie C. "Fighting the New Wars of Religion: The Need for a Tolerant First Amendment." *Maine Law Review,* 62 (2010), 23–74.

_____. "The Sins of *Hosanna-Tabor.*" *Indiana Law Journal,* 88 (2013): 981–1020.

Haberkorn, Jennifer. "Two Years Later, Few Hobby Lobby Copycats Emerge." *Politico,* October 11, 2016.

Harris, Sam. *The End of Faith: Religion, Terror, and the Future of Reason.* New York: Norton, 2004.

Hayek, Frederick. *The Constitution of Liberty.* Chicago: University of Chicago Press, 1960.

_____. *The Road to Serfdom.* Chicago: University of Chicago Press, 1944.

Herberg, Will. *Protestant, Catholic, Jew:*

An Essay in American Religious Sociology. Garden City, NY: Doubleday, 1955.

Hill, B. Jessie. "Putting Religious Symbolism in Context: A Linguistic Critique of the Endorsement Test." *Michigan Law Review,* 104 (2005): 491–545.

Horwitz, Paul. *The Agnostic Age: Law, Religion, and the Constitution.* New York: Oxford University Press, 2011.

_____. "The *Hobby Lobby* Moment." *Harvard Law Review,* 128 (2014): 154–190.

_____. "The Religious Geography of *Town of Greece v. Galloway.*" *Supreme Court Review,* 2014 (2014): 71–93.

Jablon, Robert. Press Release, Associated Press, April 30, 2012.

Jeffries, John C., and James E. Ryan. "A Political History of the Establishment Clause." *Michigan Law Review,* 100 (2001): 279–370.

Johnson, Curtis D. "Sectarian Nation: Religious Diversity in Antebellum America." *Organization of American Historians Magazine of History,* 22 (2008): 14–18.

Jones, Robert P. *The End of White Christian America.* New York: Simon & Schuster, 2016.

Jordan, Karen A. "Free Exercise Jurisprudence and Theology in the Public Square." *Trinity Law Review,* 19 (2014): 187–266.

Kanin, Max. "*Christian Legal Society v. Martinez*: How an Obscure First Amendment Case Inadvertently and Unexpectedly Created a Significant Fourteenth Amendment Advance for LGBT Rights Advocates." *American University Journal of Gender, Social Policy and the Law,* 19 (2011): 1317–1326.

Keller, Tim. "*Arizona Christian School Tuition Organization v. Winn*: Does the Government Own the Money in Your Pocket?" *Cato Supreme Court Review* (2011–2012): 149–184.

Kirk, Russell. *The Conservative Mind: From Burke to Elliot.* Washington: Regenery, 1978.

Knowles, Helen J. *The Tie Goes to Freedom: Justice Anthony Kennedy on Liberty.* Lanham, MD: Rowman and Littlefield, 2009.

Koppelman, Andrew. *Defending American Religious Neutrality.* Cambridge, MA: Harvard University Press, 2013.

_____, and Frederick Gaddis. "Is *Hobby Lobby* Worse for Religious Liberty than *Smith*?" *University of St. Thomas Journal of Law and Public Policy,* 9 (2015): 223–247.

Laycock, Douglas. "*Hosanna-Tabor* and the Ministerial Exception." *Harvard Journal of Law and Public Policy,* 35 (2012): 839–862.

_____. "Religious Liberty and the Culture Wars." *University of Illinois Law Review,* 2014 (2014): 839–880.

_____. "Substantive Neutrality Revisited." *West Virginia Law Review.* 110 (2007): 51–88.

_____, and Luke W. Goodrich "RLUIPA: Necessary, Modest, and Underenforced." *Fordham Urban Law Journal,* 39 (2013): 1021–1072.

Ledewitz, Bruce. *Church, State, and the Crisis in American Secularism.* Bloomington: Indiana University Press, 2011.

Lessig, Lawrence. "The Regulation of Social Meaning." *University of Chicago Law Review,* 62 (1995): 943–1044.

Linas, Christopher. "*Salazar v. Buono*: A Blow against the Endorsement Test's Core Principle." *Denver University Law Review,* 88 (2011): 603–629.

Liptak, Adam. "Religious Groups Given 'Exception' to Work Bias Law." *New York Times,* January 11, 2012.

_____. "Supreme Court Rejects Contraceptive Mandate for Some Corporations." *New York Times,* June 30, 2013.

Lu, Angela. "War Memorial Cross in Mojave Desert Resurrected on Veterans Day after Long Legal Battle." *Christian Headlines.com,* November 12, 2012.

Lund, Christopher. "Leaving Disestablishment to the Political Process." *Duke Journal of Constitutional Law and Public Policy,* 10 (2014): 45–57.

Lupu, Ira. "*Hobby Lobby* and the Dubious Enterprise of Religious Exemptions." *Harvard Journal of Law and Gender,* 38 (2015): 35–102.

_____, and Robert W. Tuttle. "The Mystery of Unanimity in *Hosanna-Tabor Lutheran School v. EEOC.*" *Lewis and Clark Law Review,* 2016–2017 (2016–2017): 1265–1315.

Macpherson, C.B. *Burke*. New York: Oxford University Press, 1980.

Mann, Gurinder Singh, et al. *Buddhists, Hindus, and Sikhs in America: A Short History*. New York: Oxford University Press, 2007.

Marshall, William, and Gene Nicol. "Not a *Winn*-Win: Misconstruing Standing and the Establishment Clause." *Supreme Court Review*, 2011 (2011): 215–252.

Massaro, Toni M. "*Christian Legal Society v. Martinez*: Six Frames." *Hastings Constitutional Law Quarterly*, 38 (2011): 569–629.

McAfee, Ward. *Religion, Race, and Reconstruction: The Public School and the Politics of the 1870s*. Albany: State University of New York Press, 1998.

McConnell, Michael. "The Origins and Historical Understanding of Free Exercise of Religion." *Harvard Law Review*, 103 (1990): 1409–1517.

Michaels, Laura. "*Hein v. FFRF*: Sitting This One Out." *Harvard Civil Rights and Civil Liberties Review*, 43 (2008): 213–237.

Munoz, Victor P. "Two Concepts of Religious Liberty: The Natural Rights and Moral Autonomy Approaches to the Free Exercise of Religion." *American Political Science Review*, 110 (2016), 369–381.

National Opinion Research Poll, September 2011.

Numrich, Paul. *The Faith Next Door: American Christians and their New Religious Neighbors*. New York: Oxford University Press, 2009.

Nussbaum, Martha. *Liberty of Conscience: In Defense of America's Tradition of Religious Equality*. New York: Basic Books, 2008.

_____. *The New Religious Intolerance: Overcoming the Politics of Fear in an Anxious Age*. Cambridge, MA: Harvard University Press, 2012.

Orchowski, Margaret Sands. *The Law that Changed the Face of America: The Immigration and Nationality Act of 1965*. Lanham, MD: Rowman and Littlefield, 2015.

Perry, Michael. *Constitutional Rights, Moral Controversy, and the Supreme Court*. New York: Cambridge University Press, 2008.

Pew Research Center. *America's Changing Religious Landscape*. May 12, 2015.

_____. *Religion and Public Life Survey*, July 29, 2015.

Public Religion Research Institute Polls, March 15, 2012 and June 11, 2014.

Rassbach, Eric. "*Town of Greece v. Galloway*: The Establishment Clause and the Rediscovery of History." *Cato Supreme Court Review*, 2013 (2013): 71–93.

Ravitch, Frank S. "Be Careful What You Wish For: Why *Hobby Lobby* Weakens Religious Freedom." *Brigham Young University Law Review* 2016 (2016): 55–116.

_____. *Freedom's Edge: Religious Freedom, Sexual Freedom, and the Future of America*. New York: Cambridge University Press, 2016.

Reyes, Rene. "The Fading Free Exercise Clause." *William and Mary Bill of Rights Journal*, 19 (2011): 725–750.

Roy, Lisa Shaw. "The Unexplored Implications of *Town of Greece v. Galloway*." *Albany Law Review*, 80 (2016–2017): 87–891.

Scalia, Antonin. "Originalism: The Lesser Evil." *University of Cincinnati Law Review*, 57 (1989), 849–865.

Schultz, Kevin. *Tri-Faith America: How Catholics and Jews Held Postwar America to Its Protestant Promise*. New York: Oxford University Press, 2011.

Schwartz, Aaron E. "Dusting off the Blaine Amendment: Two Challenges to Missouri's Anti-Establishment Tradition." *Missouri Law Review*, 73 (2008): 129–176.

Sloustcher, Adam. "*Arizona v. Winn*: Negative Implications for First Amendment Proponents and Possibly for Our Nation's School Children." *Hastings Constitutional Law Quarterly*, 40 (2013): 967–988.

Smietana, Bob. "Murfreesboro Mosque Fight Laid to Rest after Supreme Court Ruling." *Religion News Service*, June 3, 2014.

Smith, Hannah C. "Supreme Court Sends Clear Message on Religion." *Deseret Morning News*, January 17, 2012.

Smith, Steven. *Foreordained Failure: The Quest for a Constitutional Principle of Religious Freedom.* New York: Oxford University Press, 1995.

_____. *The Rise and Decline of American Religious Freedom.* Cambridge, MA: Harvard University Press, 2014.

Strasser, Mark. "The Endorsement Test is Alive and Well: A Cause for Celebration and Sorrow." *Pepperdine Law Review,* 39 (2013): 1273–1316.

Strauss, Valerie. "Will the Supreme Court's Trinity Decision Lead to the Spread of School Voucher Programs?" *Washington Post,* June 26, 2017.

Sullivan, Winnifred S. *The Impossibility of Religious Freedom.* Princeton, NJ: Princeton University Press, 2005.

_____, et al., eds. *Politics of Religious Freedom.* Chicago: University of Chicago Press, 2015.

Sunstein, Cass. *One Case at a Time: Judicial Minimalism on the Supreme Court.* Cambridge, MA: Harvard University Press, 1999.

Taylor, Charles. *A Secular Age.* Cambridge, MA: Harvard University Press, 2007.

Thro, William E. "The Limits of *Christian Legal Society.*" *Cardozo Law Review,* 2014 (2014): 124–128.

Townsend, Tim. "Justices Shield Churches." St. Louis *Post-Dispatch,* January 12, 2012.

Tracey, Timothy J. "*Christian Legal Society v. Martinez* in Hindsight." *University of Hawai'i Law Review,* 34 (2012): 1–23.

Tribe, Lawrence, and Joshua Matz. *Uncertain Justice: The Roberts Court and the Constitution.* New York: Henry Holt, 2014.

Van Buren, Bruce. "Tuition Tax Credits and *Winn*: A Constitutional Blueprint for School Choice." *Regent University Law Review,* 24 (2011–2012): 515–528.

Wakin, Edward, and Joseph F. Scheuer. *The De-Romanization of the American Catholic Church.* New York: Macmillan, 1966.

Waltman, Jerold L. "Church and State in the Roberts Court." *Law and Justice,* No. 171 (2013): 5–20.

_____. *Congress, the Supreme Court, and Religious Liberty: The Case of* City of Boerne v. Flores. New York: Palgrave, 2015.

_____. "*Hosanna-Tabor Lutheran Church v. EEOC:* Defining the 'Ministerial Exception' in U.S. Employment Law." *Law and Justice,* no. 169 (2012): 210–223.

_____. *Religious Free Exercise and Contemporary American Politics: The Saga of the Religious Land Use and Institutionalized Persons Act of 2000.* New York: Continuum, 2011.

Index